Lodgers, Landlords, and Landladies
in Georgian London

Lodgers, Landlords, and Landladies in Georgian London

Gillian Williamson

BLOOMSBURY ACADEMIC
LONDON • NEW YORK • OXFORD • NEW DELHI • SYDNEY

BLOOMSBURY ACADEMIC
Bloomsbury Publishing Plc
50 Bedford Square, London, WC1B 3DP, UK
1385 Broadway, New York, NY 10018, USA
29 Earlsfort Terrace, Dublin 2, Ireland

BLOOMSBURY, BLOOMSBURY ACADEMIC and the Diana logo are trademarks of
Bloomsbury Publishing Plc

First published in Great Britain 2021
Paperback edition published in 2023

A catalogue record for this book is available from the British Library.

A catalog record for this book is available from the Library of Congress.

Library of Congress Cataloging-in-Publication Data
Names: Williamson, Gillian, author.
Title: Lodgers, Landlords, and Landladies in Georgian London / Gillian Williamson.
Description: New York, NY : Bloomsbury Academic, 2021. |
Includes bibliographical references and index. |
Identifiers: LCCN 2021001512 (print) | LCCN 2021001513 (ebook) | ISBN 9781350212633
(hardback) | ISBN 9781350253582 (ePDF) | ISBN 9781350253599 (eBook)
Subjects: LCSH: Lodging-houses–England–London–History. |
London (England)–Social conditions.
Classification: LCC HD7288G7 W56 2021 (print) |
LCC HD7288G7 (ebook) | DDC 942.107–dc23
LC record available at https://lccn.loc.gov/2021001512
LC ebook record available at https://lccn.loc.gov/2021001513

ISBN: HB: 978-1-3502-1263-3
          PB: 978-1-3502-5701-6
          ePDF: 978-1-3502-5358-2
          eBook: 978-1-3502-5359-9

Typeset by Integra Software Services Pvt. Ltd.

To find out more about our authors and books visit www.bloomsbury.com
and sign up for our newsletters.

Contents

Figures

Acknowledgements

Lodgers, Landlords, and Landladies in Georgian London has been several years in the making. I began thinking about the eighteenth-century experience of life in London lodgings when I was researching my PhD thesis on masculinity in the *Gentleman's Magazine*. I was reading many published diaries and letters to get a feel for the men and women who comprised its readership. It soon became apparent that many of them had at some time lived in this way, in a stranger's home, and that this was no cause for embarrassment. It led me to thinking about what the significance of this was for the Georgian concept of home, both for the lodgers, and for the men and women who were their landlords and ladies. Out of this thinking came this study.

In bringing this book to the press I have stood on the shoulders of giants: both those scholars whose published work I have relied upon to guide me and those who encouraged me to believe this was a worthwhile subject and helped me to shape it, especially Vanessa Harding, Tim Hitchcock and Jerry White. My thanks must also go to all the friends and colleagues, too many to name but I trust you know who you are, at the Institute of Historical Research seminar, British History in the Long Eighteenth Century, and the Women's Studies Group 1558–1837. From them I have derived support, information and suggestions, and sociability. I have felt my way through my subject at conferences and workshops: 'The Working Class at Home 1770–2017' at the Geffrye Museum, the Women's Studies Group annual workshops, the British Society for Eighteenth-Century Studies and the International Society for Eighteenth-Century Studies conferences, and 'Hogarth's Moral Geography' at the Paul Mellon Centre for Studies in British Art. I am most grateful to all those who listened and offered their thoughtful questions and comments. Finally, I must thank wholeheartedly those who kindly read through my draft manuscript and offered corrections and new insights: Amanda Goodrich, Karen Lipsedge, Bloomsbury's anonymous peer reviewer, and my editors. Any errors remaining are, of course, entirely my own. Finalizing both text and images has been difficult in pandemic-stricken times. Many libraries and their services were closed and suspended. I have been impressed by, and am immensely grateful to, the independent Gibson Library on my doorstep in Saffron Walden, Essex. The depth and breadth of its historic and contemporary collections have been a lifesaver.

It is a testament to the enduring issues of lodging that I have enjoyed so many contemporary anecdotes, absurd, tragic, and heartening, from family and friends: the landlady who served up cornflakes with custard (and the occasional stray dog-hair) as a pudding to her boarders, my mother-in-law who had her house exorcised after her relationship with a student-lodger soured, the kind landlady who gave up her own bed to a lodger who needed to move in before the old lodger left, and my sister Liz, still friends with her London landlady across thirty-five years and the Atlantic Ocean. As you will see, there are eighteenth-century parallels for all these experiences.

And that brings me more particularly to family and friends. They have all once again endured with love and good humour my obsession with a project. While I have been looking back to the past there has been new life: my five granddaughters Joanie, Ivy, Clodagh, Hattie, and Avery to whom I dedicate this book.

Notes

Biographical information

Dates are included to avoid ambiguity and are taken from the *ODNB* (see Abbreviations) or from internal sources in autobiographies and biographies.

Predecimal British currency (before 1971)

One pound (£) was divided into 20 shillings (s.) or 240 pence (d.). There were therefore 12d./pence to a shilling. A guinea was worth £1 1s.

There were gold five, two, one, and half guinea coins. Crowns (5s.), half crowns (2s. 6d.), 6d., and 3d. coins were all silver, as were pennies and 2d. coins until the introduction of 1d. and 2d. copper coins in 1797. The last silver penny was minted in 1820. Farthings (¼d.) and halfpence (½d.) were made from copper.

Long-form titles

Many eighteenth-century works have very long titles. To avoid excessively heavy footnotes these have been given in a shortened form with the full title in the Bibliography.

Abbreviations

BL	British Library
BM	British Museum
CUP	Cambridge University Press
CWAC	City of Westminster Archives Centre
GM	*Gentleman's Magazine*
HUP	Harvard University Press
LMA	London Metropolitan Archives
LWL	Lewis Walpole Library
MC	*Morning Chronicle*
NPG	National Portrait Gallery
OBOL	*Proceedings of the Old Bailey* (www.oldbaileyonline.org, version 7.2, 18 July 2016)
ODNB	*Oxford Dictionary of National Biography* (https://www.oxforddnb.com/)
OUP	Oxford University Press
RCT	Royal Collections Trust
SofL	Survey of London
TNA	The National Archives (https://www.nationalarchives.gov.uk/)
UCL	University College London
YUP	Yale University Press

1

Introduction

In 1785 the junction of Compton Street, Soho, with Greek Street was a typical busy location in the parish of St Anne Soho in the West End of London. The streets were lined with shops and workshops whose occupants lived above them, interspersed with residential houses, their householders largely drawn from the commercial and professional classes. The freeholds formed part of the aristocratic Portland Estate which had been laid out on open fields from the late-seventeenth century onwards. When John Rocque published his map of London in 1746 the area had become a well-established and densely-built urban area of the genteel, terraced, and brick-fronted 'two pair stairs and an attic' dwellings we think of as quintessentially Georgian. It had already seen several phases of partial redevelopment.[1] The householders in these terraces held leases directly from the Portland Estate or were the sub-tenants of a non-resident holder of a head lease. This arrangement was typical of London more widely, though the freeholders were not always quite as grand as the Portlands.[2]

On the late evening of Thursday 16 June 1785 the sun was just setting at the end of another hot, dusty summer's day, but there was some relief from the heat as a light breeze stirred.[3] The shop doors of Compton and Greek Streets were now closed but the windows of upper floors were open to let in its fresh air. In the second-floor front room of Mrs Hannah Barker's house, milliner Mary Gay had tucked her little boy into his truckle bed and was now tidying up. She opened the closet door. Suddenly her room filled with flames and smoke. A fire had burned its way through the new partition wall that separated Mrs Barker's house from that of her neighbour, Mr Glossop the tallow-chandler. Screaming, Mary grabbed her sleepy child and raised the alarm. Two other women appeared from the rooms at the back of the same floor: unemployed servant Mary Harivin and a single lady whose proud boast was that her father was a clergyman. With no time to collect their possessions they raced down the stairs, knocking up on the way Gilbert Dring, the tailor who lived on the first floor, Hannah Barker, her three stepchildren, her sister Ann Murrray, and her maid Ann Owen. Mrs Barker unbarred the street door and they ran out.

Someone summoned the parish fire engine, and the watchmen and heroic neighbours worked through the night to evacuate people and protect their bundled goods from the light-fingered among those who gathered to watch. Ropes were used to haul surgeon Andrew Nihell from the rubble of a collapsed building. When daylight came it was a sorry scene. Fifteen houses on Compton Street and Greek Street were destroyed and others in the area left severely damaged. Fortunately, no one had died, though Mrs Gapper, who had only moved into Greek Street three days before, miscarried the next day.[4] The leading citizens of the parish immediately set about establishing a subscription fund to aid the victims of the fire. Donations large and small rolled in from individuals (including £21 from the Duke of Northumberland), adjacent parishes and churches, and institutions (the Quakers, Piccadilly Chapel, the Society of Druids). A total of £1,281 4s. was raised, a printed notice advised potential claimants of the procedure, and by 1 July the first payments were being authorized by the committee.[5]

There was nothing out of the ordinary about a house fire or a subscription charity.[6] Indeed, the Compton Street committee examined records from a similar case from 1759 in St Paul's Covent Garden.[7] Two things are remarkable about the Compton street fire, however. Firstly, the disaster was on a large scale compared to other archival survivals. There were eighty-five claims made on the charity fund, compared, for example, to fifty-five after a 1707 fire in Charles Street, Westminster, which destroyed a similar number of houses (seventeen).[8] Secondly, although full inventories do not survive for the Compton Street losses, what does survive is detailed information on the claimants, which allows us to place individuals both in relationship to one another, and in particular rooms within each house. There were sixteen claims from householders which confirm the middling-sort, commercial nature of the area. Hannah Barker carried on her late husband's composition ornament-making business (mouldings for frames and architectural details). Others included a locksmith, grocer, greengrocer, cabinet-maker, haberdasher, tailor, paper-stainer, tobacconist, and bookseller. A further twenty-nine claimants were domestic and business servants.

These numbers were dwarfed, however, by forty claims from lodgers – men and women, singletons, couples, and families – representing almost half of all claims by number. These lodgers lived in units totalling at least sixty-five people living in twenty-two affected houses. At Hannah Barker's house, Mary Gay and her child, Mary Harivin, the clergyman's daughter, and Gilbert Dring were all lodgers, as was the surgeon Andrew Nihell and his wife and child in Greek Street. They came from quite different backgrounds, but they had this in common: they all paid rent to live in a room or rooms in someone else's private home. They were not part of the 'household' or family linked by kinship, affect, and shared activity, but of the 'houseful', those who also slept under the same roof but lacked these ties – servants, apprentices, visitors, and lodgers.[9] In the case of the Compton Street fire claimants, there were more lodgers than servants.

Without in any way belittling the dreadful experience undergone by those caught up in the fire, the Compton Street papers therefore confirm an important reality of eighteenth-century London life. While the rows of near-identical Georgian front doors depicted by John Tallis in his eighty-eight pamphlet guides, *London Street Views*, suggested homogenous, self-contained, nuclear family households within, the truth was that lodging was ubiquitous in all but the most exclusive locations.[10] The London home was very likely to accommodate non-kin who were there at arm's length, on a commercial basis and at the will of the landlord or lady, rather than as members of the kinship family or socio-economic household unit. As Hannah Barker's houseful indicates, by twenty-first-century standards the London house was often a very crowded space.

Although there are no firm statistics for overall lodger numbers until the national census of 1851 – and even then the figures are imprecise – lodgers are thought to have been present in at least one eighth of households, both in London and elsewhere, at any one time since the late-sixteenth century, more in some locations and fewer in others.[11] As lodging is a two-way process necessarily entailing both a lodger or lodgers and a landlord/lady, together with family and other household members such as servants on each side, the total number of people in a 'lodging relationship' at any one time was higher. Allowing for changes in circumstances over a lifetime – lodging while a student, 'downsizing' on retirement from business, changing housing choices with rises and falls in economic circumstances – the numbers experiencing lodging on either side of the bargain at some point in their lives were higher still.[12] To understand Georgian 'everyday' life – the choices of accommodation, the private and shared space people had available to them, the relationships they enjoyed or endured – we need to understand what it was like to live in a house that included lodgers.[13] Achieving that understanding is the aim of this study.

In spite of its widespread presence both in lived experience and in representations in novels and plays such as Samuel Richardson's *Clarissa*, Frances Burney's *Evelina,* and Samuel Foote's *The Commissary,* lodging in the private house is an under-researched area of eighteenth-century social and cultural history. There is a long-standing and rich literature on the architecture of Georgian London, for example John Summerson's *Georgian London,* the many volumes of the *Survey of London,* Peter Guillery's *The Small House in Eighteenth-Century London,* and Todd Longstaffe-Gowan's *The London Square.*[14] Amanda Vickery's *Behind Closed Doors* and Karen Harvey's *The Little Republic* are just two of the recent studies which go further and populate the architecture with the lives and material culture that took place within these houses. They capture the ways in which class and gender constructed the late-eighteenth-century and nineteenth-century ideal of domesticity – the patriarchally-led house as a home and a retreat from work, rather than the economic site of labour it had been in preceding centuries.[15] The establishment in 2011 of the Centre for the Studies of Home, a joint venture between Queen Mary, University of London and the Geffrye Museum, is testament to a new awareness of the historical importance of the home and the domestic, and to the number of scholars working in the field.[16]

Household servants have received full attention from, for example, Bridget Hill, Tim Meldrum, and Tessa Chynoweth, yet the presence of lodgers in eighteenth-century houses remains relegated to articles and chapters or scattered references in general works on the period.[17] This is surprising as the presence of lodgers intruded on and refashioned the space, privacy, and domesticity of the home, its capacity to offer both material and emotional comforts.[18] For lodging entailed 'living with strangers', the title of an edited volume on modern English bedsits and boarding houses. Scottish lawyer James Boswell (1740–95), perhaps best known as a biographer of his friend the lexicographer and literary lion Dr Samuel Johnson (1709–84), used 'stranger' non-pejoratively to describe his relationship with his Downing Street landlord Mr Terrie.[19] Lodgers were not just strangers; however, they were also customers and creators of additional housework who were making their own version of a domestic world, albeit constrained in space and contingent on their relationship with their landlord/lady. For each party, these constraints rendered the home space ambivalent, creating what a modern sociological study describes as 'a situation where often neither party feels "at home"'.[20]

Among historiographical discussions of lodging, the two classic studies of eighteenth-century London by Dorothy George and Peter Earle acknowledge and discuss its role within the housing options open to Georgians living in the capital, as does Jerry White in his more recent panoramic study of London. Guillery also takes account of lodgers in considering how space, including the common parts such as stairs, was used in a small Georgian London house.[21] Joanne McEwan's and Pamela Sharpe's 2007 article 'It Buys Me Freedom' opens, like this chapter, with a house fire in St Anne Soho which revealed occupancy by the householder Mrs Band, two family members, two apprentices to Band and four lodgers. It is a good short study of lodging in middling-sort eighteenth-century London from the perspective of both landlord/lady and lodger.[22] Moving into the following century, in 'The Separation of Home and Work?' Leonore Davidoff has written on landladies and lodgers in the nineteenth and twentieth centuries. She sees the practice from the landladies' point of view as laborious work on a continuum with their general domestic labour which assisted with household income and so independence. Davidoff finds lodging as a housing solution to be in decline by the end of her period.[23] *Lodgers, Landlords, and Landladies in Georgian London* builds on all these foundations but goes further to provide the first full-length study of the practice of lodging in the period. It therefore acts as a corrective to over-simplified narratives of Georgian housing, family, and domesticity.

This study of lodging also intersects with many other aspects of social and cultural history of the period. It adds to our understanding of the impact of urbanization and of the architecture of 'ordinary' houses by introducing a more detailed consideration of the actual use made of designed spaces, especially those that were communal in a house in multi-occupation. Eighteenth-century town houses are often described as embodying an 'architecture of privacy' in which rooms were no longer *en filade*, one opening off another, but opened individually off halls, corridors, and landings.[24] Contemporary commentators such as architect Isaac Ware (1704–66) thought of these 'common houses in London' as both standardized and idealized, being:

> all built in one way, and that so familiar that it will need little instruction, nor deserve much illustration. The general custom is to make two rooms and a light closet on a floor, and if there be any little opening behind, to pave it.

These were houses planned, Ware thought, 'for the reception of a family of two or three people, with three or four servants'.

Ware considered that each room in such houses had its own distinct function: kitchen, dining-room, parlour, bed-chamber, garret for servants. He noted with some distaste the prevalence of a little shop on the ground floor, 'stealing' floorspace from a rear parlour, and also suggested that rather than two ground-floor rooms – a fore parlour narrowed by the entrance hall and a rear parlour – a better arrangement would be a large front hall and a rear parlour. Ware's idealism ignored the practical reality of the life-styles of the occupants of 'common houses' in areas such as Soho's Compton and Greek Streets. Retailers inevitably needed a separate front room for their shop, and the many households who, as we shall see, relied upon an income from lodgers, naturally preferred the 'common' layout with as many distinct rooms as possible, either to let as bedrooms or, in the case of the fore parlour, to use as a communal social space.[25] Elizabeth McKellar points out this less romantic truth about London's new houses: they were for an increasingly commercialized, mass-consumption market that assumed the continual renewal and replacement of products. They could be successful only if they met social and cultural needs and were commercially viable.[26]

Indeed, ironically it was the 'architecture of privacy' with its separation of rooms that allowed the easy taking of lodgers, with the loss of household privacy, in the first place. For rooms which opened off halls and landings could, of course, also be closed off for a lodger's use. A plan for a house in Great Russell Street could have been made with lodging in mind. There were to be 'very good' brass locks to the rooms on the middle floors, but with a master key, a door between the two second-floor rooms and a closet partition. Such a flexible house layout was perfect for the taking-in of lodgers, and its features resemble many of those met in the following chapters of this book.[27] One consequence of the presence of lodgers in houses such as this was that both hosts and their lodgers lived in more confined, shared, and multipurpose spaces than either Tallis's images or Ware's volumes suggested. This fact prompts a rethink of the indoor space available to Londoners and its implication for the life that they led outside the home in public spaces such as taverns and coffeehouses. That rethink includes a better understanding of the working practices of many famous lodgers who created art and literature while eating, socializing, and sleeping in the same one room. This is an aspect of their lives generally overlooked in, for example, the *Oxford Dictionary of National Biography*, but not in memoirs or lives written by themselves or by contemporaries who understood, and maybe shared, this way of life.

We also need to think about lodging in the context of the commercialization of society, and especially its impact on the gendering of work in the period. Economists Josiah Child (1631–99) and, later, Adam Smith (1723–90) framed accommodation provided to London's in-migrants by private landlords/ladies as both part of and vital to the nation's trade. For Child, this extended to the poor:

The Riches of a *City*, as of a *Nation*, consisting in the multitude of Inhabitants …
you must allow Inmates [i.e. lodgers]*, or have a City of Cottages* … For *the resort
of Poor to a City or Nation well managed, is in effect, the conflux of Riches to that
city or Nation*.[28]

For Smith lodging, in the broad sense of accommodation, was, with food and
clothing, one of the three necessities of life and was acquired by labour through
the essential commercial processes of treaty, barter, and purchase.[29] For both
men the lodgings market was part of a virtuous economic circle. It shared many
of the features of a newly-consumerist society – advertising, browsing, choice –
and as a 'necessity' was not freighted with the taint of the amoral luxury that
sapped the national spirit decried by eighteenth-century moral polemicists such
as Anglican clergyman John Brown (1715–66), author of the popular *Estimate of
the Manners and Principles of the Times*.[30]

Some contemporary sources (legal guidebooks for example) routinely
gendered offering or taking lodgings as a male practice, and a rich seam of
literature and images (see Chapter 2) depicted the landlady and single female
lodger as women involved in the sex trade. Closer reading of a wider range of
sources reveals that this was rarely the case. On the contrary London's many
private landladies, both single and married, were respectable businesswomen
undertaking skilled commercial work. Female lodgers did, perhaps inevitably,
include some sex-workers, but also many women for whom, as Chapter 3 shows,
lodging offered an independent way of life free from the control of their families
especially their male relatives. Writer Aphra Behn (?1640–89), businesswoman
Hester Pinney (1658–1740), poet and scholar Elizabeth Carter (1717–1806), and
actor and author Elizabeth Inchbald (1753–1821) are among the independent
singlewoman lodgers whom this study discusses.

Finally, lodging played an important and under-appreciated part in the
Georgian culture of sociability and social mixing. Social mixing is often discussed
in the contexts of public amenities such as pleasure gardens, walks, resorts,
assembly rooms, and the theatre – sites where men and women of different classes
accidentally rubbed shoulders – and of 'polite' visiting in the home, where most
socializing took place, as Benjamin Heller points out.[31] Lodgers were as sociable
as anyone else in the capital. They too visited friends and received visitors. Some
also mixed with their landlords/ladies and fellow-lodgers, drinking tea and
playing cards, and joining them and their families on trips and outings. These
were activities that again compromised the space of the home and the privacy of
all its occupants. However, leisure and socializing in this context, as we shall see,

required careful negotiation and diplomacy. Lodging often entailed a further sort of compulsory mixing within a house, that of different social classes or, in the contemporary discourse, 'sorts'.[32] This was not the mere shoulder-rubbing in public spaces referred to above. It was unavoidable and everyday. Within a house with lodgers there was often a heightened consciousness of social class: between landlord/lady and lodgers, and between lodgers in rooms of different status, especially when disputes arose. This mixing was certainly not democratizing. It could provoke bitter conflict. Whether for good or bad, it was therefore one means of transmitting knowledge of the manners and attitudes of others that informed nineteenth-century class formation.

The verb 'to lodge' and its derivatives were both broad and imprecise terms, as the 1851 census returns show (see above). The meaning could be both specific (lodging in a room in someone's house) and more general (any place where one passed the night), and even metaphorical: one can lodge a request or a complaint. Kings, queens, judges, and prisoners in the eighteenth century all had lodgings. Rooms in inns were called lodgings (and still are in the United States). In the mid-century, Samuel Johnson, who had personal experience of a range of London lodging-rooms, defined the verb 'To Lodge' as having four meanings: 'To reside; to keep residence', 'To take a temporary habitation', 'To take up residence at night' and 'To lay flat'. 'A Lodger' was 'One who lives in rooms hired in the house of another' or 'One that resides in any place', and 'Lodgings' meant 'Temporary habitation; rooms hired in the house of another', 'Place of residence', 'Harbour; covert' or 'Convenience to sleep on'.[33] For the purposes of this study a 'lodger' is a person who rents a room or rooms in the home of a resident occupant householder, much the same therefore as Johnson's lead definition. This definition therefore excludes institutional lodgings (colleges, hospitals, prisons), hotels and inns, and the buildings known as 'common lodging houses'. Common lodging houses were subdivided buildings, a room per singleton or family or even a shared room and bed. They did not always have a resident landlord/lady and were typically the dwellings of the poor. Although they are worthy of study, they are beyond the scope of this book, except where the contrast between 'private' and 'common' lodgings is important. They are also a reminder that there was more than one 'world of lodgings'. Contemporary newspaper advertisements offering accommodation were naturally aimed at the better class of lodger and frequently made this distinction between private and common lodging very clear:

it is by no means a common lodging or boarding house; none therefore who
would chuse, or are used to such places, need apply,

declared one placed in the *Morning Chronicle* in May 1772. Those advertising
their need for accommodation in the paper were equally keen to avoid the
common lodging house:

Wanted in the West-end of the town … a neat first floor and ground parlor
[*sic*] … the price must be moderate, and no common lodging house.[34]

As to the time period covered, strictly speaking 'Georgian' comprises the
116 years of the reigns of the four consecutive King Georges: 1714–1830.
Georgian is interpreted here a little more loosely, starting in the final decades
of the seventeenth century. This captures the westward expansion of the post-
Restoration, post-Fire capital, and the development of a well-understood
London lodgings market in the late-Stuart years, creating what Susan Whyman
calls 'a floating mass of lodgers crowded into rooms'.[35] Indeed, the prevalence
of lodgers from this period in the newly-built areas of London such as Soho
indicates that lodging played a part in the long chain of development financing
identified by McKellar, albeit very much at its consumer tail end.[36] As Chapter
3 indicates, without lodgers the rents demanded for the new houses would have
been unaffordable for many who colonized these districts.

The late-seventeenth century also supplies early qualitative material: both
fiction such as that of poet and playwright John Dryden's (1631–1700) comedy
The Wild Gallant, and lives such as Aphra Behn and fellow-writer William
Congreve (1670–1729), and some quantitative evidence. Recovery from the
political instability and fears generated by the Popish Plot (1678–81), Exclusion
Crisis (1679–81), and Glorious Revolution (1688), and the financing of the
wars of William III resulted in the gathering of various population lists by
the authorities aiming at 'the determination of the landed classes and of the
established church … to re-establish and maintain their economic superiority,
spiritual power and social control'. The surviving Marriage Duty Assessments
(see Chapter 3) and the work of political economist Gregory King (1648–1712)
provide a baseline, albeit a slippery one, for the scale and social character of
lodging from which eighteenth-century developments can be judged.[37]

This study is restricted to London. By this is meant the wider metropolis
within which it was possible to travel daily to and from the twin centres of the
commercial City and of Westminster, home of the Court and the entertainment
district of the West End. This was a radius of perhaps three to four miles from

these centres, at a pinch five miles which would include Hampstead. This area closely matches the perambulation of London undertaken by historian and biographer Dr Thomas Birch (1705–66). Birch set out from his house in Norfolk Street, Strand towards Chelsea, then at the waterworks turned north to Marylebone. Skirting the town, he crossed Islington Road at Angel, walked through Hoxton to Shoreditch, Bethnal Green, Stepney, Limehouse, and Poplar, took a boat to Deptford, then passed through Bermondsey on the Old Kent Road to Newington, over St George's Fields to Lambeth, crossed the Thames again to Millbank, and was back at Charing Cross and Norfolk Street. The twenty-mile route took him six hours.[38] Lawyer and music scholar Sir John Hawkins (1719–89), who recorded Birch's walk round London's perimeter, thought London had expanded by the time of his writing (1787), and indeed the area covered by John Cary's 1790 *General Plan* of London's turnpike gates (Figure 1) is greater, taking in Kensington, Paddington, Holloway, and Mile End.[39]

That this was the extent of London in the minds of its residents is borne out by the evidence of the choices lodgers made. In the early century, from April to

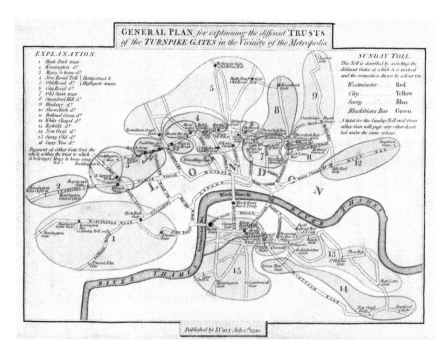

Figure 1 John Cary, *General Plan for Explaining the Different Trusts of the Turnpike Gates in the Vicinity of the Metropolis*, 1790. Author's collection, photography by Urban Picnic, Saffron Walden.

July 1711, Irish clergyman and author Jonathan Swift (1667–1745) lodged in Chelsea for its rural quality of better air and the exercise of walking to London, although he found it inconveniently inaccessible in wet weather when walking was impossible and stagecoaches hard to find, leading him to move back to more central Suffolk Street.[40] Half a century later, American Loyalist refugee, merchant Samuel Curwen (1715–1802), lived in lodgings both in the central parts of town and in Islington, Battersea, and Knightsbridge while in London during the Revolutionary War.[41] Artists Benjamin Haydon (1786–1846) and George Morland (1763–1804) each lived in 'humble' lodgings in Paddington when down on their luck.[42] For these lodgers London very definitely included the semi-rural former villages at the very edge of Richard Horwood's late-century map, the places traversed by Birch and mapped by Cary.[43] Some *Morning Chronicle* advertisements for rooms to let and rooms wanted referred to connectivity between the peripheral villages and suburbs and central London. A thirty-year-old 'Single Gentleman' sought lodgings for two nights a week within two miles of St Paul's. An advertisement in 1794 for board and lodging in Pentonville referred to the hourly coaches to the Royal Exchange and Strand, as did one for rooms in Chester Place, Lambeth.[44]

Over the Georgian period to 1830 London had indeed grown substantially from a population of around 490,000 in 1700 to one and a half million by the time of the 1831 census, absorbing many of the surrounding villages in the process as the Cary map suggests.[45] It had also become qualitatively different. By the nineteenth century it was firmly established as the capital city not just of a nation but of an empire built largely on the spoils of war. There were cultural and commercial institutions in new buildings which announced this, many of them in the classical style reminding their viewers of the earlier great empires of Athens and Rome: Sir John Soane's (1753–1837) Bank of England in the City, Sir Robert Smirke's (1780–1867) British Museum, and William Wilkin's (1776–1839) National Gallery and University College, London, to the West, and James Johnson's and Smirke's Royal Mint and docks to the East. At the same time some elements of old authority were breaking down – the power of the City livery companies over the apprenticeship system, and church courts, for example – to be replaced by the more private morality identified by, among others, Faramerz Dabhoiwala. This in turn saw a shift towards new attempts at social control, such as the charities, societies, and campaigns variously aimed at reforming 'manners', often entailing clearing the streets of prostitutes, idle poor, and the generally profane.[46] This study explores the continued prevalence of lodging as an essential part of the housing market against this background of change.

The reason for studying London is a practical one: a national study would be so large as to be unwieldy. Indeed, even for the metropolis a search for 'lodgings' between 1700 and 1830 in Old Bailey Online produces an unwieldy 5,013 results.[47] London was by a huge margin the largest city in Britain. It constantly drew in men and women from across the British Isles and beyond. Much of their demand for housing was met by the largest and most vibrant lodgings market in Britain. Of course, London cannot stand in for England, let alone Britain. There were swathes of rural Britain where lodgers were few and far between. But there were plenty of lodgers in many of the nation's expanding cities and towns of all sizes. Kevin Schurer's analysis of the Marriage Duty Assessments from 1695 to 1705 in six different regions found lodgers were by far the most numerous in London (a mean of 1.7 per houseful of mean size 6.1), but were also present in Shrewsbury (a mean of 0.5 per houseful of 4.5), Bristol (0.2 in 3.9) and Southampton (0.2 in 4.0). In rural areas – Kent and Wiltshire – on the other hand, the figures were 0.1 (in housefuls of 4.7 and 3.9).[48] S. J. Wright has written about lodgers in eighteenth-century Ludlow, a market town of 2,500–3,000 by 1750, concluding that lodgers were present in one in seven households, constituted between 8 and 10 per cent of the adult population, and were largely short-term residents with a bias towards 'the elite', although the poor were also represented.[49] Di Cooper and Moira Donald have considered the evidence for 'hidden' kin lodging in early-nineteenth-century Exeter.[50] London lodgers discussed in this book sometimes spent periods away from the metropolis lodging in provincial cities and towns in much the same way as they did in London. Curwen lodged in Exeter and Bristol, for example. Some provincial urban centres developed specialist lodging markets: the English and Scottish university towns, districts around hospitals with medical schools, spas, and tourist resorts – Bath, Buxton, Margate, and Scarborough, among others. In these centres new houses were sometimes developed specifically for letting in this way.[51] These lodging markets are also outside the scope of this study, but there are some features they shared with London lodgings. A provincial example will therefore occasionally be used to make a general point and, conversely, scholars of the provinces and regions may find much in the discussion of London's housing arrangements that is also relevant to them.

The aim throughout has been to use a large number of varied sources in order to paint as broad a picture of lodging practices as possible. They include such local censuses as exist, the lists of lodgers that arose from serendipitous events like the Compton Street fire, wills and inventories, crime reports, civil legal cases and guides, published letters and life-writing, articles and advertisements in the press – especially the leading London daily, the *Morning Chronicle* (the 'Chronicle') – fiction, drama, and images. All these sources have their problems. In the first place there is, of course, the general historical problem of the chance nature of record survival. There is in addition no record series that allows a quantitative or qualitative comparison of lodging across time. The closest to a qualitative series is probably the approximately 400 advertisements placed in the *Chronicle* by London landlords/ladies and prospective lodgers in the thirty years 1770–1800.[52] Letters and life-writing tend to privilege male authors over female and the socially advantaged over the less so, though a particular effort has been made to include as many voices as possible of the great variety of Georgian Londoners who sought a degree of respectability in their accommodation: the genteel and the artisan, temporary residents, women, those whose origins lay in the provinces, Ireland, or abroad, the estimated 15,000 non-white population.[53] Fiction (including drama and images) is exactly that; it is not strictly factual but does delineate a 'horizon of expectations' about lodging that was culturally dominant in eighteenth-century society and which can be compared to the lived experience recovered from life-writing.[54]

However, the sheer volume and density of available material on London lodgings overcomes some of these issues, allowing the creation of a thick description of the practice that can help us understand what it was like to live in a house with lodgers. Life-writing is invaluable as a source for mundane details that are often overlooked by, for example, biographers. Its limitation is an inherent class, occupational, and gender bias. It over-represents certain occupations. Artists, actors, and authors, for example, are all perhaps more able and willing than the average person to put pen to paper and write about themselves – and maybe to embellish a little in the process. There are also very few examples of life-writing by a landlord or landlady. Taking in lodgers may have been something they preferred to gloss over but probably they had little reason or time to record it. Exceptions to this are actor Charlotte Charke (1713–60), writer Thomas Holcroft (1745–1809), advocate of women's rights Mary Wollstonecraft (1759–97), Radical tailor Francis Place (1771–1854), and Essex tailor Thomas Carter (b. 1792). These men and women experienced lodging on both sides of the bargain, though they are more reticent about their time as landlords/ladies. The landlord/lady experience and viewpoint must therefore be obtained by careful reading against the grain of lodgers' accounts.

Novels, plays, and images are used as a historical source to provide a cultural setting for the Georgian audience's understanding of lodging. Many authors had, as subsequent chapters show, considerable personal knowledge of life as a lodger. They mined the familiar relationship between landlord/lady and lodger as a rich vein of dramatic tension and comedy that reflected a reality of London life. Those among their contemporary audience who had experienced lodging acted as an 'interpretive community'. The depiction had to be true enough to produce 'nods of recognition' from them.[55] It also encouraged them to interpret their future experiences through the lens of these representations. For those who had not, or not yet, experienced lodgings these representations were an equally powerful set of scenarios and stereotypes. Conduct guides were another important Georgian genre. They helped an increasingly geographically and socially mobile population manoeuvre without embarrassment through the events and situations they might encounter. There were guides for servants, for ladies and for the newly-genteel.[56] There was little in the way of advice to the etiquette of lodging, however. In their absence, the scenarios and stereotypes of lodging in fiction presented a range of possible occurrences and of means to resolve them.

The chapters that follow are arranged to follow the process of taking, living in, and leaving lodgings. This mirrors the lived experience of lodging for both landlords/ladies and lodgers as a cycle not dissimilar to the eighteenth-century genre of novel known to us as the 'It Narrative'. Produced throughout the century, an It Narrative followed the circulation of an object (sometimes an animal) and told the history of its passing from owner to owner. Lodging often played a part in these narratives, as it did in other fictions of the period. Both the It Narrative and lodging were also products of the commercialization of eighteenth-century English life that the economists Child and Smith praised. This chapter arrangement also enables a descriptive approach to the world of lodgings not readily available elsewhere, alongside an analytical one. This study is in itself a guide and by the conclusion readers should feel equipped to tackle the Georgian lodging market for themselves.

Chapter 2, 'Making the landlords, landlady, and lodger', looks at how texts, both fictional and factual, and images created offered cultural interpretations of these three stock characters and the relationships they created. These cultural concepts were often encountered by the reader or viewer before any actual attempt was made to find either a room or a lodger. Chapter 3, 'Meet the landlord, landladies, and their lodgers', moves from the realm of the imagined to the real to consider available evidence for the class, gender, and life-cycle stage of landlords/ladies and lodgers. It also establishes the importance of place: the inhabitants of the West End *versus* 'Cits', the respectable *versus* the less so ('sailortown' in the eastern parishes around the docks, for example). In Chapter 4, 'Matchmaking', the means by which the parties met, negotiated, and made their bargain are reviewed followed by Chapter 5, 'Moving in and rubbing along', which examines the ways in which the lodger made a home of his/her room(s), and the small pleasures and frictions that arose as host and guest learned to live alongside one another. Sometimes this led to an acrimonious parting of the ways. Other lodgers were long stayers – American Founding Father and ambassador to England Benjamin Franklin (1706–90) in Craven Street – or moved on when their circumstances changed, perhaps when affluent enough to take a lease of their own – the historian of Rome Edward Gibbon (1737–94) and tailor Francis Place. It was quite possible to remain on good terms, friends even, after parting. All these endings, good and bad, are the subject of Chapter 6, 'Moving out, Moving on'.

Finally, in Chapter 7 the Conclusion draws all the findings together to consider the role of lodging within Georgian society. It argues that lodging was a key means of accommodating the swelling population of the capital. It facilitated the in-migration and visiting for business that was essential to London's continued economic growth. At the same time, it satisfied landlords' and ladies' needs for additional cash income and financial security. It was well-placed to do both these things as it was almost infinitely flexible, each lodger contract being unique and capable of variation as the lodging term progressed. Analysis of lodging also uncovers the independence of many Georgian women: both those who, like Behn, lodged, and the thousands of landladies, working women who were making a significant contribution to the market economy while often remaining hidden from view as 'housewives'. It reveals too the increasingly sharp class differences in society and the acute awareness of them. Finally, it is a reminder that the attractive rows of Georgian terraces were often very densely occupied and not only by the householder's family. A house was a home, it was domestic, but equally it was a prime asset exploited to the maximum for money.

2

Making the landlord, landlady, and lodger

This chapter looks at the preconceptions that eighteenth-century people brought to their experience of lodging relationships. Before they took rooms or a lodger, while a lodging relationship endured, when it ended and even if they never were or took a lodger they were surrounded by representations of landlords, landladies, and lodgers in a range of situations both fictional and real. Lodging played a central part in novels and plays, and in satirical prints. It also featured in non-fiction: in published life-writing, in press reports and in guidebooks to London and to the law of landlord and tenant. All these representations supplied a range of stereotype characters and situations that could then be used by their audience to interpret, guide, and measure the actual lodging relationships that they experienced.

Some representations were realistic, others fanciful, exaggerated, or comic. In order to do their cultural work, however, they had to resonate with the audience. Author Clara Reeve (1729–1807) defended the role of the novel on this basis, saying in *The Progress of Romance* (1785): 'the Novel gives a familiar relation of such things, as pass every day before our eyes, such as may happen to our friend, or to ourselves.'[1] J. Paul Hunter explains that in many of these novels (it is true of plays and images too) the narrative 'usually reflected the values of "modern" London life and represented to those – especially the young – who aspired to migrate to London what sophisticated lives could be like.'[2] For migrants to London, many of whom were young, that 'sophisticated life' was perforce led, at least at first, in lodgings (see Chapter 3). As in life, fictional lodging was so prevalent in texts and images of the period that of necessity this chapter can only cover a small number of works, the well-known and the less so. These have been arranged chronologically within genres. While these genres were not always as recognizable to their writers as to the modern reader, it assists in demonstrating the historical nature of the themes that emerge and the changes in them during the eighteenth century.

———————

Stock representations of lodging were of long-standing and very deeply embedded in English culture. Geoffrey Chaucer's *Miller's Tale*, one of the *Canterbury Tales* (*c.* 1387–1400), is an early vernacular text about a landlord, landlady, and lodger. The tale has an urban setting (Oxford), contrasting social classes (John, a carpenter, and Nicholas, his poor scholar-lodger), a nosy landlord (John spies on Nicholas through a hole in the door), and, a result of introducing a stranger-lodger to the household, an illicit sexual liaison (between Nicholas and the carpenter's much younger wife, Alison).[3] Class, sex, nosiness, and the poor scholar were themes that persisted to the eighteenth century and beyond.

In the late-sixteenth century London experienced rapid population growth.[4] Much of this was in-migration and was accommodated by householders opening up their spare rooms to lodgers, sometimes called 'sojourners'. It is no coincidence that these years also saw the establishment in autobiographical works of the impoverished scholar-lodger, of whom Chaucer's Nicholas was the ancestor, as a standard character in English literature.[5] The lodgers in these texts were always men. Though women were lodgers too, they were rarely either scholars or writers.[6] The scholar-lodger was strongly identified with London, and with garret-living in particular. His 'vagabond lifestyle' introduced further elements that would remain culturally familiar in the Georgian era: the suggestion of impermanence and debt, and a perceived association between lodgings and brothels.

The persona of the reprobate poet was adopted and adapted from their own lives by a cluster of English writers: Robert Greene (1558–92), Gabriel Harvey (?1550–1631), and Thomas Nashe (*c.* 1567–*c.* 1601). Harvey, a lodger himself, sneered at Greene's 'continuall shifting of lodgeings' and his 'beggarly departing in every hostisses [i.e. landlady's] debt'. He alleged Greene could afford only one shirt and that his landlady Mrs Isam lent him both money and a spare shirt while his was in the wash. When Greene died at her house in the Thameside ward of Dowgate she paid for his winding-sheet and burial.[7] Reading between Harvey's unkind lines there is, therefore, a hint of caring affection between Mrs Isam and her celebrity lodger. Thomas Nashe positively revelled in self-referential display of his spartan, yet roistering, life. He and his alter-ego 'Pierce Penniless' were habitués of the seedy districts on the City's outskirts, lodging in places like a 'Chamber in Cole-Harbour, where they live in a continuall myst between two Brew-houses'.[8] Cole [Cold] Harbour in Upper Thames Street in the City had the right of sanctuary and so was associated with debtors. Here Nashe/Penniless allegedly shared his bed and one pair of

breeches with his colleague Lusher.[9] Thomas Middleton (1580–1627) wrote a
sequel to *Pierce Penniless*, in which he vividly described Nashe's pitiful room
at Mrs Silverpin's in Pickt-Hatch Walk (an area of Clerkenwell notorious for
prostitution), up two dark pairs of stairs and where:

> the sullen blaze of a melancholy lamp that burnt very tragically upon the narrow
> desk of a half-bedstead … the bare privities of the stone-walls were hid with two
> pieces of painted cloth, but so ragged and tottered … the tester, or the shadow
> over the bed … made of four ells of cobwebs.[10]

Harvey, Greene, and friends were primarily writing for their own circles. The
garreteer and landlord/lady stereotypes were taken up in non-autobiographical
writing which aimed at a wider audience. Dryden's *Wild Gallant* (first performed
in 1663, and not a particular success) continued the tradition. The Bibbers, a tailor
and his wife whose surname implies fondness for a drink or two, are landlord and
lady to the eponymous wild gallant, Mr Loveby. His failure to pay for rent and
board and, a hint of sexual impropriety, 'many a good thing besides, that shall
be nameless', sees him threatened with the cheaper room in the garret 'where the
little bed is'. Mrs Bibby thinks he knows the room already – another hint of sex.
Loveby describes it as a 'little ease' (a tiny cell) that recalls Penniless' lodgings:

> A penny Looking-glass cannot stand upright in the window; that and the Brush
> fills it: the Hat-case must be dispos'd under the Bed, and the Comb-case will hang
> down from the Seeling to the Floore. If I chance to Dine in my Chamber, I must
> stay till I am empty before I can get out: and if I chance to spill the Chamber-pot,
> it will over-flow it from top to bottom.[11]

Moving into the early-eighteenth century, Daniel Defoe (?1660–1731)
continued this exploitation of the literary potential of a life spent shifting from
lodging to lodging in his 'proto-novels … rogue histories, scandal chronicles
and romantic novellas'.[12] Defoe used his characters' shifting accommodation,
including lodgings, more dynamically than his literary predecessors to mirror
and so emphasize the ups-and-downs of their lives. In Defoe lodgings can,
therefore, be alternately low-life one minute and changed for something
respectable the next. He is always quite specific about their geography within the
metropolis to make this point. Locations are both real and serve to define social
status and morality. Orphaned boy Colonel Jack 'lodges' while homeless, in the
summer 'about the watch-houses and on bulkheads and shop-doors' and in the
winter by the warmth of glass manufactories to the east of the City. But Jack is

ambitious, aiming for a 'society lodging', as he ironically puts it. He achieves his goal when he becomes a pickpocket's accomplice and the pair lodge together in 'a little garret fit for our quality'. He later establishes himself in a room of his own.[13] Jack is upwardly mobile and this lodging at last provides a degree of stability and privacy: it is to him a home.

In *Moll Flanders* (1722), Defoe depicted lodgings and their locations in even greater detail to indicate the volatile turns of her life. Moll's picaresque career entails a seemingly endless cycle through a variety of rooms in London and elsewhere – the latter a reminder of the vibrant market for lodgings outside the capital. Some lodgings are clearly respectable: as a young widow she lodges at a London linen draper's, and after her second husband absconds she takes rooms in the Mint as 'Mrs. Flanders, widow', the title, like the rooms, a claim to gentility. However, she later lodges with a friend at Rotherhithe in the docks and at a house of dubious repute in Bath (already a rising spa town under Master of Ceremonies Richard 'Beau' Nash, 1674–1761). Here Moll lives rent-free in the winter low season and, come spring, entertains a fellow 'gentleman' lodger in her bed, later retrenching by moving to the cheaper second floor and one room rather than two. This episode picks up the thread of the lodging as brothel or house of ill-repute. The pair then spend six quieter years in rural Hammersmith living as husband and wife, she unaware that he is married with a house in Bloomsbury. After this is revealed, financial hardship leads Moll to move to the cheaper north, then back to London and St John's Street, Clerkenwell, at 6s. a week (£15 12s. a year). Moll considers this rent so low that the landlady must be making her profit on the 'extras': bringing to childbed 'ladies of pleasure', again a sexual element to lodging in a location hard by the seedy haunts of Thomas Nashe 150 years previously. She has five years of respectable housekeeping married to a banker but after his bankruptcy and death returns to lodging and low-life subsistence plying her needle and thieving in the same fringe districts Nashe knew: Smithfield, Newgate, Little Britain, Stepney, Whitechapel.[14] As she leaves Hammersmith Moll describes the portable material poverty of this transience:

> what little I had in the World was all in Money, except as before, a little Plate, some Linnen, and my Cloaths; as for Household stuff I had little or none, for I had liv'd always in Lodgings.[15]

For Moll, then, lodging is an integral part of the flexible and opportunistic economy of make-shift, which may include but is not defined by sex work. It is only broken by the improbable: a chance meeting while in Newgate prison awaiting the death sentence with a former husband, their reconciliation, commutation of their sentences to transportation and sailing off together to a fresh start in the New World.

Defoe returned to the themes of high and low, respectability, and sex work in *Roxana* (1724).[16] Moll's and Roxana's stories, popular in new editions throughout the eighteenth century, were dominated by notions of circulation and flow: of lovers, accommodation, and money. His heroines note the price of their rooms, and Roxana takes regular inventories of the wealth she has acquired. For Defoe moving through lodgings was a microcosm of the fast-spinning world of commerce and trade, a subject on which he also wrote.[17] The political debate on the economic benefits of wealth amassed through trade in 'luxuries' *versus* the traditional Christian virtue of thrift was captured by his contemporary, Bernard Mandeville, in the *Fable of the Bees* (1705), a firm assertion of the former case. Mandeville (?1670–1733) was personally aware of the role of lodging in providing flexible accommodation in this new world – he had himself lived in 'obscure lodgings' while struggling to establish a medical practice in London.[18] The passage, or circulation, of an individual or individuals through lodgings was, then, both a consequence of and a form of commerce. Whereas in the sixteenth and seventeenth centuries London's civic authorities had attempted to limit and control lodging, they now proved powerless to halt it. By the eighteenth century lodging was, as Josiah Child proposed, increasingly deemed necessary and so socially acceptable.

Unsurprisingly, therefore, lodging continued to feature in eighteenth-century fiction of all types, just as it did in real life. The stereotypes established from Chaucer onwards were expanded and developed: venal, prying, artisan landlords/ladies, lodgers down on their luck, low-life and impermanence, the social geographies and distinctions of East End, City and West End, and the sex trade or, at the very least, a sexual frisson. However, eighteenth-century writers and artists now introduced into their work a greater variety of more rounded middling-sort characters and their moral values. The 'middling sort' was a segment of British society increasingly evident from the seventeenth century onwards, 'sort' rather than 'class' being the usual contemporary term. Middling-sort people did not fit neatly into the traditional binary classifications of the landed interest and the rest, of patrician and plebeian. It was a broad category and hard to pin down precisely, but can perhaps be best defined as 'independent persons' engaged in 'the translating of work into money' – professionals, dealers, and retailers such as those found in Compton Street in 1785, for example – with an annual income of somewhere between £40 and £200. These middling people accounted for around 1 million people in a British population of approximately 8 million and were especially associated with towns and cities. They can also be defined by their cultural outlook, based on the shared values of domesticity, hard work, and self-improvement identified by Margaret Hunt.[19] The middling sort not only featured in these new-style novels and plays, they were a key audience for them.

Many authors now went beyond the old, simple trope of the garret to locate their lodgers with precision on particular floors of a house. This 'language of floors' was so well understood as to be the butt of satire in *Olla Podrida*, a short-lived magazine published by Revd Thomas Monro (1764–1815):

> the Lodger in the first floor scarcely designs to return the bow of the occupier of the second in the same house, who, on all occasions, makes himself amends by speaking with the utmost contempt of the Garretteers over head, with many shrewd jokes on Sky Parlours. The precedency between the Garret and the Cellar seems evidently in favour of the former, Garrets having time out of mind been the residence of the Literati …
>
> Besides the distinctions of Altitude, there is that of forward and backward: I have heard a lady, who lodged in the fore room of the second story [*sic*], on being asked after another who lodged in the same house, scornfully describe her by the Appellation of the Woman living in the back room.[20]

Before looking at some of this fictional writing, we turn first to the art of William Hogarth (1697–1764). Hogarth's work both provides a link to earlier representations of London's garreteers and was also a profound influence on many later artists and writers. Prints of Hogarth's work were a popular purchase and were also used on decorative objects such as fans.[21] They were therefore as important as text in creating impressions of lodging for men and women of the middling sort and above. Prints were vivid and could reach lower in the social spectrum too: literate and illiterate, rich and poor, all Londoners could see for free these and the other images discussed below displayed in print-shop windows.[22]

Hogarth set many of his characters in a London of circulation through lodging-rooms. The six paintings/engravings in his *Harlot's Progress* series (1731) depicted the life story of naïve country-girl-come-to-town, Moll Hackabout, in part through the stages of her lodgings. As in Defoe's work, these reflect the vicissitudes of life, but they were not just amusing. They now pointed a moral about the importance of 'proper' work and sexual continence that was so important to the middling sort and underlay the various reformation of manners movements (Chapter 1). For Hogarth's Moll, unlike Defoe's, her lodgings map a relentlessly downward trajectory, underlining firmly the popular association between the woman lodger and sex work. Picked up by a notorious brothel-keeper even as she steps from the York coach, in Plate 2 she begins her career as a kept woman in the sumptuous surroundings of a drawing room which of course implies the luxury of a separate bedchamber, descends in Plate 3 to the messier multipurpose lodging-room of a common prostitute and, after a stint in Bridewell, ends her life in Plate 5 in a bare room even further down the lodging pecking order.[23] The *Distrest Poet* (*c.* 1736) is, at first blush, a close cousin of the early-modern literary representations of the garret-poet. Hogarth gives us a struggling writer in a gloomy, ill-furnished garret, the cupboards are bare and an angry creditor (a milkmaid) stands at the door (Figure 2).[24] What Hogarth adds, updating the stereotype in tune with the rising culture of domesticity and the family, is an industrious wife and a child for whom the poet is signally failing

Figure 2 William Hogarth, *The Distrest Poet*, 1740 (engraving from painting of 1736). Courtesy of the Lewis Walpole Library, Yale University: 812.00.00.92.

to provide. His fruitless attic toil, like Moll Hackabout's sex work, is not a fit occupation. In the *Industry and Idleness* series (1747) Hogarth again portrays the consequences of masculine morality and immorality.[25] Virtuous, hard-working apprentice Francis Goodchild marries his master's daughter, grows rich, and serves as Sheriff and then Mayor of London, independent in his own house (Plates 6, 8, and 12). His lazy boyhood workmate, Thomas Idle, chooses a reprehensible career path which leads him to contrasting domestic instability in the arms of a common prostitute in a garret lodging-room (Plate 7). Hogarth emphasizes insecurity – the door is propped shut with planks and even the bed is collapsing. Apart from the street, the only place lower than this is the night-cellar (Plate 9), the last resort of the depraved and homeless and so impermanent that a bed might be charged by the night for a penny or so.

Garreteers continued to appear in prints throughout the century. Most lacked the dense story-telling and moral impact of Hogarth, but they did continue to underline the long-running connection between artistic suffering and miserable accommodation. In *The Brain-Sucker; or the Miseries of Authorship* (1787), attributed to Thomas Rowlandson (1756–1827), the shabby room is so small the bed is turned up during the day to make room for working at the table. A furious employer, probably a publisher (he holds a book titled *Odes*), is conspicuously better-fed than the poet.[26] *The Lottery Ticket*, an anonymous pair of prints of 1792, conveys a Hogarthian warning of the danger inherent in seeking a quick fortune without the virtue of labour, and genders this as female, an Eve-like temptation.[27] A carpenter, his wife, son, daughter, and cat dwell in a live-work lodging-room. The first print shows a happy, industrious, domestic scene. Male paid work jostles with the female work of laundry, food provision, and education. It is an idealized microcosm of the virtuous, patriarchal family. Centre-stage, however, the wife brandishes a lottery ticket offering an easy £30,000. The second print assumes that the ticket was a blank. The once-prosperous family is reduced to ragged and starving destitution in a room stripped of everything that can be sold. *A Gentleman of Moderate Income: Making Himself Decent to Dine Out* (Laurie and Whittle, 1796) adds a late-century note of political panic to the well-explored conventions of the attic-lodger. The young man's attempt to present himself respectably through (tattered) clothing is at odds with his room (Figure 3). An advertisement for bug destruction denotes its unsavoury nature and a second poster of Thomas Paine suggests the dangerously radical views such an impermanent room and its tenants might also harbour. Temporary lodgers with no solid roots in their parish now summon all the fears induced in the middling and ruling classes by the French Revolution. As the author of the *Rights of Man*

A GENTLEMAN OF MODERATE INCOME.
Making himself decent to dine out.
Published 28 Nov.1796 by LAURIE & WHITTLE 53 Fleet Street London.

Figure 3 *A Gentleman of Moderate Income, Making Himself Decent to Dine Out*, 1796. This is a sparsely furnished lodging-room, probably a garret judging by the beam. The simple bed, mirror, and razor on the window-ledge and shabbiness of the lodger are reminiscent of the rooms described 200 years earlier. Courtesy of the Lewis Walpole Library, Yale University: 796.11.28.01.

(1791), Paine (1737–1809) was regarded by conservative-minded men and women as a traitor introducing labouring Britons to notions of egalitarianism. The poster aligns Paine with the vermin that the 'bug doctor' professes to kill, and this lodger with a potential fifth column of like-minded radicals moving silently and unobserved through London's hidden garrets.[28]

Other images played more broadly than Hogarth, and again without his moral compass, on the sexual connotations of lodging. Matthew Darly's 1777 *A Lodging House Lady of Bath* (Figure 4) with her elaborate and fashionable

A LODGING *HOUSE LADY OF* BATH.

Figure 4 Matthew Darly, *A Lodging House Lady of Bath*, 1777. Courtesy of the Lewis Walpole Library, Yale University: 777.07.16.01.2+.

clothing, lapdog, and novel is, if intended to represent a landlady, far from practical and business-like in appearance and so and perhaps a madam. If intended to represent a singlewoman lodger she is probably on the hunt for a husband or lover.[29] In his *Cries of London* series of 1799, Rowlandson depicts a watercress-seller, accompanied by her two children, accosting a leering elderly gentleman as he knocks at the street door of a Mrs Burke. Leaning from the first-floor window are two young women, one of them half-naked.[30] The set-up would have been obvious to the contemporary viewer. Watercress was regarded then (and still is) as an aphrodisiac, Mrs Burke is a madam, the gentleman her customer, and the

Figure 5 George Hunt, *Lodgings to Let Alone*, ?1825. One of the comic prints that suggest that a landlady was as available as her rooms, though here the 'joke' is turned on its head: she is too ugly to be of interest. Note the 'To Let' sign in the right-hand window. Courtesy of the Lewis Walpole Library, Yale University: 825.00.00.63.

young women her lodgers working from her first floor. Rowlandson's setting is specific. The house is on (Great) Portland Street, where since the mid-eighteenth century development had edged northwards onto virgin land. It was respectable, characterized by relatively modest houses used for retail and business.[31] Sex might well be one of the trades found there, according to Rowlandson. His print therefore follows the long-standing trope of the female lodger as sex worker.

An eager expectation or 'mis-understanding' that women in lodgings meant sexual shenanigans supplied the long-running 'joke' in three prints spanning 1798–1825.[32] In each of these an attractive young landlady shows a gentleman over a lodging-room, and in each case the man, ogling and touching her, openly regards her person as part of the deal. 'No Sir, I am to be let alone!' she cries. In the George Cruikshank (1792–1878) version the gentleman replies, 'Oh! very well, if you are to be lett alone! I'll hire you, & d–n the lodgings!!!' A twist on the joke is *Lodgings to Let – Alone* of 1825 (Figure 5), where an older, ugly, and over-dressed landlady offers to 'do for ye'. The gentleman cannot exit the situation fast enough.[33] In these prints, landladies are either sirens or undesirably old matrons. As working women, the prints imply, they cannot be taken seriously.

Returning to fiction after this diversion, *Low-Life: Or One Half of the World Knows not how the Other Half Live* is an anonymous satirical hour-by-hour account of a June Sunday in London in the early 1750s. Explicitly descended from Hogarth, it opens with an address to the artist.[34] It describes scenes that Defoe would have recognized. Sunday is no day of rest and worship but a dizzying round of debauchery and dishonesty in which impermanent and dubious lodgings and lodgers play an integral role. These are, unsurprisingly given the title, drawn from the lower end of eighteenth-century society where lodgers are constantly shifting, frequent pawn brokers, and are evicted for non-payment of rent. Garret dwellers climb not only the stairs to their rooms but the social ranks as they struggle to maintain an outer gentility in the circumstances endured by Dryden's gallant, Loveby, or the later *Gentleman of Moderate Income*:

> boiling water in Earthen Chamber-Pots and Pipkins, to wash their sham Necks, ruffled Sleeves, and worn-out roll-up Stockings, that they may make a genteel Appearance in the public streets.

Poverty-stricken authors have temporarily escaped the family noise of confined rooms leaving behind 'poor honest women' who, like Hogarth's poet's wife, darn, wash and iron while awaiting their no-good husbands' return, alternately soothing and scolding their crying infants. Coiners are hard at work counterfeiting the currency while fellow-lodgers sleep. Kept mistresses and landladies sit up until the small hours to unlock the doors for rakes and ruffians who have been on the town. Those who are locked out sit with the constables in the city's watch-houses. There is, however, a touching observation of poorer lodgers as a genuine community:

> going to each other, and after paying their aukward [*sic*] Compliments, borrowing Saucepans and Stewpans, for the dressing Peas, Beans Bacon and Mackerell for Dinner.[35]

In 1806, James Beresford (1764–1840) again imagined such low lodgings for a middling-sort audience in his hugely successful comedy dialogues *The Miseries of Human Life*. His readership was only likely to experience such rooms, if at all, 'on a sudden and desperate emergency' – thrown out of the home by an angry wife perhaps. It is not far from Pierce Penniless two centuries before:

> no fire-place – one crazy chair … All about your bed – a litter of sleepless brats in the hooping-cough hard by, with only a half-inch panel between their throats and your ears – one quarter of an inch of farthing candle … No soap … but one towel … Triangular scrap of looking-glass … No one coming to open your windows … No bell.[36]

These representations of lodging interpreted for the middling-sort reader the disorderly lives of those below them in the pecking order. This is the world of the common lodging house as viewed by a social superior, a world that fascinates the reader, perhaps, but which that reader is now implicitly invited to avoid.

Defoe was not the only writer of fiction interested in the commerce and circulation that drew the attention of the economic writers Child, Mandeville, and Smith. A popular eighteenth-century fictional genre already discussed in Chapter 1 was the It Narrative. The changing fortunes of the circulating object, the 'It', purported to reveal truths about society in much the way that Moll Flanders's and Roxana's histories had done.[37] Samuel Johnson, who had seen his fair share of London lodgings, created an alternative It Narrative in a 1751 *Rambler* article, 'The Revolutions of a Garret', where a rented room is the setting through which characters pass. The *Rambler* lodging-room is avowedly society in miniature – 'a single house will shew whatever is done or suffered in the world' – a panopticon from which Johnson surveys, albeit in a higher literary style, much the same territory of debt, cheating, crime, and sex as *Low-Life*. A tailor is the first tenant. He stays a month, pays for a week, and does a flit with a customer's cloth. A Moll-Hackabout-type, just arrived from the country, follows but is let go when too-frequent visits from a Cheapside 'cousin' threaten the reputation of the house. After her comes an elderly gentleman of apparently good character, keeping himself to himself, but who (again like *Low-Life*) is revealed to be a coiner. Next an author fills the garret room with books. Although he sleeps until noon, he proves noisy from evening to midnight as he paces and rages over his work until evicted for setting fire to his curtains. That lodgers were careless around fire since the house was not their asset was a standing joke in an age when house fires from unattended candles or hearths were common. In Rowlandson's 1799 print for use as a wallpaper border a watchman shouts 'Master your House is on Fire'. From an upper storey a bleary night-capped man replies, 'Don't make such a bawling Fellow. I'm only a Lodger.'[38] Several more short-lived and unsatisfactory lodgers later the *Rambler*'s landlady finally takes in two single women, sisters, one sick, the other her nurse. When the former dies the second pays her debts and leaves.[39] In Johnson's version of the It Narrative it is the room that seems to speak but in effect we, unusually, see lodging from the point of view of the landlady. Johnson suggests her hard work of monitoring and enduring the quirks (and worse) of lodgers, and the reader is left feeling that she has probably seen enough of society in the round.

The *Rambler* lodgers came from a rich variety of backgrounds, just as did Hannah Barker's lodgers in Compton Street in 1785. It is the nuances of social class that form a crucial plot element in Henry Fielding's *Amelia* of the same year. Amelia and William Booth constantly change their lodgings. This is the consequence of precarious financial circumstances, for they are otherwise genteel. There is a moral content here: Booth is irresponsible and foolish. Like Hogarth's poet he is a failed paterfamilias. He has neither provided for nor protected his young family with a proper, permanent home. They are instead compelled to lodge in the Verge of the Court, a Crown area around Whitehall which, like Cold Harbour for Thomas Nashe, provided sanctuary from arrest. But it is not only the Booths who are down on their luck. The taking of lodgers is also depicted as the resort of the genteel of reduced means. Landlady Mrs Ellison is a clergy widow obliged to let out rooms to survive but she is, she constantly reminds the Booths, 'of a very good family ... Few of my lodgers, I believe, ever came of a better'.[40]

The lodger's social mobility is, on the other hand, upwards in Samuel Foote's (1721–77) comedy, *The Commissary* (1765). Protagonist Zachary Fungus, newly-arrived back in London from India, is a *nouveau riche*, a nabob in miniature. His fortune stems from service as a commissary, a non-combatant army officer responsible for supplies: bathetic rather than heroic. He is contrasted both with his own origin (a driver of carts) and with his plain-speaking and -living tallow-chandler brother Isaac. As a first step in his self-reinvention Fungus lodges with Mrs Mechlin, in Covent Garden, a fashionable location but also the heart of London's sex trade (see below). His lodging is a base where he can acquire gentlemanly skills: riding, poetry, music, oratory, fencing. He has, moreover, a French manservant with him to underline his pretentious social-climbing. His landlady is a businesswoman apparently dealing in lace and silk (mechlin was a high-quality Flemish lace) and is possibly a widow, though her marital status is never made clear. As she has a daughter, Dolly, she may be an unmarried or deserted mother. This is made more probable by her secondary business of match-making, dangerously close to working as a procuress. Foote shows lodging used to gain a foothold in a good district of town but cannot resist the landlady-as-bawd stereotype.

This cultural connection between lodging and sex was made most explicit in every sense by John Cleland (1709–89) in *Fanny Hill* (1749). Fanny is yet another country girl in London lured into sex work. Her story is, however, not one of decline into misery and death but of the happy pursuit of sexual pleasure, even when it is driven by economic necessity, until she eventually marries her first lover Charles and lives happily (and affluently) ever after. It is, as many have observed, narrated in Fanny's voice, yet entirely viewed from the standpoint of an elite man. 'Lodge' is as likely to be used by Cleland/Fanny to refer to the act of sexual penetration, underlining the understood relationship between this accommodation and sex for sale. Much of the action also takes place in lodging-rooms, where Fanny is a kept woman. Sexual activity is depicted as something accepted by commercially-minded landlords/ladies, whose overriding concern is to see the rent paid on time. Fanny lives with Charles in two second-floor rooms and a closet for half a guinea a week at Mrs Jones's in D—Street, St James's. Jones is the now-familiar social-climbing, garrulous, mercenary landlady. She boasts of the ambassador living on her first floor and lives 'entirely on what she could squeeze out of her lodgers'. She overlooks the young couple's antics in return for their cash – and indeed has a somewhat colourful past herself.[41] Charles is tricked into going abroad and Fanny takes up with Mr H. He understands the language of floors and sets her up in a more expensive first floor of a 'plain' tradesman's house. This landlord too is tolerant of the social round the pair enjoys, and of Fanny's exuberant love-making with Mr H's country servant Will.

Fanny is compelled to move on not by the landlord but by Mr H who catches her *in flagrante*. Her next lodgings, less fashionable but half the price, are at a brush-maker's in R—Street, Covent Garden, which effectively doubles as a brothel where once again 'provided the rent was duly paid, everything else was as easy and commodious as one could desire'. Unlike Fielding's Mrs Ellison, Foote's and Cleland's landladies are mercenary to a fault. We must remember, however, that the authors were not men who needed to earn extra cash from their home. They could afford to be disparaging.

From the mid-century onwards the position of the single female lodger was given a fresh interpretative twist in novels of sensibility. 'Sensibility' had its roots in the science of nerve theory expounded by natural philosophers Isaac Newton (1642–1727) and John Locke (1632–1704). It privileged the sensations and feelings of the individual.[42] Novelists of sensibility laid claim to realism. They developed their characters by exploring their internal psychology and reaction to believable events. Taking 'conventional situations, stock familial characters and rhetorical devices', they reworked them to arouse sympathy in the reader.[43] Lodging was one of those conventional and 'real' situations, and landlords, ladies, and lodgers were again among the stock characters.

Novels were much-associated at the time with the female reader and have been described as depicting a greater freedom for women, especially when it came to choosing a marriage partner.[44] It was a trammelled freedom, however, since this independence required them to negotiate their way in a reshaped, commercialized patriarchal society without the traditional networks of support and discipline.[45] Margaret Doody considers the figure of the 'autonomous and commanding male' too strong to permit much contingency of plot-line around him. Contingency was therefore centred around the female characters, rendering them lustless, frail, buffeted by chance and the machinations of men, in constant need of protection from seduction.[46] In this context a woman's move to lodgings, to living in a stranger's house, marked a new independence from family ties but was also symbolic of imminent danger, of 'virtue in distress'. The socially inferior landlord/lady and the sex worker remained powerful images, but the robust, buccaneering, and shameless Moll Flanders or Roxana was replaced by the troubled nubile and genteel female lodger who excited the readers' pity at her vulnerability in a merciless world of sex and money. The association between a house lodging single women and a brothel remained, and was now typically associated with a milliner's shop (a business gendered as female where male shopkeepers were the subject of ridicule), but the psychological treatment in the novel of sensibility rendered this association more sinister.[47] These novels therefore both opened up vistas of new possibilities for the female reader, and at the same time dispensed cautionary advice.

The classic of the genre is Samuel Richardson's *Clarissa* (1748) and its heroine Clarissa Harlowe the classic chaste woman undeserving of her fate. The family home, Harlowe Place is apparently stable, permanent and materially comfortable, but appearances deceive. Her *arriviste* family is intent on Clarissa's marriage against her inclinations to the odious but moneyed Mr Solmes. For Clarissa, Harlowe Place therefore lacks emotional comfort and becomes a cruel prison. London lodgings, by contrast, appear to offer a vision of freedom and choice. She writes enthusiastically to best friend Anna Howe of the various rooms there proposed by the Dolemans, accomplices of her rakish gentleman admirer, Robert Lovelace. Shall it be the first floor over a mercer's in Bedford Street Covent Garden, or Norfolk or Cecil Streets with their views over the river to the Surrey Hills, or the respectable army widow's in Dover Street, Mayfair? All are, as Chapter 3 will show, wholly credible locations. She fixes upon the last, which was heavily promoted by Doleman.[48] Although initially pleased with her accommodation (less so with the vulgar landlady Mrs Sinclair), it is a sign of her underlying anxiety about privacy and security in this new setting that one of Clarissa's first actions when alone in her rooms is to inspect 'the doors, the windows, the wainscot, the dark closet as well as the light one'. She only settles to write after 'finding very good fastenings to the door and to all the windows'.[49] She is right to be concerned: the house is a brothel, Mrs Sinclair is a bawd, and Lovelace plans to lodge in the same house, something which as a mere lodger she is powerless to prevent. Her lodgings here, at Hampstead during her brief flight from Sinclair's, and as an involuntary lodger arrested for debt in the Rowlands' sponging-house (a place of temporary confinement for debtors) are all prisons just as was Harlowe Place. Both landladies – Sinclair and Mrs Moore at Hampstead – prioritize economic self-interest, agreeing readily to the wealthy Lovelace's schemes, as he books up all the rooms at the latter's house and contrives Clarissa's rape at the former's. In fact, over her five months as a lodger Clarissa is always vulnerable until her final days with the homely Smiths, honest, middling shopkeepers in King Street, Covent Garden, and their other lodger, widowed Mrs Lovick. Here in a simple room on the first floor appropriate to her gentle status, she at last finds a loving if surrogate family, and the reader can only watch and weep as she declines and dies in the presence of her waiting coffin, sure of Heaven as the only and eternal safe home.[50]

A similar plight, that of the fallen woman of good family, was central to a series of fund-raising fictions purporting to be four autobiographies: *The Histories* of *Some of the Penitents in the Magdalen-House*, published in 1760 with the involvement of Richardson.[51] The Magdalen Hospital for repentant prostitutes had opened in 1758 in Goodman's Fields to the east of the City. It was one of the charitable moral reform institutions discussed in Chapter 1.[52] The *Histories* was a publicity tool for the Hospital's aims, deploying the well-trodden storyline of Hogarth's *Harlot's Progress* and the same tropes of sensibility as *Clarissa* to elicit pity and donations. All employ the tragic narrative of destruction by male seduction in stories that were also potentially titillating to a middling-sort readership with its moral code of restraint, decency, and family. The first and fourth narrators cite a catastrophic move into lodgings as a turning point in their slide from grace. Emily, orphaned daughter of a clergyman, takes rooms after she is seduced by the son of a friend with whom she lives, bears a child, and is evicted. The elderly landlady proves a bawd, the house a brothel. A second lodging, chosen for its cheapness, is no better. The landlord and lady are as unconcerned as Cleland's characters about the activities of their young female lodgers, maybe even sympathetic since they entertain Emily and her child to tea on her birthday. Emily expresses some agency, maintains her respectability as far as possible and demonstrates her deserving character by keeping her room clean and taking in paid needlework.[53] The family of the fourth, anonymous, storyteller, like Clarissa's, attempts to force her into a loveless but financially shrewd marriage. Like Clarissa, she escapes but unlike Clarissa it is to live as the mistress of her lover Captain Turnham, in lodgings in the centre of London. The lodgings have a secretive air: in the busiest part of town where taking lodgers is unremarkable (see Chapter 3) the couple are a 'commodity' and pass without notice. Towards the end of her narrative the storyteller is once again in lodgings, over a little shop and, like Emily, by working at her needle demonstrates her underlying virtue.[54]

Henry Mackenzie's (1745–1831) *The Man of Feeling* (1771) marks the high watermark of the novel of sensibility. Its protagonist Harley is moved to tears by a series of vignettes of human suffering, among them the plight of another fallen Emily (Atkins), reduced to garret-lodgings unchanged in style since the sixteenth century:

> up three pair of stairs, into a small room lighted by one narrow lattice, and patched round with shreds of different-coloured paper. In the darkest corner stood something like a bed, before which a tattered coverlet hung by way of curtain.

Emily's person is similarly in disarray: 'Her hair had fallen on her shoulders! her look had the horrid calmness of out-breathed despair!'[55] Both room and person move Harley to action and rescue. Yet there was by now something time-worn, even absurdly excessive in the depiction of Emily and in Harley's reactions. Seven years later, in *Evelina*, Frances Burney (1752–1840) returned to the comedic potential of lodgings while never losing sight of her eponymous heroine's realism as an individual. Burney's own family background was of assistance here: she grew up close to ways of life where lodging was more commonplace than she probably wished to admit.[56] Her mother Esther Sleepe ran a fan-making business in the City with her mother and sisters. Many shopkeepers and craftspeople took in lodgers as a side-line (Chapter 3). If the Sleepes did not do so, their neighbours almost certainly did. Burney's parents had married in haste and began life together in straitened circumstances. Frances was vague about their accommodation at this stage. Was it perhaps in a lodging-room or rooms? Or might they have taken in lodgers to ease financial pressures?[57]

It is tempting to read Evelina as an avatar of Burney the social climber. The novel is certainly highly conscious of social class, and its depiction of lodgings is no exception. Evelina's embarrassingly common relatives, the Branghtons, live over their silversmith's shop on unfashionable Snow Hill just north of Holborn and have two lodgers, both of whom are sought after by women in the plot as possible husbands, and both of whom woo Evelina. Mr Macartney is a troubled but gentlemanly Scottish poet who, naturally, inhabits their garret up three pair of stairs. He reminds us of Hogarth's *Distrest Poet*. Indeed, poverty compels him to withdraw from his agreement to board with his hosts. Like teenaged Bristol poet Thomas Chatterton (1752–70), who in real life came to London, failed, and died at his own hand in a garret room, Macartney attempts suicide. Unlike Chatterton he is rescued by Evelina's intervention, an emasculating reversal of the usual gender roles in the novel of sensibility. On the prestigious first floor lodges Mr Smith. Like Foote's Zachary Fungus he keeps a servant and is, according to Miss Polly Branghton, 'quite like one of the quality, and dresses as fine, and goes to balls and dances, and every thing [*sic*], quite in taste'. However, as Polly's social superior Evelina perceives, he is in truth infinitely coarser than the garreteer Macartney. A lodger's superficial appearance could be deceptive if one did not have right interpretive skills.[58] Burney's unpublished 1779 play *The Witlings* certainly shows an understanding both of the life of the shopkeeper (a milliner's, where, unusually, the play opens) and of the comings and goings in landlady Mrs Voluble's house where the poet Dabler lodges.[59] Voluble is presumably not a pen-portrait of any Burney-Sleepe family member for, like Foote's Mrs Mechlin and as her name implies, she is another garrulous, nosy, scandal-monger who feels no qualms over rummaging through her lodger's possessions while he is out. Like Mrs Ellison in *Amelia* she is eager to claim a certain social standing. She assumes a personal prestige from those who visit her 'Poet of Fashion' – 'whoever passes through her hall to visit him, she claims for her acquaintance' – and seeks to establish herself as embedded in a network of landladies of respectability in recommending various 'very genteel apartments' as suitable for the heroine, Cecilia's, accommodation.[60]

It was not only the fictional characters and settings of novels, plays, and prints that built a set of cultural expectations of lodging for the Georgian audience. There was also a wealth of factual material purporting to represent and interpret the reality of lodging. This included published life-writing, stories in the press, guides to London (and other towns and cities), and handbooks on the law for the layperson. Some of this material was presented in a format very close to its fictional counterpart such that there was a constant reciprocation between the two forms – fiction and fact – which were therefore mutually reinforcing.

A sub-genre of life-writing, that by 'scandalous women' and sometimes dubbed 'whore biographies', relied upon this blurring of the boundaries between, on the one hand, novelistic and image representations of life in lodgings and, on the other, lived experience. Its authors exploited familiar understandings from the former to frame the latter in a manner known to appeal to a paying readership.[61] The most obvious example of this blurring of boundaries is in Scottish author Tobias Smollett's (1721–71) novel of 1751, *Peregrine Pickle*, into which Smollett inserted *The Memoirs of a Lady of Quality*, the unvarnished autobiography of Frances, Viscountess Vane (1715–88), who passed through lodging-rooms as fast as she moved from lover to lover.[62]

Unlike the fictionalized and almost exactly contemporary Magdalen penitents' stories, the 'whore biographies' were designed purely to exploit middling-sort ambiguity over shocking, yet titillating, immorality, especially that of the rakish upper echelons of British society.[63] However, they were also triumphant demonstrations of the agency of their undefeated female authors, and therefore posed a challenge to sensibility. To take just one example in greater detail, the partly fictional *Memoirs* of beautiful 'courtesan' (the *ODNB* designation) Frances Murray (1729–78) are divided into chapters, exactly like a novel. Murray began her London career after her relationship with lover Jack Spencer, grandson of the first Duke of Marlborough, broke down. Like Hogarth's Moll Hackabout, she was picked up and exploited by a City bawd. Unlike Moll her professional trajectory was upwards: to lodging and sex work in the West End and to living 'kept' by, among others, the Earl of Sandwich, Sir Richard Atkins and Lord _____. It culminated in a married happy ending (to actor-manager David Ross).[64] Murray celebrated her life as a cross between the now-dated picaresque of Defoe and a *bildungsroman* in which her individual effort and perseverance, qualities admired by the middling sort, overcame early life difficulties. To illustrate this she deployed the full range of lodging accommodation and geography from a garret over a chandler's shop in the Old Bailey living on 'small beer and sprats', to polite 'apartments' with a servant and two maids in Pall Mall, and with stints in between at more middling-sort Charing Cross and Leicester Fields (now Square).[65]

Lodgings were similarly associated with sexual misdeeds in two further non-fiction genres in the *Trials for Adultery*, reports of divorce cases and of 'criminal conversation' law suits, in which a husband sought damages from her lover for a wife's consequent reduction in value, and in *Harris's List of Covent-Garden Ladies*, a pocket-sized annual 'directory' of central London prostitutes published annually between 1760 and 1795.[66] Like 'whore biographies', both profited from the prurient fascination with single women living in lodgings, again with the added piquancy of class. The *Trials* and *Harris's* provided yet another window into the amoral behaviour of the aristocracy and elite, which in lodgings collided with the workaday world of the middling-sort landlord and lady. In 1772, for example, Catherine Cade's husband Philip, an officer in the Exchequer, brought an action for divorce. The previous year Catherine, only sixteen when they married in 1766, began an adulterous affair in the marital home with Irish peer Lord Aylmer. The Cades separated and she moved into the Pinner home of her father Sir Charles Wentworth, MP for Minehead, then went into lodgings, first at Pinner at the house of a carpenter-joiner and his wife, the Travethans, and next at Hampstead at one Mrs Tully's. Mrs Travethan and Tully's daughters all deposed that she was visited regularly by Lord Aylmer, in Hampstead posing as her brother, and that the couple spent the nights together in one bed. The lodgings depicted in the *Trials* are places of illicit rendezvous, deceit, subterfuge, and surveillance. In Catherine's case, it bought her into intimate contact with both a noble and an artisan household, where she mixed across class boundaries both above and below her own position.[67]

While the authenticity of its entries is debated, what is certain is that for thirty-five years *Harris's List* perpetuated the notion that single women living in lodgings were engaged in sex work and defined the locations in which they were deemed likely to live and operate. It was an association captured metaphorically in a cant phrase recorded by dilettante antiquarian Francis Grose (1731–91) in his popular *Dictionary of the Vulgar Tongue*. This for several decades enlightened and entertained the literate from a *de-haut-en-bas* perspective with definitions of over 9,000 colloquial and rude words and phrases omitted from Johnson's *Dictionary*:

> ROOMS: She lets out her fore room and lies backwards, saying of a woman suspected of prostitution.[68]

Harris's origins lay in manuscript lists circulated by Harris, a pimp, in the 1740s.[69] Frances Murray's *Memoirs* include an account of her physical examination at his hands and her first entry in his books, to which she attributed an increase in custom and in the price she was able to charge. Based in the first floor of a Charing Cross milliner's, again picking up the idea of the milliner's-cum-brothel, she was 'a new face', described as 'A fine brown girl, rising nineteen years … will shew well in the flesh market'.[70] *Harris's* was laid out in columns imitating the format of street and trade directories and gazetteers, implying a knowable 'geography of pleasure', complete with prices. Richard Newton's etching of 1794 depicts a punter actively using the guide. A copy of *Harris's* is open in his hand at the page for 'Miss Love' as he stands before a house of ill-repute.[71] Many of the most frequently occurring streets in *Harris's* lie beyond the Covent Garden of the title, in the angle of Oxford Street and Tottenham Court Road, south of Fitzroy Square. From 1758 to 1772 this part of the Berners Estate was, like Great Portland Street to its west, one continuous building site on the northern fringe of London where town met countryside. Over 200 houses 'ran through the gamut of larger mid-Georgian terrace house types' which accommodated both the fashionable and a range of households of traders, artists, and musicians, some of them lodgers (see Chapter 3).[72] As with Rowlandson's watercress-seller, it seems a common belief that the trades in this new suburb included sex.

Some of the ladies in *Harris's*, like the penitent Magdalens, had allegedly been reduced to this way of life after a seduction by a gentleman of superior status. Miss Les—r, of 23 Upper Newman Street, was a servant from Holborn 'debauched' by a lawyer who had spied her innocently walking in Gray's Inn Gardens with her little ward. On desertion, she was thrown out of her place, took lodgings near Red Lion Square and resorted to prostitution. Others were jolly in the mode of Fanny Hill or the two women in Rowlandson's watercress-seller print. The Misses D-vis and Godf—y, also of Upper Newman Street, occupied respectively the parlour and first floor, while the Misses Towns—d and Char-ton had a similar arrangement at 12 Gresse St and shared a carriage. None of

Harris's ladies lived as desperately as the young Murray had done in her garret (though some were described pejoratively as ugly, pox-ridden, drunk, etc.), but the *Olla Podrida* hierarchy of floors applied. Some of Harris's 'frail sisterhood' only earned enough for a second floor and were looked down on by those on the floor below.[73] In 1773 Charlotte Benevent was living at Princes Street, on the corner with Lisle Street, where 'above lodges Miss Boothby … with whom she has no connection, thinking herself much superior to any on a second floor'.[74] Rowlandson represented the same hierarchy. In *First and Second Floor Lodgers* (*c.* 1790) two women leaning from the upper floor of a house in Union Street (now Riding House Street) on the Berners Estate are noticeably less fashionably and more immodestly attired than the pair on the first floor. But all four have this in common: they are advertising themselves from lodging-rooms.[75]

If *Harris's* purported to be a specialist guide for the connoisseur of female flesh, there were also genuine guides for the visitor to or newly-arrived resident of what was an increasingly vast and unknowable metropolis that had to be 'learned'. The guides had origins that lie before the period of this study, an early example being Henry Peacham's *Art of Living in London* (1642). Peacham advised taking private lodgings as having fewer temptations to spending on drink, tobacco and gambling than an alehouse or inn.[76] These guides proliferated in the eighteenth century as London grew and the population became ever more mobile and somewhat more literate.

Revd John Trusler's *London Adviser and Guide* contained, according to its full title, 'Every Instruction and Information Useful and Necessary to Persons Living in London and Coming to Reside There': some 200 pages of practical information. His first chapter was 'Houses'. It outlined the best areas for housing and the likely cost. On lodgings he advised that there were rarely unfurnished rooms in the prime districts (St James's, Charing Cross, the squares, Covent Garden and the theatres, St Paul's, Cheapside and the Royal Exchange).[77] Samuel Leigh's *New Picture of London*, first published in 1818 and revised and reissued several times to 1830, tucked the accommodation chapter towards the end of a massive 500 pages aimed more at the 'stranger' in the tourist market. Leigh regarded lodgings as an alternative to hotels, taverns, inns, and coffeehouses and listed nine boarding house addresses. Like Trusler he offered advice on prices and the need for careful negotiation.[78]

Where Trusler and Leigh differed was in the tone of their guides. Trusler's work sounded many notes of caution, creating an image of a city and its world of lodgings pregnant with risk and danger, and of a disorderly society in need of reform. He warned of the danger of taking unfurnished rooms: that lodgers' goods could be distrained for their landlord's debts. Some landlords removed troublesome lodgers by raising the rent and then threatening to sue for non-payment. They might also lock a lodger out of his/her room, detaining their goods in lieu of overdue rent. Indebted lodgers could also be up to tricks, especially in the Verge of the Court where Fielding placed the Booths and where Trusler warned that 'most' houses let lodgings to men and women with money difficulties. He claimed one debtor had been accustomed, when he needed to leave the safety of the Verge, to take a boat on the Thames, as the river was also a privileged area.[79] Some entries in Grose's *Dictionary of the Vulgar Tongue* also warned of the trickery rampant in lodgings. There was the 'Dining Room Post': a mode of stealing in houses with lodgers by rogues pretending to be postmen who sent up sham letters to the lodgers, and, while waiting in the hall for the postage to be paid, went into the first room they saw open, and robbed it. In the 'Lodging-Slum' lodgers hired ready-furnished lodgings, and stripped them of plate, linen, and other valuable articles. In Wales landlords/ladies were allegedly accustomed to employ the 'Welsh Ejectment' (unroofing the house to force out a bad tenant).[80] That these were real risks was confirmed for readers of an Old Bailey case reported in 1806. Two men called at Bynon and Elizabeth Wilkinson's home and saddler's shop in South Molton Street, Mayfair on a late January afternoon when the light must have faded. While Elizabeth showed one of them the second-floor bedroom the other stayed below and stole three silver teaspoons.[81]

Later in the nineteenth century the sense of danger seems to have receded. Leigh's guide was a work of promotion, even puffery, on behalf of the capital – the guide was 'luminous', with illustrations and descriptions of attractions and improvements. However, while it might not have been necessary to go quite so far as the Welsh Ejectment to remove a mere lodger rather than someone with a lease, an 1835 lawsuit just beyond the period of this study and reported in both the press and in law reports, legal digests and textbooks revealed the lengths to which an unscrupulous landlord might still go. Plaintiff Mr Underwood, a tailor, and his wife lodged in four rooms on a first and second floor at 3 Leicester Street, Leicester Square, taken by the year at £28. Underwood both worked from the premises and sublet a pair of the rooms to two gentlemen at 14s. a week, thereby more than covering his own rent. His jealous and angry landlord, plumber and glazier William Burrows, 'bedaubed' the banisters with 'filthy and adhesive matter' (tar), blocked up the skylight to the stairs and removed the water-closet, door-knocker and bell-wire. The court found for Underwood, awarding him £50 damages on the grounds that he had a 'clear' right to these amenities whether or not they had been specifically mentioned at the time of taking the lodgings. It seems unlikely that the lodging arrangement between Underwood and Burrows survived the dispute. Burrows, however, paid the price for his poor business acumen and was declared bankrupt in 1841.[82]

Another suit that caught the popular imagination and established in Georgian minds, as well as in law, the position of lodgers and landlords was that of Lieutenant General William Gansel (sometimes Gansell, 1715–74) in 1774. 'Gansel's Case' (comprising the civil case *Lee v. Gansel* and an Old Bailey trial) was so well known that Prussian visitor to London Johann Wilhelm von Archenholz (1741–1812), writing eleven years after the events and Gansel's death, recorded that 'All England was attentive to the decision on the question, whether a lodger enjoyed the same rights as the owner of a house?'[83] The judges' decision upheld that most fundamental tenet of 'liberty and property', expounded by judge William Blackstone (1723–80) in his influential *Commentaries*: that an Englishman's home is his castle, a place of immunity from arbitrary intrusion and which he is entitled to defend even to death.[84] But was a lodging-room in itself a castle, a 'mansion' in its own right?

Gansel was a long-term London lodger, as an army officer presumably on a rather on-and-off basis, living for thirty-eight years (twenty-eight years in some contemporary sources) at Craven Street, between the Strand and the Thames (overlapping with Franklin who also lodged long-term in the street). Gansel had two rooms on the first floor, two on the second and use of the kitchen for himself and his two boy servants. His resident landlord and lady, Mr and Mrs Mayo, ran a clock- and watch-making and jewellery business from the ground-floor back room (where Franklin had been a customer in 1767, buying a ring for his daughter Sally).[85] The Mayos had 'inherited' Gansel on moving to the house sixteen years previously. There was 'nothing magnificent' about the set-up; Gansel's rooms were 'like other lodging-rooms'.[86] Gansel, however, had a long history of financial troubles on account of his 'life of gaiety'.[87] In the early afternoon of 26 August 1773 surgeon Samuel Lee, to whom Gansel owed £134, obtained a warrant for his arrest and sent in the bailiffs. The front door, which served the Mayo family, their business and the lodgers, stood open. Lee and the bailiffs' men entered, spoke to Mrs Mayo in the parlour, then raced up the stairs. After an altercation with Gansel's servants they arrived at the second-floor room inside which Gansel, armed with pistols, had locked and barred himself. They broke down the door and forced their way in. During the fracas Gansel fired two shots. The first grazed the hair of one man, the second passed through the hat of another, but Gansel was eventually overpowered and arrested, although he continued to put up a fight. As they dragged him downstairs, he hung on to the banisters with such strength that they broke. At his criminal trial for felonious shooting Gansel spoke eloquently in his own defence referencing Blackstone:

> Had I not a right to defend myself in my own house? I always understood, and I understand now from the authority of Mr. Justice Blackstone, that the house of an Englishman is his castle; and that a room which a man has for a certain time is his house.[88]

The jury agreed and acquitted him. Gansel remained in the Fleet debtors' prison and in the new year brought a civil case against Lee alleging that his arrest and imprisonment were illegal as the officers had broken into 'the apartment where he lodged'. Lee in his turn applied for a ruling on the matter. Lord Mansfield delivered judgement on 27 January 1774. He upheld the general rule that an Englishman's house was his castle, that it was illegal to breach its outer defences of external doors and windows. However, in this instance, the single, common street door, and not his chamber door, led to Gansel's castle. The bailiffs had entered this peaceably and legally, and the arrest was therefore also legal. As Clarissa Harlowe found in fiction, so Gansel found in fact: a lodging-room was never entirely secure. Gansel was to have no further lodging than the Fleet, where he died six months later in July 1774. The Mayos must have faced considerable repair bills but continued to trade from Craven Street until at least 1777.[89] Whether they ever took lodgers again after this experience is not known.

Gansel's Case continued to reverberate into the nineteenth century in guidebooks written by barristers and elucidating the law on landlord and tenant for the layman and woman. John Irving Maxwell, for example, made it clear that an apartment in a house divided into tenements was only a 'distinct mansion' if it had its own front door. Where the householder was resident, then the apartment was part of his or her 'mansion'. William Woodfall's *Law of Landlord and Tenant* (still the standard textbook on landlord and tenant today) advised similarly.[90] The guides' audience was both landlords (in the guidebooks it was never a landlady) and tenants and lodgers, also imagined as male. It was a potentially lucrative market: three-quarters of the inhabitants of Great Britain were believed to fall into one of these three categories.[91] They instructed the hosts on how to 'conduct themselves legally and securely' and enabled tenants to 'guard against encroaching landlords'.[92] The chief focus of the guides was leases for a term of years and lodging typically only filled a page or two, at most a short chapter. Nevertheless, and despite their largely practical nature, the guides contributed to the cultural perception of lodging. They gendered the practice, and they followed Trusler and press reports in conveying a degree of anxiety about the problems that could arise, with one author regarding London as especially subject to lodging-room frauds.[93]

Several guides counselled, therefore, as for a lease, an inventory of a room's contents and condition, and printed standard templates for a written lodging contract and other notices, implying a formality to the process. There is virtually no evidence of written contracts in the life-writing sources, however (Chapter 4). It is likely that many lodging contracts were in fact oral only. In all of the guides' proformas both parties were men. Maxwell indeed reminded readers that where lodgings were let jointly to a man and wife, in law (that of couverture) the transaction was that of the husband alone.[94] John Paul's 1778 version imagined a grocer landlord with a gentleman lodger taking the second-floor front room in a house with other lodgers, each of whom could call upon the landlord's maid servant when she could be spared.[95] All contained the same general advice that lodgings taken for a short period were exempt from the rule that notice to quit had to expire on the Quarter Day on which the tenancy had begun. 'Reasonable notice' on either side was instead sufficient. This was typically taken to be one week where rent was paid weekly and so forth. Landlords were cautioned that a lodger might be a thief in thin disguise, setting up the 'Lodging-Slum' to which 'persons letting furnished lodgings are much exposed'.[96] A 1691 statute had made this 'frequent practice' (theft from a lodging-room) a felony, and so in theory punishable by death, punishments under common law being thought insufficiently deterrent.[97] Lodgers too were cautioned. Those taking unfurnished rooms needed to be aware that if the landlord were himself in arrears with his own rent (which was of course difficult for the lodger to ascertain), then the lodger's goods might be subject to distraint (seizure) by his creditors.

The anxieties lurking in the guides and in Grose's *Dictionary* were reinforced by reporting of crimes in the press and in publications such as *The Proceedings of the Old Bailey* and the *Newgate Calendar*, which in its many editions kept particularly notable crimes and criminals in the public eye long after the event. Gansel's Case was reported in each of these. Anyone reading these texts could be forgiven for thinking that the world of lodgings was rife with theft, violence, even murder.

Theft from lodging-rooms continued undeterred by the 1691 Act. At the Old Bailey, prosecution under the Act was so routine that John Styles has used the evidence to examine the sort of possessions, including furnishings, that working people in inexpensive but not desperately low lodgings in London either owned or had 'the use of'. His search of the Old Bailey on-line database found

265 cases involving 1,682 objects generated by this act in the 1750s and 1790s alone.[98] It is not surprising that most the of stolen items were relatively portable: bedding, chamber pots, candlesticks, table- and cookware, usually belonging to the landlord/lady but sometimes the property of fellow-lodgers. In 1723, for example, lodger Thomas Saunders was found guilty of stealing gold pieces, coins, spoons and other goods from his landlord and lady, the Wheelers, while they were out. Mrs Wheeler tugged at the court's heartstrings with an account of their middling-sort industry and thrift. The stolen goods were 'all that they had been working for all their Life, to keep them when they were old'.[99] Readers of the *Proceedings* might well have taken the view that the less well-off were a risky proposition as lodgers and that anyone who ran a common lodging house had only themselves to blame.

Gansel's Case involved a degree of violence against a lodger where public sympathy was largely on his side. Many reports of crimes of violence involving lodgers concerned the threat to landlords/ladies from their lodgers. In spring 1761 the press eagerly reported the sensational story of the gruesome murder of landlady Anne King by her lodger, noted Swiss miniature painter Theodore Gardelle (1722–61), in the respectable location of Leicester Fields. Indeed, the Hogarths lived at The Golden Head, number 30. The case was also reported in the *Proceedings* and *Newgate Calendar*.[100] Gardelle had killed King during a row. He subsequently dismembered her body and burned or concealed its parts. He was convicted and hanged in the Haymarket, near the scene of his crime, and his body displayed in chains. The monthly *Gentleman's Magazine* reported the crime in its March edition and in April, after the execution, returned to the subject of Gardelle, lodger and murderer, filling seven pages (one seventh of the magazine). It presented Gardelle as a classic itinerant, rootless, and immoral lodger (he had lived an irregular life in Paris with a woman whom he never married and whom he had deserted together with their two children). Crueller, however, was its criticism of victim Anne King. The landlady was no longer an object of pity but was characterized, like Darly's *Lodging House Lady of Bath* perhaps, as 'a gay showy woman, of a doubtful character, who dressed fashionably, and was chiefly visited by gentlemen'. In this version of the crime Anne King was a loose woman, almost a sex worker, and therefore the friendless author of her own misfortune.[101]

However, most of the headline-grabbing violent crimes in lodgings took place far away in terms of social class from respectable districts such as Craven Street or Leicester Fields. The reporting served to underline for a middling-sort readership the notion that cheap lodgings made some parts of London and other large cities inherently dangerous, no-go areas that were the resort of a threatening underclass. This was especially so by the end of the Georgian period, when the turmoil and horrors of the French Revolution had revealed that it was possible for the *status quo* to be totally overturned to the detriment of the propertied classes. Fear of this contagion spreading to England lay behind the Thomas Paine poster in the *Gentleman of Moderate Fortune* print (Figure 3). There was too fear of literal contagion: that disease might spread from the unhealthily overcrowded quarters of cities where the poor dwelt into adjacent respectable neighbourhoods.[102] Two notorious cases that terrified the public were the December 1811 Ratcliffe Highway murders in east London and the Burke and Hare murders of 1828 in Edinburgh. Both occupied column inches in the newspapers and inspired illustrated 'true crime' pamphlet accounts.

Ratcliffe Highway (now simply The Highway) connects the City of London to the docks around Limehouse to its east. It was described by Thomas De Quincey (1785–1859), forty-two years after the events, as 'a public thoroughfare in a most chaotic quarter of eastern or nautical London … a most dangerous quarter' where 'every third man at the least might be set down as a foreigner'.[103] It would be more accurate to say that in 1811 it ran through a mixed area occupied by professionals, shopkeepers, and tradespeople, cheek-by-jowl with De Quincey's transient sailors and low-life of the busy docks. At the time of the murders it was acquiring something of a reputation through press reports and the *Proceedings* as a street associated with crime, but for theft rather than violence.[104] The shockingly brutal and apparently random murders were in fact completely out of place.

The first was the night-time massacre of four members of the Marr household – young couple, baby, and apprentice – at the Marrs' linen draper's shop, followed twelve days later by that of the Williamsons, publicans at the respectable King's Arms, New Gravel Lane (now Garnet Street), and of their servant Bridget. The inn shutters had been closed but it was the Williamsons' practice to leave the street door unlocked 'as well for the accommodation of the neighbourhood as of the lodgers'.[105] Their lodger John Turner, a sawyer who for eight months had occupied the front garret on the second floor, woke and, using knotted bedsheets, escaped via the window to raise the alarm. Amazingly, the Williamsons' fourteen-year-old granddaughter slept through the carnage and survived. The press was full of the story, there was widespread public panic, and a reward of £500 was offered by the government. The first suspect was Silvestor Driscol, a lodger at Pratt's Buildings, New Gravel Lane, who had blood on his white duck seaman's trousers but was exonerated by a milk-woman. She slept in the same room, evidence to shocked and voyeuristic readers alike of overcrowding and loose living.[106] Eventually another local lodger, twenty-eight-year-old Irish sailor John Williams, was arrested on information laid against him by a former shipmate. Williams hanged himself in Coldbath Fields prison before he came to trial. Nonetheless his body was paraded on a cart round the streets of east London before he was buried, with a stake through his heart, at a crossroads outside the churchyard of St George in the East. It was easy to portray Williams as a drunken, shiftless man, living transiently in cheap digs. By his own account, a sailor's life here was one of dancing, singing, drinking, fighting and late nights.[107] That he was Irish probably counted against him too, as did the rumour that he had changed his name twice: from Murphy to avoid detection in a previous crime, and to Williamson in 1810 when signing up for a voyage on the *Dover Castle* East Indiaman.[108]

The 1828 case of William Burke and William Hare was reported across the nation and inspired unanimous revulsion. Although taking place in Edinburgh, it could just as easily have been in east London or St Giles. These two notorious labourers, also Irish by birth and in their thirties, lived in the cramped alleys of Edinburgh's Old Town that were, said one commentator, 'the resort of every sort of vagrant'.[109] Hare's wife ran a lodging-house for beggars in a one-storey building in Tanner's Close, West Port, where a bed costed a mere 3d. a night.[110] Two rooms were full of beds, one of which was the 'home' of Burke, a cobbler, and his partner Margaret McDougal. It was chaotic and insanitary:

> a disgusting picture of wretchedness; rags and straw, mingled with implements of shoemaking, and old shoes and boots … A pot of boiled potatoes was a prominent object … The bed was a coarse wooden frame, without posts or curtains.[111]

In this dismal setting the pair murdered sixteen men and women, most of whom had come as lodgers, selling the corpses to the eminent Edinburgh surgeon Dr Robert Knox (1791–1862) for anatomization.[112] Outrage, but also curiosity, was so great that Hare's squalid house became a tourist attraction, as did Burke's executed body (Hare had turned King's evidence). Burke's skeleton, a death mask with the noose mark of hanging visible, and a pocketbook allegedly made of his skin remain on display at the Surgeons' Hall Museum in Edinburgh.[113] There could not be a better illustration of the growing class-consciousness provoked by middling-sort knowledge of the lodging practices of the poor.

———————————

The extent to which lodging penetrated the cultural consciousness of Georgian readers and observers was extensive, so much so that this chapter has of necessity only covered a small percentage of all the texts and images depicting landlords/ladies and their lodgers. The setting was invariably urban, and the stereotype characters portrayed were represented from the point of view of the middling-sort or elite potential lodger. Plebeian lodgers and landlords/ladies rarely spoke for themselves in their own voices except in accounts of trials, and even here they were mediated by a clerk.

Many of the stereotypes were of very long-standing, as far back as Chaucer. Landlords, and landladies in particular, were social climbers from the trading classes, were mercenary and nosy, and turned a blind eye to or were engaged in the sex trade. By the eighteenth century lodging was no longer perceived as in itself a threat to the civic authorities but lodgers were still represented as shiftless and irresponsible. Singlewoman lodgers were tantamount to sex workers, a reputation harnessed for their own ends by the 'whore biographers'. Poorer lodgers were thought liable to disappear with the bed-sheets owing rent. In extreme circumstances lodgers, as strangers in the private family home, were cuckoos in the nest, posing a personal threat to their hosts.

Some aspects of the representations did change in the eighteenth century, however. Towards the end of our period, awareness of the gender and class distinctions of lodging practices was sharper. The singlewoman lodger was no longer the spirited, independent heroine of Defoe but was sentimentalized in novels and in tales of redemption such as the Magdalen *Histories* as a damsel in distress and in need of rescue. To the hierarchy of prestige of the floors in a house receiving lodgers, Hogarth and others added a moral message, that the impoverished male garreteer was failing in his duty to support himself and his dependants through proper work. Reporting in the press and pamphlets underlined the class gulf between respectable and non-respectable lodgers and the districts of London and other cities where they might each be found. In London, these reports played their part in inventing the dangerous East End with its swarming multitudes of the lawless and diseased who threatened the very existence of the respectable population living so close by.

Meet the landlords, landladies, and their lodgers

The previous chapter considered how representations in fiction, images, and in the press and other sources built a widespread set of beliefs about landlords, landladies, and their lodgers. It identified a number of stereotypes, many of them less than flattering. This chapter analyses the evidence for lodging in London and looks at examples of real landlords/ladies and lodgers in order to uncover any defining characteristics, and the extent to which these matched the stereotypes.

As Chapter 1 explained, there was no systematic census identifying lodgers in households until 1851. There was little administrative need to list them: lodgers were not liable for most taxes or to serve in parish offices, nor were they enfranchised at the parish or national level.[1] Any official statistical evidence from the pre-census era was therefore produced for diverse purposes and is patchy, partial, and varies in the details included. Early-modern surveys of lodgers were driven by national panics over, for example, Catholic plotting, and by localized concerns over overcrowding and pressure on the poor rates. Under certain circumstances it was even possible for lodgers' servants and some lodgers to gain settlement under the Poor Laws.[2] National panics had abated somewhat by the end of the seventeenth century, though they were occasionally revived at times of crisis (see Chapter 1). In 1680, for example, the large and socially-mixed parish of St Martin-in-the-Fields undertook a survey of 'Lodgers being Foreign, or reputed Papists'. From the 1680s there had been a notable influx of French Huguenot refugees into England. Many settled in St Anne Soho. While Huguenots were safely Protestant there was clearly some anxiety about these new foreign residents and their socio-economic status. In 1711 the Commission for Building Fifty New Churches asked the parish vestry for information on their numbers. The vestry replied that of a parish population of 8,133, there were 962 French 'inhabitants', children, and servants but a massive 3,318 'Lodgers who are chiefly French, their children and servants', 41 per cent of the total population.[3] Later in the century French émigrés remained congregated in this parish, and after the 1789 Revolution in more-recently built-up Marylebone, while many of the French nobility were clustered in Richmond-upon-Thames.[4]

Valuable late-seventeenth-century sources for lodging are a reinstated national poll tax of 1692 and two new taxes introduced to fund wars in Europe. All three were assessed and raised locally and provide some listings of lodgers among those liable, although these lists were not compiled to a consistent formula across parishes. This is in large part attributable to the uncertainty about the exact status of lodgers discussed in Chapter 1: were they a subsidiary part of the main, i.e. landlord's/lady's, household or were they households unto themselves?[5] Under the Four Shillings in the Pound Aid introduced in 1693 (a 20 per cent tax levied on the rental value of real property, income earned in public service and stock or ready money within personal estates) householders were obliged to list all lodgers in their household. Those with real property valued at under £1 were exempt and the assessments do not therefore capture poorer householders and lodgers. Surviving lists cover wards and parishes in the Cities of London and Westminster and some of urban and rural Middlesex.[6] For 1695 there are the Marriage Duty Assessments, listings of inhabitants under a 1694 Act imposing taxes on burials, births, and marriages, and annual dues upon bachelors over twenty-five years of age and childless widowers. These are more helpful in identifying lodgers, who were taxable alongside householders. Lodgers were therefore included in the assessments, though again not consistently. Surviving assessments are more geographically limited than the Four Shillings in the Pound Aid lists as no records survive for the expanding Westminster suburbs.[7] This chapter makes use of the digitized records for sixteen parishes scattered around the centre, north, and west of the City, which have been alphabetized by surname but do include details of lodgers and some landlords/ladies ('The Marriage Duty Survey').[8]

By the eighteenth century metropolitan authorities had given up the attempt to control the spread of London's built envelope, and relative political stability reduced the hysterical searching for fifth columnists. There are consequently no equivalent series of listings to those of the late-seventeenth century for comparative purposes. Nevertheless, the late-seventeenth-century sources do provide a valuable baseline from which to explore the phenomenon of lodging in the Georgian era using the later more serendipitous and anecdotal sources. These – the Compton Street fire of 1785, advertisements placed by both landlords/ ladies and lodgers in the *Morning Chronicle*, and the personal biographies found in memoirs, life-writing and letters – are then used to supplement and enrich the picture derived from the early statistical surveys.

Writing in 1696, Gregory King estimated that there were 1.3 million inhabited houses in England, 105,000 of them within the metropolitan area. He calculated an average London household size of 4.57 giving a population of 479,850 (479,600 persons according to King) with 'sojourners' (lodgers) accounting for 8 per cent of this population, 38,388 persons (incorrectly calculated by King as 42,400). This proportion was higher than in 'other cities and great towns' (5 per cent) and 'villages and hamlets' (3 per cent).[9] Indeed, the number of London lodgers estimated by King was larger than the entire population (between 25,000 and 30,000) of England's second city, Norwich, and its hamlets at this date.[10] King also believed sojourners to be older than the national average: thirty-five compared to twenty-seven years old, probably because lodgers were largely an adult population whereas the wider population, as in developing economies today, included a high proportion of children.[11] King used the Marriage Duty Assessments as a basis for his estimates, but he had nothing to say about the heads of the households with lodgers, the landlords, and landladies. Writing one hundred years later, towards the end of our period, Giuseppe Graglia, of whom little is known, estimated that there were 'in the kingdom' 300,000 'independent people, that pay rent in furnished houses, or in furnished apartments', a lower percentage of the population (3.6 per cent of the population of England in the 1801 census) than that arrived at by King. Graglia appears to have plucked his figure out of the air, however.[12] As an end point, lodgers accounted for 5 per cent of the total national population in 1851 and were found in 12 per cent of households.[13]

Turning next to the available evidence from the Poll Tax, Four Shillings Aid and Marriage Duty Assessments, it would be pointless here to retrace the comprehensive work of Craig Spence.[14] Spence found that 47 per cent of City households in the 1692 Poll Tax records contained a lodger or lodgers. Most of these (61.7 per cent) were single lodgers concentrated in wealthier parts of the City: Coleman Street and Broad Street wards, and western wards within the walls. Many lodgers were affluent themselves, members of the gentry even. There were slightly more male lodgers than female and markedly fewer widowed lodgers (10.9 per cent) than widowed householders. Where a household contained a second lodger, in 12.7 per cent of cases this was a servant and in 10 per cent a child. City lodger households were therefore most likely to be relatively well-to-do single persons or a couple with no co-habiting children. There were relatively few instances of a household containing more than two lodgers (11.3 per cent), and households with lodgers only rarely contained apprentices (0.8 per cent), perhaps for reasons of space.[15]

The Marriage Duty Assessments did not routinely make clear the relationship between individuals at an address.[16] However, the Marriage Duty Survey contains 2,268 surname entries, of which 325 (14 per cent) are noted as lodgers or households containing unnamed lodgers. Removing duplicates (i.e. where the landlord/lady and lodger(s) appear separately in the listing) gives 317 discrete entries for households engaged in lodging in some way. Within these 317 entries there are over 479 individuals in sub-households headed by a lodger, giving an average lodger-household size of 1.5 persons.[17] These are minimum figures. There may be lodgers in the list not described as such. It is also a snapshot: there may be households on the list that sometimes took lodgers but did not accommodate any at the time the assessment was made (the summer months). In line with Spence's Poll Tax findings, St Stephen Coleman Street (the largest parish) had by far the largest number of lodger entries at ninety-nine (30 per cent of the total). This was followed by St Olave Silver Street (forty-seven/14 per cent) and St Swithin (twenty-nine/9 per cent). These figures can be further nuanced by the detail from the Four Shillings Aid data which again reveal the presence in certain locations of wealthy lodgers with personal wealth over £12 10s. These lodgers were most prominent by far in St Sepulchre (near St Paul's cathedral), where there were 105 such lodgers in 39.7 per cent of households. There were other clusters in the fashionable and expanding Westminster districts of St Anne Soho, Covent Garden and to the south of the Strand, and in the City in Cheapside, Cornhill, and Fenchurch Street.

All of these were areas of higher than average rents, where lodgers were part of the long tail of financing described in Chapter 1.[18] Individuals who took rooms on the City in the late-seventeenth and early-eighteenth centuries include Cheshire-based Roger Whitley (1618–97), MP and former Civil War Royalist. Whitley visited London regularly in the 1680s and 1690s for business, generally lodging with shopkeepers in the City, but also in the Strand area and, on one occasion, further out in semi-rural 'Kinsenton' (Kensington, lower left, no. 1 on Cary's map, Figure 1).[19] Thomas Wale (1701–96), a Cambridgeshire merchant trading with the Baltic states, also lodged at various addresses in the City.[20] Yorkshireman James Fretwell (1699–1772) was educated for a career in trade and moved to London in winter 1717 to live and gain work experience with his maternal uncle John Woodhouse, an attorney in the Sheriff's Court. Woodhouse was thirty-one, single and, unlike Whitley and Wale, a permanent London resident but not yet a householder (though he was shortly to become one). In 1717 Woodhouse was himself lodging at a Mr Reed's near Threadneedle Street and then at an apothecary's shop in the Poultry.[21]

These districts of the City and of Westminster around the Strand were what can be termed 'nodes' of respectable lodging. They map closely onto the fictional setting of lodgings in novels and plays of the period. Their popularity with lodgers can be seen in the St Martins-in-the Fields 1680 Return of Lodgers for Suffolk Street Ward, covering the district between Coventry Street and Cockspur Street, bounded by the east side of Haymarket, and Whitcomb Street and Hedge Lane to the west. John Strype's 1720 edition of John Stow's 1598 *Survey of London* described Suffolk Street as 'a very good Street, with handsome Houses, well inhabited and resorted unto by Lodgers'.[22] Here in 1680, 114 households contained over 258 lodgers. Like Spence's City lodgers and as implied by Strype, some of these lodgers were of gentry status or above: Sir Thomas Slingsby, MP for Knaresborough, and Lady Delarivier and her family. There were military and naval officers: Captains Charles Harwood and Jenkyn Morgan. Others are untraceable in the historic records but can be assumed to be part of London's growing population of men and women, artisans, labourers, and servants, being both themselves and the streets in which they lived 'of no great account'.[23] This data therefore reinforces the message that lodgers came from across the social spectrum and were not necessarily impecunious.

Later, in the eighteenth century, lodgers had a greater choice of locations as the capital expanded ever-westwards. Nonetheless, the evidence of lodging advertisements placed by both landlords/ladies and lodgers in the *Morning Chronicle* between 1770 and 1800 indicates that the City and Strand area remained favoured locations throughout the century. Many of the almost 400 advertisements did not give a precise, or even any, location. Where they did, the commercial heart of the City remained popular, mentioned in thirty-five advertisements placed by landlords/ladies. Here the Royal Exchange was the most frequently mentioned location (twenty-one landlords/ladies, sought by fourteen lodgers). Other named City locations included St Paul's, Bank, Cornhill, Fenchurch Street, Finsbury Square, Leadenhall (one lodger noting his need to be within ten minutes of the East India Company headquarters), Mark Lane and St Sepulchre.[24] In the 1770s, American merchant Joshua Johnson (1742–1802) thought that lodging in the City close to the heart of the business district gave him a commercial advantage over rivals who, lured by the siren call of London's recreational possibilities, were 'running to the other end of town to lodge'.[25]

As well as being a commercial centre drawing in lodgers with business to transact, the City was a place of arrival in London either by ship or for travellers by coach. Coaches from the north terminated in Bishopsgate (as Hogarth's Moll Hackabout's had done) and those from the south travelled over London Bridge.

Recently-arrived lodgers often stayed close to such points at least for a week or two, finding their feet in a strange city before moving elsewhere. Armenian immigrant Joseph Emin (1726–1809) arrived as a sailor on the *Walpole* in 1751 and lodged initially in the docks at Wapping, next in Dowgate Hill, then in Cheapside at an attorney's.[26] In August 1775 Curwen began his English lodging career in Drapers Court, Princes Street, between the Poultry and Lothbury.[27]

Notably, there was never more than a handful of *Chronicle* advertisements for anywhere east of the City – one a-piece for Tower Hill and the Minories, three in Clapton and Hackney and the following:

> One or Two Ladies may be accommodated with BOARD and LODGING, and an Extra Parlour and Servant's Rooms if required; in a respectable family in the neighbourhood of Mile-end.[28]

At this period Mile End New Town, no. 12 on the extreme right of Cary's map (Figure 1), was under construction but only on a piecemeal basis. Along with Clapton and Hackney to its west, it retained something of a peripheral, semi-rural character.[29] Clearly the poorer suburbs of east London, including Wapping where Emin had spent only two weeks before moving gradually westwards to greater gentility, were not a part of the lodgings market represented by these advertisements or by most life-writing.[30] They were, however, along with the riverside settlements on the south bank, inevitably popular with the large number of sailors of all nationalities: temporary residents with a little money in their pockets awaiting a voyage out, men like merchant navy officer John 'Rambling Jack' Cremer (1700–74) who decided with a cousin to blue twenty guineas a-piece on 'a Gentelman's [*sic*] life' for a fortnight.[31] As Chapter 2 explained, novels like *Moll Flanders* and news and crime reports, culminating in the Ratcliffe Highway murders, underscored an impression that this was an anarchic, vicious part of town and not for the respectable. In November 1782, for example, a notice was placed in the *Chronicle* informing the public that the Middlesex justices in Whitechapel had issued warrants for the searching of lodging-houses for 'rogues, vagabonds, and idle and disorderly persons'.[32] The docks and the divided dwellings for poorer workers in Spitalfields were increasingly understood by middling-sort contemporaries as 'other' and as socially problematic.[33]

There was sufficient anxiety, and racism, among the better-off to prompt an early 'reform' of the squalid *ad hoc* private arrangements that lay behind the pitiful 1793 death of John Dullen, an ill black sailor. On a cold November night

Dullen was dumped in the street and left to die by his landlord Jacob Jeggett, who ran a cheap lodging-house for sailors and 'common girls of the town' in tiny Catherine Wheel Alley, just east of Bishopsgate. Jeggett was tried for murder but acquitted on grounds of good character.[34] Reform was attempted when a barracks was established in Ratcliffe Highway to accommodate over 1,000 'Lascar' (Asian) seamen (from 1814 run at the East India Company's expense), though by 1815 the barracks was itself the subject of a critical report into the conditions there.[35]

There were areas west of the old City walls which were similarly never found in *Chronicle* advertisements or life-writing. In the 'Rookery' of St Giles-in-the-Fields 'if there is no more than one bed in each room, there are usually two or three, and sometimes even four occupiers of that one', said an article in *Olla Podrida*.[36] There were too plenty of lodging-houses in the narrow streets, alleys and courts around Old Pye Street, Westminster. This was also increasingly seen as a low district, its accommodation described by a parish official as 'little Hutts, little low Huts 2 or 3 Rooms', their inhabitants common soldiers, sellers of old clothes, beggars, 'ragged people'.[37] These, with their eastern counterparts, were the lowest end of 'common lodging houses', and 'common lodging houses' of any description were much disliked by the *Chronicle*'s would-be lodgers. There were twenty-four who requested that no such place reply to their advertisement. Equally, eighteen landlords/ladies promised that theirs was not such an establishment or that they were a 'private family (fifty-four), were 'new to lodging' (five), had no other lodgers (thirty) or only one other (three). It was important to be certain that the lodging situation was one of respectability and gentility, words that recur frequently in the advertisements, as we shall see.

However, the rest of Westminster featured prominently in *Chronicle* advertisements reflecting both supply – a century of westwards expansion onto green fields – and demand. Over 100 rooms offered were in the bustling 'centrical' area, the district between the western extremity of the City and the seat of government in Westminster and its West End (essentially the uncoloured area at the centre of Cary's map, Figure 1).[38] Johnson, famously a lover of London, thought that 'the full tide of human existence is at Charing Cross'.[39] The Compton Street fire took place in its heart and locations here occur time and again in life-writing.

Thomas Bowles's engraving of the Strand in the 1790s shows a busy shop-lined street that was popular with lodgers (Figure 6). Many thought the hubbub was worth it: the Strand and other similar streets offered the perfect blend of access to business to the east, to the publishing and bookselling businesses of Fleet Street

Figure 6 Thomas Bowles, *A View of Somerset House with St Mary's Church in the Strand, London*, after 1794. The Strand was a key route between City and West End. Lined with shops and businesses, it was a wide, well-paved thoroughfare constantly busy with pedestrians and vehicles but ever-popular with lodgers. Courtesy of the Lewis Walpole Library, Yale University: Topos L847 no. 96+.

and St Paul's, to the Inns of Court, to leisure facilities, such as theatres, and to the Court district of the West End. The *Chronicle* advertisements included sixteen landlord/lady offers of rooms in the West End, eighteen described as 'near' the park, playhouses and St James's; seven in Soho; five in Pall Mall and the Strand. Other named locations were Red Lion Square, Craven Street (where Franklin and Gansel lodged), Fleet Street, Bond Street, Leicester Fields (location of Anne King's murder), Covent Garden, Oxford Street and 'near' Somerset House, the Adelphi and Cavendish and Fitzroy Squares. Lodgers sought rooms in similar locations: near St James's, Cavendish Square, The Haymarket, Gower Street, Strand, Portland Place. 'Near' is the weasel word in these advertisements (as it is with estate agents today). The least likely location for a house with lodgers was actually in these grand developments, squares and streets, as Trusler noted in his guide. Here there was no economic imperative to let out rooms.

'Near' followed the standard style of addressing a letter. However, it also implied that a lodger could hope for distinction by proximity to the grandest parts of town. Landlords/ladies seemed only too happy to pander to this desire when promoting rooms in the middling-sort side streets close by. Although timber-framed buildings survived across London to the early-twentieth century, houses in these districts were likely to be relatively new-built and, as one advertiser ('near' Hanover Square) put it, 'fitted up in an elegant stile and modern taste'.[40] They were situated on relatively clean, paved and lit streets, with nice proportions and details to the main rooms, modestly handsome doorcases and stairways, and glazed sash windows.[41] Their layout with entrance hall and landings was, as Chapter 1 explained, perfect for taking in lodgers.[42] It was, then, hardly surprising that the Westminster suburbs gradually became one of the most attractive lodging locations in the capital.

For advertisers, the key in all these locations was to define the situation in terms that differentiated it from the common lodging houses of the poor. Landlords and ladies were keen to stress the respectability/reputability and gentility of their situation, words that occurred more than any others (apart from 'airy') in their advertisements: thirty-nine and 111 times respectively. 'Airy' was promised in forty-one advertisements, and 'healthy' in twenty. These terms also featured in many advertisements for lodgings wanted: genteel fifty-six, respectable/reputable twenty-nine and airy twenty-one. Many advertisements combined two or even all three terms:

> A RESPECTABLE LADY may be accommodated with Board and Lodging in a small genteel family, in an airy situation at the west end of the town.[43]

'Airy' may have hinted at a first-floor location, since the first-floor windows and ceiling in a Georgian terrace were usually taller than on other floors. Above all it suggested somewhere removed from the stink of manufacturing or the dark, ramshackle and overcrowded tenements that one Westminster overseer of the poor feared to visit: 'a little blackguard place I was over my shoe to get to it.'[44] It conjures up light, a breeze, and the possibility of a view, which was increasingly used to sell rooms in the *Chronicle* of the 1790s. Lodgings in Knightsbridge enjoyed 'one of the most beautiful prospects in Hyde-Park'; a 'small genteel family' sought a lodger for an 'airy' situation with a view of 'London behind, and Surry-Hills [*sic*] on the front'; a room in Cecil Street, Strand, benefited from 'healthful air from the Water'.[45] The teeming lodging-houses around the docks were near the water, but no one lived there for the view, or would have described the setting as healthy. Social class and differentiation were again everything.

Diaries and memoirs confirm the attraction of these respectable and genteel districts and rooms to respectable and genteel lodgers. The central area close

to the houses of publishers suited writers and habitual lodgers such as Johnson
and his fellow author and friend Oliver Goldsmith (?1728–74), who lived in
shabby, probably timber-framed, Green Arbour Court (Figure 7) and then more
respectable Wine Office Court. Actors lodged close to the London theatres (and

Figure 7 S. Rawle, The *Residence of the Late Dr. Goldsmith in 1758*, 1803. Oliver
Goldsmith lived in Green Arbour Court in 1758. The houses may well have been
old-fashioned timber-framed structures, which were generally cheaper. The area was
comprehensively redeveloped as Holborn Viaduct in the 1860s. Courtesy of the Lewis
Walpole Library, Yale University: 803.02.01.01.

also lodged in other cities when on tour): Charke, Inchbald and Tate Wilkinson (1739–1803) and his many friends, for example.[46] Their accommodation was the predecessor of the theatrical 'digs' of the nineteenth and twentieth centuries. Artists, generally at the struggling end of their profession, lodged as near as affordable to wealthy patrons, Hogarth's St Martin's Lane Academy (founded 1735), the Royal Academy (opened in Pall Mall in 1768 and from 1780 at New Somerset House, Strand), and other West End exhibition spaces. A 1797 advertisement in the *Chronicle* headed 'TO ARTISTS' advertised a genteel, furnished first floor at 41 Jermyn Street (now number 36) as having light 'particularly well adapted for that profession'. In addition, it boasted (truthfully) two rising stars and future presidents of the Royal Academy, Thomas Lawrence (1769–1830) and Martin Archer Shee (1769–1850), as previous occupants.[47] The young Haydon lodged in the Strand, Carnaby Market, Rathbone Place, and Marlborough Street, and Scottish artist David Wilkie (1785–1841) in Marylebone with a coal merchant – inconvenient since it involved 'a good long walk twice a day' to the Academy and soon exchanged for Solls Row at the southern end of Hampstead Road (near Farthing Pye Gate, no. 4 on Cary's map, Figure 1) – and then from 1808 at clergy widow Mrs Coppard's at 84 Great Portland Street.[48] From 1803 to 1821 engraver, artist, and poet William Blake (1757–1827) and his wife and collaborator Catherine (1762–1831) lived, worked, and socialized in two modest rooms above a shop at 17 South Molton Street, between Oxford Street and Piccadilly in Mayfair. Their decision to downsize from an eight-room house in Lambeth may not have been entirely motivated by the price of rentals. Mayfair was well located for clients, galleries, and other artists.[49]

The central district of Westminster also suited visitors to London. Some, like Jonathan Swift and Americans Franklin and future president Thomas Jefferson (1743–1826), had business in Westminster with the great and good of the Court and Parliament. Between 1710 and 1713 Swift occupied central lodgings in Pall Mall, Bury Street, St Alban Street, Leicester Fields, and Rider Street. He found, as we have seen, that Chelsea and Kensington, though better for health, were too far out of town for one who travelled in almost daily.[50] From 1757 to 1775 Franklin was periodically in London as a diplomat and always lodged in 7 Craven Street, Strand (modern number 36, Figure 8) with widowed Margaret Stevenson and her daughter Mary, known as Polly. When Polly and her family took over the house in 1772, Franklin moved with Mrs Stevenson to another house in the same street.[51] Jefferson, as Minster Plenipotentiary to France, came to London in 1786 for seven weeks at the invitation of another future president,

Figure 8 Frederick Adcock, *Benjamin Franklin's House, Craven Street*, 1912.
36 Craven Street, where Benjamin Franklin lodged between 1757 and 1775. It is a
'classic' Georgian townhouse typical of many in streets popular with respectable
lodgers. It was built in 1730 and altered after Franklin's time in 1792 when the fourth
storey was added. The only surviving house either side of the Atlantic where Franklin
lived, it is now a museum. Author's collection, photography by Urban Picnic, Saffron
Walden.

John Adams (1735–1826), his counterpart in England. Jefferson stayed one night with Adams in Grosvenor Square and then took accommodation of his own in Golden Square, Soho, at a Mrs Conners's. His accounts show that he enjoyed shopping, especially for gadgets, and travel while in England.[52] Visitors whose stays were more purely for pleasure included Yorkshire gentleman and bachelor John Courtney of Beverley (1734–1806), who, often with his widowed mother in tow, travelled and lodged in York, resort towns, Cambridge and London. In early summer 1759 the pair took three rooms and two closets at Mrs Denham's, Featherstone Buildings, Holborn for 25s. a week. The house was well-placed for sightseeing: over a month and a half they took in Vauxhall, Marylebone and Ranelagh Gardens, Drury Lane and Sadler's Wells theatres, a lottery draw, spied members of royal family, and met William Hogarth. In 1761 Mrs Denham had no rooms available, so they made do with Mrs Powell's in Cecil Street, Strand (a parlour and two lodging-rooms on the second floor at 28s. a week), returning however to Mrs Denham's in summer 1765.[53]

Overseas visitors were advised to take private lodgings rather than an inn or hotel on grounds of cost.[54] Virginian landowner William Byrd (1674–1744) lodged in 1717–21 just off the Strand, convenient for his sex tourism as well as the more official variety.[55] The Mozarts came to London for a year in April 1764 when Wolfgang was eight and his sister thirteen years old. Although here to work, the family also found time for the sights and lodged at 'the house of Mr. Cousin, haircutter in Cecil Court, St. Martin's lane, at London' and later (after a period in Chelsea for health reasons) at 15 Frith Street (current number 21) the house and shop of Mr Thomas Williamson, stay-maker and wax-chandler.[56] Also in 1765, French man of letters Pierre-Jean Grosley (1718–85) lived by Leicester Fields in a little, irregular-shaped house where very few of the small rooms were not let out to lodgers, and in 1786 German novelist Sophie von la Roche (1730–1807) lodged in Portland Street, one of the newest developments in Westminster.[57]

Some lodgers were prepared or preferred to lodge at a slightly great distance from the centre of London, especially in the semi-rural villages that were gradually being subsumed within the capital's sprawl and were within walking distance – typically a greater distance than the twenty-first-century pedestrian would countenance – or were linked to the capital by a regular coach service.[58] Antiquary Daniel Lysons (1762–1834) in his *Environs of London* (1795) recorded the growth of the outer parishes and the concomitant rise in the number of lodgers there. The population of Putney's 440 houses, for example, was 2,294 of whom 274 were lodgers, a proportion (12 per cent) close to that for central

London. In Wandsworth the figure was even higher: 4,554 inhabitants and 843 lodgers (18.5 per cent).[59] Reasons for the decision to lodge on the periphery included not only health but economy, discretion, having friends in the neighbourhood, and the desire for fresher air and some peace and quiet away from the busy streets of the capital. These locations – Kensington, Richmond, Windsor, Islington, Hampstead – some of them off the edge of Cary's map, were all included in *Chronicle* advertisements. Private lodging therefore grew and spread with London, though landlords/ladies made sure to draw attention to the connectedness of their premises to the centre: 'within five miles of Hyde Park Corner, where Stages pass every hour', for example.[60]

The cleaner urban fringe was popular with those whose health was delicate: Swift, the Mozarts, and Wilkie, who moved to Hampstead when ill. Other health reasons – an embarrassing pregnancy that evoked Moll Flanders's Clerkenwell landlady, a diagnosis of lunacy or a sexually-transmitted disease – necessitated discreet, secluded accommodation. Facilities for treatment of these conditions were often located around the urban periphery and were advertised in the *Chronicle*. The Medical Lunatic Asylum was 'in the vicinity of London', though patients could be advised in the first instance at 193 Strand.[61] The 5 October 1795 number carried two advertisements for specialist lodging: an asylum in Paddington for ladies suffering from insanity and apartments 'in town or country' with medical attendance for 'Ladies who suffer from the consequences of indiscretion'. Scottish biblical scholar Alexander 'the Corrector' Cruden (1699–1770) was twice removed from central lodgings to private madhouses in Bethnal Green (1738) and Chelsea (1753). These seem to have been organized rather as lodging-houses. Cruden's first-floor Chelsea room, was, he said, as pleasant as any lodging-room but for its involuntary nature: 'a neat well-furnished apartment that might have served a prince; but it was made to serve as a prison for the *Corrector*'.[62] Charles Lamb (1775–1834) and his sister Mary (1764–1847), both of whom were born in and adored London, also spent periods on its fringes, in Hoxton, Dalston, Enfield and Edmonton, during Mary's bouts of mental ill-health.[63]

For others, the urban fringe offered respite from hectic city life. Over summer 1727, while their townhouse was redecorated, melancholic Midlands gentlewoman Gertrude Savile (1697–1758) and her mother lodged in Wandsworth after a search which took in Kew, Richmond, Petersham, and Brentford. Her pleasure in the garden at Wandsworth indicates that perhaps it was for a quieter, greener setting in the heat of summer that they sought more rural rooms.[64] For Goldsmith remote lodgings allowed him to work without the distractions of town and friends. During 1767 he lodged, largely at the behest of his publisher Newbery (who sensibly deducted the rent at source from his salary), at Canonbury House, Islington, and in 1771 he took rooms at a farmhouse near the 'six mile stone' on Edgeware Road to concentrate on his *History of Rome*.[65] Curwen, who had many lodging addresses in central London and the western edge of the city, tried Islington for six months from October 1775, Brompton in early 1781, and Battersea in the summer of the same year. He walked across the metropolis from all these locations.[66] Later in life Inchbald lodged in a more retired style at Turnham Green, almost seven miles from central London, and then at the Salterellis' large boarding-house, Kensington House, Kensington Road, where she died.[67] Lodgings away from the centre were often cheaper. At one point Curwen even considered Croydon for 'the cheap rate of £30 per year full board', and it was for urgent reasons of economy that both Morland and Haydon each retreated to Paddington, no. 3 on the western fringes of Cary's map (Figure 1).[68]

Having established the geography of the London lodging market, this next section reviews the evidence for the individuals who decided to take lodgers into their spare rooms, using the limited statistical data available supplemented by other sources such as advertisements and diaries. It looks both at what sort of people they were and, as far as possible, at their motives for becoming landlords and ladies.

The late-seventeenth-century Marriage Duty Survey identifies with certainty only twenty-eight landlords and ladies with something over fifty-five lodgers between them.[69] There were seventeen landlords, eleven of them married. Almost 100 years later, of the seventeen landlords involved in the 1785 Compton Street fire, five are known to have lived with a wife, and of those where no wife is named four had at least one servant. Operating both a shop or trade and lodgings was obviously easiest if done as team-work. In 1762–63 the young Boswell's landlord and lady were Mr and Mrs Terrie in Downing Street, Westminster. Terrie was Chamber-Keeper to the Office for Trade and Plantations and Boswell dealt with both husband and wife. Curwen similarly often lodged with married couples and dealt with the wives at least as much as the husbands.[70] Managing lodgers was, even where a man's name appeared on lists of householders, often in practice gendered as female work, as Amanda Vickery has shown.[71] All too often this work is literally only accidentally visible in sources, after a fire or crime for example, hardly considered as work by contemporaries and economic historians alike since it is so closely related to unpaid housework outside the market economy.[72]

However, if we redefine taking lodgers as work in a highly active marketplace (Graglia based his calculations on lodgers moving twice a year, and Curwen moved at least thirty-four times in his nine-year exile), the private lodgings business can be fitted neatly into Hunt's category of the eighteenth-century middling-sort family enterprise with its attendant ethos.[73] Taking lodgers represented thrift, maximizing one's assets and opportunities. It provided a buffer of extra income against future expenses or difficulties.[74] *The Economist*, a little pocket-sized book of household budgets in its 15th edition by 1781, described a range of frugal strategies (such as home baking and brewing and doing one's own hair) to make money go further while still making a genteel appearance, noting that taking in lodgers had not been allowed for but could be used to increase income.[75] In 1725 'A German Gentleman's' satirical description of London captured just such a family, a shopkeeper, his wife, and eighteen-year-old daughter, 'extraordinary Oeconomists', living in St Anne Soho on £70 a year, a typical, modest, middling-sort income for a retailer. Not only did they make a joint of meat last two days and a shift (shirt) three, they 'let three Parts of their House ready furnish'd'.[76] In 1797, Francis Place and his wife, who now had four rooms 'en suite' on a second floor for £16 a week, took the same cautious approach. They 'intended to lodge some respectable single man and thus reduce the amount of the rent which was more than my circumstances warranted me to undertake to pay without such aid'.[77] Caricaturist George Cruikshank (1792–1878) and novelist Charles Dickens (1812–70) each recalled their mothers taking in lodgers to supplement the male household income when times were tough in the early-nineteenth century.[78]

Indeed, as the legal case *Underwood v. Burrows* revealed, the rent from letting lodgings might fully cover the lease rental, leaving the net shop or other income as pure profit. A 1778 advertisement for a bankruptcy auction of the furniture, possessions, and lease of bookseller Samuel Beacroft advised that his Charing Cross premises 'were excellently calculated to make the rent by lodgers'.[79] Taking lodgers was therefore a sound financing strategy. It enabled shopkeepers and other middling-sort Londoners to live reasonably securely (though Beacroft had evidently not managed to do so) in an otherwise too-expensive area of affluent customers. One would-be lodger well understood this. He and his wife wanted to lodge near the Royal Exchange and expected that their rent would 'ease the expence [*sic*] of housekeeping' for a landlord or lady.[80] Some householders, like the Kennington landlady advertising in the *Chronicle* in 1795, deliberately fixed up their houses for the taking of lodgers: freshening up the paintwork, furnishing the rooms with beds and other necessary furniture, maybe providing a communal parlour, and acquiring a sufficient stock of linen, crockery, cutlery, and so forth.[81] There was a plethora of adaptable furniture that could be moved as lodgers came and went, such as folding and sofa-beds and curtains that could be put up and taken down quickly and easily by the householder or a servant.[82]

Lodgers, for their part, seem generally to have been unconcerned about the shopkeeping and other trades taking place on the ground floor provided it was not a 'noisy, dirty, offensive' business.[83] Both Teresia Constantia Muilman (another *ODNB* 'courtesan', 1709–65) and author Laetitia Pilkington (*c.* 1709–50) were slightly disappointed in lodgings where entry was via the shop: 'there was but one Inconvenience, which was, that there was no Passage into the House, but through the Shop', said Pilkington.[84] It was a stipulation made by some lodgers in *Chronicle* advertisements that there should be a private entrance: 'if at a reputable shop (which would not be disliked), a separate door would be wished'.[85] Some shops were probably adapted in this way, and later developments sometimes incorporated shop fronts with a trade door and a second, private door, an open acknowledgement of the part lodgers played in funding the occupation of such premises. A surviving example is Woburn Buildings (now Walk) built in 1822 and where Scottish writer Thomas Carlyle (1795–1881) lodged when first in London (Figure 9). Such doors permitted the admission of lodgers and their visitors without the need to mingle 'in common' with customers as they did at Hermin's (Hemmings?) Row, St Martin-in-the-Fields, where in 1755 William Storey had a barber's shop and landlady Mrs Arundell let upper rooms.[86] It was another important nod to the maintaining of gentility, here of the paying guest.

Rooms that could be spared were also an important resource for landlords/ ladies in times of greater need. A sub-set of fourteen *Chronicle* advertisements uncovers a strategy whereby taking lodgers could be used to raise a capital sum upfront to pay off debts or finance an enterprise. In these cases, the lodgings came in return not for a weekly rent payment but a loan from the lodger:

> A real Gentlewoman of unexceptionable Character wants to borrow Forty Pounds for Six Months, at five per cent. and good security, and as a compliment perfectly legal, she will accommodate the Lender with Board and Lodging, free from expences till the money is paid.[87]

The sums proposed ranged from this £40 to £300 for three years.[88] A lodger in such a deal was tantamount to a leverageable asset that could be used to improve

CARLYLE'S LONDON LODGINGS, 5, WOBURN BUILDINGS.

Figure 9 *Carlyle's London Lodgings, 5 Woburn Buildings*, 1895. 5 (now 6) Woburn Buildings (now Walk) just south of the New (Euston) Road was Thomas Carlyle's first London lodging. He lived here with his brother who was also a lodger. Woburn Buildings was a new street, built in 1822 on virgin land belonging to the Bedford Estate by Thomas Cubitt (1788–1855). It consisted of two terraces of shops with accommodation over, and, as this image illustrates, they had the crucial two doors for separate entry to the shop and the living quarters, indicating that the likelihood of lodging was probably in the mind of the architect from the start. Author's collection, photography by Urban Picnic, Saffron Walden.

liquidity as much as was the house in which he or she lived. It was a deal, however, that from the outset created an imbalanced relationship, locking the lodger into accommodation that might prove unsatisfactory. It is also difficult to see how some of the capital sums proposed were reasonable given the prevailing level of rents (see Chapter 4). Indeed, no arrangement of this sort has yet come to light in life-writing and similar sources.

Across the whole time period of this study all the sources establish that landlords/ladies operating private lodgings were largely drawn from the broad group of the middling sort, typically the shopkeepers or skilled craftsmen and women depicted in contemporary fiction. The strong association between the retail trades and the taking-in of lodgers is confirmed by other studies. In their sample of eighteenth-century shopkeepers in London and York, Hoh-Cheung and Lorna Mui found that 42 per cent in the former and 31.8 per cent in the latter city took lodgers.[89] Shelley Tickell's analysis of shopkeepers' finances makes clear the importance of supplementing retail income with rent from lodgers.[90]

Most of the ten late-seventeenth-century Marriage Duty Survey landlords where an occupation is given – an attorney, watchmaker, porter, scrivener, packer, clothdrawer (finisher of cloth), joiner, oilman, weaver, and the City Crier – fall within the category of middling sort as do the landlords/ladies who made claims after the 1785 Compton Street fire (see Chapter 1). *Chronicle* advertisements, on the other hand, were usually reticent about the landlord's/lady's trade, preferring, if anything was said at all, the catch-all 'tradesman'. Among those named were various teachers and physicians whose lodgers were also their clients (see below), a bun-baker, merchant, clergyman, and artist (M. Charles, miniaturist, Strand, who also advertised 'strong likenesses' painted in one hour).[91] Although few in number, all again fit comfortably into the category of the middling sort. Life-writing also confirms the middling-sort, retailing character of the lodgings business across London as a whole. Several writers' landlords/ladies have already been introduced. Others include Anglo-Irish clergyman and author Laurence Sterne (1713–68), who from 1765 lodged when in London (and died) above widowed Mary Fourmantel's up-market and discreet Bond Street bag-making (i.e. silk bags for hair 'queues') shop. Back in London in 1768 Boswell lodged with an upholsterer, and in 1769 with a milliner. One of Inchbald's landladies, Miss Baillie, was also a milliner. The doomed poet Chatterton (see Chapter 2) lived in a sack-maker's (dressmaker's) garret, and artist, writer and journalist William Hazlitt (1778–1830) at a tailor's at 9 Southampton Buildings, Holborn.[92]

As we have seen, many hosts operated as a married couple, with the wife often assuming responsibility for the lodgers. Other landladies were single women, like Inchbald's Miss Baillie. There were nine singlewoman landladies in the Marriage Duty Survey, seven of them described as widows. Of the twenty-two households with lodgers in the Compton Street fire records of 1785, five were headed by women. We have already met Hannah Barker of Compton Street, the widow carrying on the composition ornament-making business of her late husband. She also looked after three stepchildren. Mary Death (Church Street) was also a widow, Ann Turner (Frith Street) was a milliner and for Mrs Elizabeth Barrett and Mrs Stephenson (both Greek Street) no further information was given. Only Barker and Turner definitely had live-in servants to help with the work of servicing their lodgers (and in Barker's case assisting with her trade).[93] The gender of most *Chronicle* advertisers with rooms to let is not known, but where it is the genders are evenly balanced: twenty-three were placed by men and twenty-four by women, of whom only seven declared themselves widows. The evidence of the life-writers, where widowed landladies of all ages are found very frequently, suggests that widowed landladies were in fact more numerous than is immediately evident from such surveys as exist. Some women may have chosen not to focus on their widowhood in advertisements, out of discretion or to guard against the various lodging scams perhaps.

The task of servicing lodgers without a partner or live-in help must have been onerous and not undertaken lightly. If these single landladies, widowed or otherwise, do not seem to have been women in dire need, neither was their income likely to have been as high or secure as that of their male counterparts.[94] Their decision to take lodgers was probably based on a similar, but more urgent, prudent economic rationale to that of couples. Curwen described a prospective London landlady, Mrs Smithson, as 'in the plan of keeping a boarding house, wants me for one of her family'. She was apparently struggling financially.[95] It allowed widows, the separated, and the abandoned to remain in the family home. Jane Hogarth (bapt. 1710, d. 1789), for instance, stayed at Leicester Fields after William's death in 1764. At first, she was able to make a sufficient income from sales of prints, but when this dried up she 'was then absolutely living by her lodgings'. Her lodgers included the Scottish painter Alexander Runciman (1736–85).[96] For all single women, becoming a landlady was a means to financial independence in an environment with limited opportunities for well-paid genteel work, running a school being another option as several lives in this study testify. Wilkie's landlady Mrs Coppard can probably be seen in this light since she became a landlady in the year of her husband's death. Mary Wollstonecraft, her sister Eliza and friend Fanny Blood, all unmarried, created an independent life for themselves when they became landladies in Newington Green in 1785, setting up a school of twenty pupils and taking in two families of lodgers in addition.[97]

For singlewoman hosts, lodgers provided a little company, even security. *Chronicle* advertisements promoted this idea of company rather than hard cash as an important motive. Among landlords/ladies, twenty-eight made 'society', sometimes adding that this was 'select' or agreeable', an express part of their offer. In 1783, for example, a 'Widow Lady' offered a spare room:

> for the sake of society, and wishes for an agreeable companion, can genteelly accommodate a lady with Board and Lodging, on very moderate terms.

Similarly, in 1795 a 'Middle-aged single Lady, with a genteel independence' wished 'to accommodate a Lady or Gentleman of fortune ... her only inducement is society'.[98] Protestations that money was not the object may have been made in order to protect the advertisers' sense of their own gentility. It may also have been tactical – too-evident desperation placed the host in weaker position when negotiating over rent. There is evidence in memoirs that company could, however, be a supplementary factor in the decision to rent out rooms. When working as a young journeyman printer in 1720s London, Franklin had lodged with an elderly widow in Duke Street, by Lincoln's Inn Fields. She let the room to him cheaply at 3s. 6d. a week (reduced to 1s. 6d. when he announced he planned to leave) 'as she said from the protection she expected in having a Man lodge in the House'. She was lame from the gout and unable to move around the house much:

> so sometimes wanted Company; and hers was so highly amusing to me; that I was sure to spend an Evening with her whenever she desired it ... the entertainment was in her conversation.[99]

Nevertheless, much as they genuinely sought company, most landlords and ladies were of course letting rooms for money. After all, the 'Middle-aged single Lady' cited above did want a lodger of fortune and was charging the high price of one hundred guineas a year. We should not lose sight of the fact that these men and women took lodgers as a deliberate strategy in a commercial, competitive and sometimes ruthless business. When Wollstonecraft was about to travel to Lisbon in 1785 she (rightly as it turned out) feared that she would lose her lodgers to rival Newington landlady Mrs Cockburn.[100] A landlord or lady might well be prepared to reduce their terms to keep a good tenant rather than risk a vacancy and the total loss of cash, something Franklin and Boswell both exploited, but this did not necessarily mean they were friends with their lodgers.[101] Nevertheless, despite lodging being a business, across all the sources examined here few landlords/ladies took more than one, two, or three lodgers at a time. One, two, or three maintained the semblance of genteel company in a private home. Any more might have smacked of the common lodging house.

This was a point of continuity. In the late-seventeenth century most of the landlords/ladies in the Marriage Duty Survey had only one or two lodgers. There were, however, three households, all headed by a married man, containing a much larger number.[102] In St Nicholas Acons, Timothy Simms and his wife accommodated an unspecified number of shoemaker lodgers, suggesting a specialized business of possibly itinerant workers in the craft. A century later Charles Newham (b. 1799), a carpenter and builder from Rochester, Kent, lived like this. He arrived in London aged eighteen with £1 and 'my kit upon my shoulder' and found work at £1 a week: 'We all lived and lodged, together with our master [Mr Goff] and his family at No. 16 Waterloo Place, St James's, which was then in course of being completed.' He moved several times, lodging with other hands with the master or foreman of a site on which they were working.[103] In 1785 there were two households with similarly large numbers of lodgers in Compton Street: Hannah Barker accommodated, as we have seen, five individuals (one of them with a child), and John Batchellor, a haberdasher on the corner of Compton Street and Star Court, had seven lodgers in five lodger-households, one with a servant. Both had let some rooms to lodgers of lowly standing. In Barker's case they were servants out of place and in Batchellor's a dealer in oil and vinegar in the garret, probably therefore a street-seller. Those responsible for distributing the charitable funds singled Batchellor out with the comment that he 'let the greatest part of his house unfurnished', which sounds like criticism. Batchellor was noted as having children and a servant, but there is no mention of a wife. Without a partner, he may have been struggling to cope with shop and family and have resorted to the large number of lodgers, for whom he could not afford to provide furnishings. The committee's deliberations reveal that Barker was 'much embarrassed' even before the fire. Her husband had 'embarked on many Schemes which did not answer his Expectations' and she had a number of creditors.[104] These two examples suggest that for some landlords/ladies the prime motive was the mitigation of financial strain, but they hint too at the risk of some loss of social status where there were too many lodgers. Barker and Batchellor, and perhaps Timothy Simms before them, had strayed a little too close to the common lodging house and in the process had compromised their gentility.

There were, though, limited circumstances in which the taking of multiple lodgers was acceptable and respectable, and where lodgers may even have shared rooms with others. These were the various lodgings which operated as educational establishments, both formal and informal. The Norland military academy in Kensington offered as a unique selling point a guaranteed single bed per lodger, an indication that rivals did not. Its board, lodging, and officer-training programme was also advertised as being cheaper than central lodgings and at a distance from the dissipation so tempting there.[105] Medical students often lodged communally in houses near their hospital in the households of medical staff. Father and son Richard (1751–1823) and Hampton Weekes (1780–1855) of Hurstpierpoint, Sussex, each lived in lodgings with four or five other students when training at St Thomas's. In 1815 poet John Keats (1795–1821) lodged at a dresser's house with other students while studying at Guy's.[106] Inchbald's later lodgings were more like retirement homes with large numbers of mature lodgers. In 1803 she lived at Mrs Wyatt's Annandale House, Turnham Green, where, like the Salterellis' Kensington House, the accommodation was specifically for Roman Catholics (it too had a chapel). There were twelve other paying guests, as well as the twenty scholars attending Wyatt's school. In 1816 she lodged at Miss Hodge's, 4 Earl's Terrace opposite Holland House in Kensington, where four other older ladies lodged:

> All the old widows and old maids of this house are stretched upon beds or sofas with swoln legs, nervous head-aches, or slow fevers, brought on by loss of appetite, violent thirst, broken sleep, and other dog-day complaints.[107]

As already touched on above, lodging was also integral to some medical practices. 'German gentlewoman' Anne Levenst specialized in female ailments from her home in Arundel Street, Strand, where patients 'may be lodg'd at my House, and accommodated with all things necessary, at a Reasonable rate'.[108] Multiple lodgers were accommodated in some of these medical establishments. These lodgings all had in common a degree of professional specialization which underpinned their respectability and avoided the taint of the common lodging house.

———————————

It is now time to turn to the lodgers, to consider what sort of men and women they were. Living as a lodger in someone else's home has sometimes been described either as a life-cycle phenomenon or as a mark of failure for the middling sort and above. That is, lodgers have been deemed most likely to be young adults not yet in a position to form a household of their own, the single elderly no longer willing or capable of taking on the burdens of housekeeping, or men and women down on their luck.[109] This implies that for the genteel, and those aspiring to gentility, lodging was more a matter of temporary expedient than of free choice. It also assumes that the goal was a house to call one's own, which for most eighteenth-century urban men and women would have been a house held on a lease for a term of years rather than a freehold. Eighteenth-century legal guides, as we have seen, gendered lodging as a male practice, and literature and prints associated female lodgers with sex work. The reality was more complex.

Spence suggests that for some late-seventeenth-century lodgers (City gentry, mercantile, and service groups), renting rooms with services provided was preferable to the burdens of housekeeping.[110] This may well have been the case for single persons and for those who spent only limited time in the capital and did not want or could not afford the expense of keeping a London townhouse (some members of parliament, provincial merchants, and tourists for example), and would have applied equally in the eighteenth and indeed nineteenth centuries. As British commerce expanded during the eighteenth century, both in scale and geographically, so the population of the capital and the number of business and other visitors grew. There was a constant influx of people into London, especially of the single young. Young women came primarily for employment in domestic service (as did Hogarth's Moll Hackabout) and young men for apprenticeships and as casual labour. Around a sixth of the national population spent some of their life in the metropolis. The pressure of demand for accommodation was immense and lodging was an important part of the solution for those looking for a home.

Moving into a lodging-room or rooms in someone's private home was usually a deliberate choice on the part of the lodger. There were alternatives for both short and long stays. It was possible, for example, to rent an entire house, to stay with family or friends, as gentrywoman Elizabeth Freke (1642–1714) often did, in an inn or coffeehouse, in chambers in the Inns of Court or apartments at the Albany (converted from York House in 1802–03 but retaining its palatial appearance).[111] From the second half of the eighteenth century there were hotels, such as Hudson's, Osborne's and Sheffield's in the Adams brothers' Adelphi complex constructed in 1764–68, Lowe's family hotel (founded by a hairdresser), or the York Hotel in Blackfriars.[112] Gentlemen's clubs also offered rooms.[113] All these forms of accommodation had drawbacks which affected the decision. Not everyone had family and friends with room to spare or who were willing to put up visitors. It could be an awkward arrangement. Elizabeth Carter 'considered herself more independent in lodgings [in Clarges Street, Mayfair], as well as more at her ease, than she would be in visiting at any friend's house', for example.[114] Renting an entire house was more expensive and more of a commitment. Clubs were, in addition to the high cost of membership, deliberately exclusive.[115]

Poet Percy Bysshe Shelley (1792–1822), no master of budgeting, stayed in London hotels as well as lodgings and in 1812 did so because he regarded a hotel as 'more convenient for negotiations [with his estranged father] than lodgings'.[116] For merchants and businessmen and women, lodging in a coffeehouse was a natural and convenient extension of doing business there. James Bond kept the Baptist Head coffeehouse in Aldermanbury in the City, 'much frequented by gentlemen of the law, &c.' and where Commissioners of Bankrupts sat.[117] In December 1789 he had at least two 'gentleman' lodgers: a Mr Robinson from Scotland who had been there for three months and a Mr Hickling 'from abroad'.[118] However, most people considered that inns, coffeehouses and hotels were too expensive over the longer term. One 1835 guide warned men of £100 a year, a decent but not large sum:

> Don't go to a hotel; leave your luggage behind the counter of the office for two-pence, and start off for a lodging … by this simple manoeuvre you save a seven or nine shilling bill, (nearly a week's lodging!).[119]

In hotels, regular tipping was often expected and they afforded little privacy with more noise and all the distractions of the 'irregularity that a public-house superinduces in persons of sober habits'.[120] On the other hand, coaching inns, some hotels, the Adelphi and Albany had stabling and carriage houses, which private lodgings generally did not (although one West-End advertiser did, unusually, offer use of the family carriage).[121] Accommodation in clubs was reserved for members and, along with the Adelphi, and Albany, were only available to elite men for whom they provided full servicing at a high price. The Albany regulations also forbade any 'Profession Trade or Business' to be carried out from apartments without express prior permission of the trustees.[122]

Chambers in the Inns of Court were also serviced, but they were less elite and not restricted to members of the Bar as barristers over the eighteenth century became less likely to 'live in', especially once married.[123] The Lambs had lived in the Temple with their parents until 1792 when Samuel Salt, the barrister for whom their father clerked, died. After this reversal of fortune, the Lamb family lived peripatetically in lodgings. Charles and Mary later returned to the Temple in 1801 as lodgers in 16 Mitre Court Buildings, staying until 1808.[124] Johnson's lodgings included rooms in Staple Inn and Inner Temple. His friend Goldsmith also lodged in the Temple, variously on the library staircase, and in Garden and Brick Courts where, in 1768, he took two rooms when flush with £400 from the success of *The Good-Natured Man*.[125] For Johnson, Goldsmith and the Lambs, chambers in the Inns and private lodgings were broadly interchangeable and chambers are found advertised on the open market in the *Chronicle*.[126]

Yet, despite the greater choice of accommodation by the late-eighteenth century, private lodging was still the predominant choice of accommodation for most people, and not only because it provided a far larger number of rooms. So, apart from the generalities covered above, what were the reasons lodgers had for choosing to lodge privately in a household? Outside the areas of London notorious for the overcrowding of poverty, the decision to lodge seems to have been related primarily to the lodger's own household size, and to the unsalaried and mobile nature of many occupations, as well as to a general desire for a degree of independence within the comfortable setting of a family home. Again, there is considerable continuity over time. Of the 325 lodger households in the Marriage Duty Survey the single largest category of lodgers was that of single persons (229, 72 per cent of the total). Married couples without resident children accounted for a further fifty-seven lodging households (18 per cent of the total) and eighteen more consisted of a single woman and her child or children, and two of a single man and child. In the 1785 Compton Street fire records twenty-six out of forty lodger households (65 per cent) were men or women living alone, with married couples without children accounting for a further four, and one instance each of a brother and sister lodging together, like the Lambs, and of two single women lodging together. Only six lodger households contained children. An obvious reason for this preponderance of singleton lodgers is that larger families who could afford it would almost certainly have preferred less restricted quarters, shunning the shared facilities that a lodging-room or rooms in someone else's house entailed. We can assume, for instance, that ribbon weaver William Farmer, a Compton Street fire victim, who lodged with his wife and six children in Greek Street (in a house where there was another lodger to boot) could not afford more space. Like the carpenter in the *Lottery Ticket* print, he must also have worked in these cramped lodging-rooms since the fire consumed his looms leaving the family destitute.[127]

The life-cycle and hardship did sometimes drive the choice. Both the single young and the single elderly might lack the financial resources and enthusiasm for the responsibilities of housekeeping which they might embrace at other life-stages. Gibbon and Place were, in terms of social rank, very different men, but both were conscious of respectability. Each moved into a home of his own as soon as this was possible (see Chapter 1). Boswell lodged in part because his father kept him on a relatively short financial leash for a man of his background: an allowance of £25 every six weeks (£216 a year). Sir John Soane, struggling to establish his architectural practice, lived from 1781 as the lodger of Miss Cecil at 53 Margaret Street, by Cavendish Square, just north of Oxford Street. He courted and married Eliza Smith while a lodger and all their children were born in Margaret Street. It was a stroke of good luck – an inheritance from his wife's uncle – that enabled them to move to premises of their own in 1790.[128] At the other end of the life-cycle we have the houses in which Inchbald lived when older. Indeed, some landladies held themselves out as experienced in care of the infirm and elderly, such as the widow who advertised in the *Chronicle* that she had 'devoted the best part of her time lately to illness in her own Family' and being without 'incumbrance', could 'pay every attention possible'.[129]

A sub-category of the young was students. London had no university until the establishment of University College in 1826, but young men came to London to study medicine, law, and art. One late-seventeenth-century family taking in lodgers in the Marriage Duty Survey was that of John Green, attorney of St Nicholas Acons. Green was a prosperous man in no need of supplementary income (assessed under the Four Shillings in the Pound Aid Green to pay £7 6s. on rentals and £2 4s. on personal property and with stock valued at £200). The unnamed lodger was probably a law student or clerk working for Green, a lodging phenomenon that continued throughout our period. It was to read for the English Bar that future politician John Philpot Curran (1750–1817) moved in 1773 from Ireland to lodgings in St Martin-in-the-Fields.[130] A 'room wanted' *Chronicle* advertisement of 1792 was placed by a young gentleman student at the Temple, and a second in 1795 sought a 'Youth of reputable parents' to be articled to an attorney and solicitor 'in genteel business' with board and lodging included.[131] Hampton Weekes' letters home reveal the rich tradition of medical students' communal lodgings. His father had also trained at St Thomas's and Hampton (himself lodging in St Thomas's Street) wrote home of a visit he had made to his father's old rooms in Castle Street. The landlord, a baker called Messenger, was no longer there, but Hampton had talked to the neighbours. What his father had remembered as a turkey skeleton hanging from the ceiling was in fact the fin of a whale.[132]

Other young people lodged while undertaking 'work experience', as James Fretwell had done in 1717. This was a sufficiently growing phenomenon that in

1724 Defoe decried it in *The Great Law of Subordination*, as one way in which London was changing. These youths, he declared, were not as subject to the hierarchical discipline of 'Family-Oeconomy' as traditional apprentices, and ought rather to be called lodgers.[133] In addition to lodging in London himself, in 1775 Thomas Wale placed his fifteen-year-old son Gregory as a boarder with a with a Spitalfields merchant, Mr Rivaz, to acquire business and personal skills, including French. Rivaz was presumably a Huguenot, perhaps the John Francis Anthony Rivaz (1730–1808) naturalized in 1764/5.[134] The Fretwell and Wale families were not unusual in this practice of finding lodgings that would enhance life prospects. Before his descent into mental ill-health, Cruden lodged for a period with Mme Boulanger of Crown Street, Soho to improve his French.[135] Several examples of lodging advertisements in the *Chronicle* offered or asked for French or other skills as part of a similar educational lodging 'package'. Educationalist Louis Huguenin Du Mitand (1748–?1816) moved to London from Paris in 1777. From the 1780s for some twenty years he regularly advertised to men and women alike his 'easy and expeditious' conversational method of learning French, 'which Reading alone can never impart', while boarding and lodging with his family at his various addresses around central Westminster.[136] Theatrical entrepreneur Anthony Le Texier (*c.* 1737–1814) offered a similar service, and an advertiser in 1795 was looking for lodgings with this particular 'extra'.[137]

In addition to languages, other skills which could be acquired while lodging were dancing, fencing, painting, music, and drawing, all rather reminiscent of Foote's Zachary Fungus.[138] For girls and young women there were no professional opportunities (just one *Chronicle* advertisement for an apprentice to a mantua-maker where lodging was provided) but young women were targeted by small boarding schools and, alongside men, by some of the lodging advertisers who offered tutoring in music, drawing, and languages.[139] Such lodgings could be part of a desirable process of 'finishing' with 'general improvement and information' a young lady between school and marriage, as sought by one 1796 advertiser.[140] It is also the implication behind 'a good opportunity for any guardian to place a young lady who had quitted school'. The situation here was 'near' Hampstead and so sufficiently far from the centre of London to avoid the risk of impropriety that Burney's fictional heroines Evelina and Cecilia had to negotiate.[141] Anna Maria ('Nancy') Woodeford (1757–1830), niece of and housekeeper to Norfolk parson-diarist James (1740–1803), noted in her diary for 2 June 1792 that her friend Miss Pausett was staying in London for three weeks at a Mr Webb's, Tudor Street, Blackfriars 'where she went on purpose to have Masters instruct her in

Music'.[142] In all these examples, male and female, the student was using lodgings as more than a temporary stepping stone, as 'digs'. It was, as McEwan and Sharpe point out, a consciously-chosen means of acquiring skills and networks that set them up for adult, professional, social, and married life.[143]

Lodging as a young, or not-so-young, adult could also provide a sense of freedom from parental or other family control.[144] 'Happy period! – painting and living in one room, as independent as the wind – no servants, no responsibilities, reputation in the bud, hopes endless, ambition beginning – friends untried', wrote twenty-one-year-old Haydon of his Rathbone Place days. At the time of writing he was, of course, unaware that his life would end in 1846 in financial and artistic failure and suicide.[145] William Mawhood (1724–97) was a woollen draper living by the gateway to St Bartholomew-the-Great, Smithfield. He lamented in his diary that his wayward son William (b. 1760), a half-pay junior officer returned from the American War, did 'not like Trade at all' and had no desire to go into the family business. Indeed, William junior passed on through his younger brother Charles the threat that he would live separately in lodgings at 10s. 6d. a week rather than stand behind a counter (though he was not so independent as to shun demanding a £50 a year allowance). No doubt William thought that away from his father's disapproving gaze he would be able to enjoy more of the drinking, spending and sex that was causing inter-generational difficulties between him and his father.[146] There is too a sense of this longing for independence in a diary entry made by artist Joseph Farington (1747–1821) for 6 July 1799 after a visit from the much younger artist Joseph Turner (1775– 1851): 'He talked to me of removing from his father's house in Hand Court, Maiden Lane.' Wisely, the older man advised him 'to take lodgings at first and not to encumber himself with a House'.[147] Young bachelors Boswell, lackadaisical law student William Hickey (1749–1827) and the restless sometime student Sylas Neville (1741–1840) were all seduced by Joshua Johnson's 'siren call' and certainly made the most of what London had to offer young men free of parental control.

To be sure, necessity of the kind met with in novels and in images of the troubled author is apparent in some life stories and press reports. Apothecary Simon Mason (b. 1701) encountered both financial and marital difficulties which at times forced him into lodgings, often apart from his wife and children. The year 1747 found him living at the Stone Kitchen tavern, Tower Hill: 'But still this was an unhappy settl'd life; I, in one Lodging, my good wife in another, and my Children at the Parish.'[148] In 1785 surgeon Andrew Nihell was rescued from the rubble of the Compton Street fire. He was living with his wife and child as a lodger on a mere second floor at William McGuire's greengrocer's shop, his medical reputation presumably in tatters after his 1776 trial for murder.[149] Death notices in the *Gentleman's Magazine*, which in the final quarter of the eighteenth century generally hymned rags-to-riches success stories, sometimes associated death in lodgings with the downward spiral of moral and financial failure that Hogarth depicted.[150] Mr Eustatius Foulcq had written a 'very elaborate and ingenious' botanical treatise but after his manuscript was accidentally burnt gave up the ghost and died in 'an obscure and mean lodging near Bishopsgate-street' in the City – perhaps the 'near' indicated the East End. William Elliott had been an 'eminent distiller' but after bankruptcy and a wandering career gambled away a £10,000 lottery win and ended his days aged ninety-seven and a beggar in an Old Street garret (Cary map no. 7, Figure 1). Thomas Fletcher had enjoyed prosperity as a Cambridge bookseller and printer but was less successful in London, made bankrupt and died in a Leather Lane lodging. Another bookseller Thomas Evans died in lodgings near St Paul's after separating from his wife in a dispute over her 'partiality' for their wastrel son.[151] These were masculine narratives, but there is also the case of Jane Mosseneau (or Mossineau), a milliner working in Berkeley Square. After a capital conviction for theft from her employer she received a royal pardon but, like a Hogarthian anti-heroine, her life was ruined by her moral lapse. Penniless through lack of work, her children were taken from her by Marylebone parish and she died alone in her lodging-room by Oxford Market.[152]

More significantly, for many Londoners well above the poverty line of these obituaries, for men and women, young and older, there was no such thing as a regular income. As Corfield points out, advancement and security were by no means guaranteed even in the professions.[153] Some higher-status occupations demanded the mobility which lodging on or near the job had offered Kent builder Charles Newham. Thomas Wiffen and his wife, who claimed from the Compton Street fire fund, had in 1785 recently returned to London from a diplomatic mission to Vienna with Sir Murray Keith and lodged in tobacconist Benedict Blume's first floor while reorienting their lives.[154] Precarity plus mobility explain why so many creative men and women – writers, actors, and artists – lived in lodgings. The temporary expedient of lodging was also attractive to army and navy officers whose regiments were not seeing active service, the half-pay men like young Mawhood. It placed them close to the centre of both the military establishment and the delights of the West End, especially its gambling clubs. For them lodging could be a long-standing arrangement, as in the case of Gansel or the near-legendary devotee of 'deep play' (heavy, high-stakes gambling), Major Baggs, who in January 1792 died at his Jermyn Street lodgings, aged seventy, of a cold caught in the round-house where he had been carried from the gaming tables of St James's.[155] The presence of these clubs was also a magnet for Pilkington who chose rooms close to elite locations where potential patrons dallied: Grosvenor Square and St James's, where she sat writing in a window 'exactly' opposite White's.[156]

There are no identifiable 'creatives' in the Marriage Duty Survey, but plenty of examples in other later sources, partly because these men and women were professionally inclined to write memoirs or, if they achieved celebrity, be written about. In the late-seventeenth century, for example, we have seen singleton playwrights and poets Congreve and Behn both lodging. Congreve spent forty years in and around the Strand, for the final twenty-three years of his life with lawyer Edward Porter and his wife in Surrey Street.[157] From 1669 Behn lived in London. She does not appear in any householder lists but in 1683 was included as 'Mrs. Bene' in a list of lodgers in St Brides parish in the house of a Mr Coggin. She is a good example of the non-fictional female lodger who was neither in peril nor a sex worker.[158] Victims of the Compton Street fire included a musician Thomas Adams, his wife and two children.[159] In addition to those already mentioned, creative eighteenth-century London lodgers included such diverse characters as painters George Romney (1734–1802) and Mauritius Lowe (1746–93), actors Dorothy Jordan (1761–1816) and Richard Suett (1755–1805), and writers Richard Savage (1697/8–1743) and Mary Hays (1759–1843).[160] All continually adapted their accommodation to such considerations as budget and health. Lodging afforded flexible living quarters that matched their flexible incomes and lifestyles. It was easy, as Pilkington, Boswell, Inchbald, or the Place family did, to move vertically or horizontally within a house, or elsewhere to a cheaper or better area as one's income expanded or shrank, usually with only the one week's notice. In this respect Defoe's depiction of Moll Flanders was an accurate one. For men, the wide variety of coffeehouses, inns, and taverns where they could eat, drink, and socialize meant that a steady address to which friends could be invited was not a paramount consideration:

> You might live in a garret at eighteen-pence a week, as few people would enquire where you lodge; and if they do, it is easy to say, 'Sir, I am to be found at such a place',

Boswell recorded Johnson as saying.[161] Irish playwright Paul Hiffernan (?1719–77) carried this out to the letter, keeping the exact location of his squalid lodgings a secret from his circle.[162] A term often used of these lodgings never visited by friends was 'obscure'.

London was above all a city where many were strangers who had moved from elsewhere. Most lodgers, as we have seen, were single. Lodging therefore offered the compensation of company in a domestic setting to those otherwise living alone, just as it did to their hosts. In the Marriage Duty Survey fifteen lone male lodgers were described as merchants, for example. They were probably men like Thomas Wale, in London temporarily on business. Many genteel men and women turned to private lodging rather than impersonal inns as the solution to accommodation on a working trip to London for reasons of cost, but also for comfort and company. In summer 1703 Catholic landowner Nicholas Blundell of Crosby, Lancashire (1669–1737), lodged with a Mr Plumber, location unspecified, when in town to finalize his marriage arrangements, paying £3 16s. 6d. for two rooms for seven nights.[163] Roger Whitley also falls into this category, as do Jefferson, the Mozarts, Swift, and Scottish poet and philosopher James Beattie (1735–1803), all of whom lodged in London while conducting business official or personal. Women were also business visitors. Sussex diarist Sarah Hurst (1736–1808) and her father travelled to London in connection with the family tailoring business and shop, and while there stayed in lodgings.[164]

Visitors from overseas were far from home and their own culture and so had particular need of the company and advice available in lodgings. Those of a scholarly bent also used it as an opportunity to 'anthropologize' the natives, generally agreeing that English homes were very clean – a major advantage they had over inns and coffeehouses. 'Men and especially foreigners live in furnished apartments and take their meals in eating-houses. You can have rooms from six-pence to half a guinea a head,' wrote Swiss travel writer César De Saussure (1705–83) in the 1720s, having previously noted that it was the practice in a well-ordered house to scrub it thoroughly from top to bottom twice a week.[165] In 1782 German author Carl Philipp Moritz (1756–1793) lived at a tailor's widow's where he felt so much at home that he could do 'just as I please'.[166] Another German author, this time a woman, Johanna Schopenhauer (1766–1838), captured the home-from-home atmosphere yet privacy that living in a family gave a foreigner or indeed any lodger:

> Usually a housekeeper or the lady of the house herself will look after the cleaning of the rooms and will also cook, so that one is made to feel really at home, at one's own hearthside, between one's own four walls.[167]

London was not dull and gloomy as rumoured, said German scholar Christian Goede (1774–1812), who lodged in Southampton Row for two years in around 1802:

let a man domesticate in London, and form a free and extensive acquaintance with the inhabitants and he will assuredly form a different opinion.[168]

For Goede domestication was clearly associated with social mixing. In *Chronicle* advertisements the high value placed by lodgers on the comfort of 'agreeable society' matched that already noted as offered by landlords/ladies. There were twenty-three lodgers looking for a private family setting, and twenty-seven hoping to be part of that family or their companion. They explained how they would themselves fit in, either generally (being 'no trouble' and keeping regular hours, for example) or more specifically: reading to the family, playing music, or helping out in their business.[169] Maybe they hoped too that some of these pleasures might reduce the rent that was likely to be charged.

Curiously, however, given the clear desire on the part of lodgers for a family setting there is evidence of a countervailing wish on the part of some to avoid the presence of children; the ultimate purpose and patriotic duty of the nuclear family at the centre of eighteenth-century ideals of domesticity.[170] While some lodgers appreciated children as a joyous part of the household they had joined, others thought them nothing but a nuisance. In real life in 1704 writer Joseph Addison (1672–1719) was composing his poem *The Campaign*, addressed to the Duke of Marlborough, while lodging in a Haymarket garret above a 'little shop'. As an essay-journalist, he later created a London-lodger *alter ego* who enjoyed playing with and reading to his widowed landlady's many children and their friends.[171] In 1758 Goldsmith played his flute to amuse neighbourhood children in Green Arbour Court.[172] Inchbald doted on George 'Pretty' Brooks, her landlord's and lady's baby son whom she claimed to have helped to wean and with whom she kept in touch after moving out.[173] For such lodgers, children in the household helped to remove the sneaking suspicion that they were there merely on an arms-length, commercial basis. It reinforced the sense that 'agreeable society' and being fully a part of the household were integral to the lodging transaction.

The childless Curwen, on the other hand, saw children as a cause for complaint. In January 1780 he was looking for new Bristol lodgings because a young child was 'too troublesome an Inmate. I hate the squall arising from maternal overfondness and indulgence', and in February 1782, now in Knightsbridge, he attributed poor sleep to a 'caterwalling [*sic*] child crying, trampling overhead … '.[174] He was not alone. Among *Chronicle* advertisements for rooms wanted, sixteen would-be lodgers made the stipulation that there be no children. It was matched by forty-one landlords and ladies making the same specification.

Perhaps they were anxious to avoid the disruption that children might have on the prime market of singletons and couples without children. Perhaps too they sought to avoid the reputational damage that single mothers or large numbers of lodgers might bring. For others they were a potential distraction from their own ease. These advertisements and experiences are a reminder that not all Georgian men and women were invested in the concept of the tender family of husband, wife, and children. Given that fourteen lodger-advertisers wanted to be the sole lodger in the house, were they instead expressing a longing for family? Did they hope, however subconsciously, to be the landlord's/lady's substitute only child?

Finally, women, who outnumbered men in the capital, were, as we have seen, excluded by regulations and social convention from some of its accommodation choices.[175] Inns, for example, were considered unsuitable for respectable lone women. In 1687 Hester Pinney (1658–1740), an unmarried lace trader from the West Country, had moved for business reasons to London and was living alone in a City inn. Her father (to no avail) reprimanded her by letter and offered to pay her way 'home':

> but I ame not satisfyed w[i]th yo[u]r living in a taverne a place of so many temptations and dangers.[176]

Elizabeth Carter's independence in desirable lodgings was made possible by the 1758 success of her translation from the ancient Greek of Stoic philosopher Epictetus. She was lucky. Women's earned income was on average lower than men's, their occupations summarized by George as 'overstocked, ill-paid and irregular'.[177] Where women lacked means, they might have been expected to choose the literal and reputational security of living with a relative, or domestic service – which could include the more genteel occupations of governess or housekeeper – over living as a lodger. This was far from being always the case, however. While the Marriage Duty Survey data appears to confirm the gender bias of the legal guides – two-thirds of lodger households were headed by a male – within the category of singletons the ratio of men to women was far less marked: 123 single men to 106 single women, of whom eighteen (compared to two men) had a child or children, and ten were widows.

In the 1785 Compton Street fire records there were twenty-one lodger households headed by a woman, half the total. Two of these singlewoman lodger households contained children and one single woman lodger was described as a widow. Like their male counterparts, they spanned a wide range of positions on the socio-economic spectrum. Isabella Morrison, Mary Harivin, and the unnamed daughter of a clergyman were all servants out of place, and Hannah Barker's sister, formerly an 'upper servant' lodged with her. Milliner Mary Gay, who had discovered the fire and lived with her seven-year-old son, was perhaps deserted by her husband, who was described as 'absent'. Fanny Desseran was John Batchellor's oil-and-vinegar-dealer garret-lodger, and greengrocer McGuire's lodger Genevieve Dumenil washed and mended silk stockings. Neither of these latter two women can have enjoyed a lucrative trade. In October 1780, for example, Inchbald paid just 4d. to have an unspecified number of silk stockings washed.[178] Some of these women lodgers' claims were very small, even allowing for the fact that the furniture of their rooms may have belonged to their landlord/lady, or that they may have managed to escape with the greater part of their goods. Mary Starling, one of the garreteers, claimed only 16s. 6d. for linen and Alice York 16s. for household furniture, for example.[179] They are reminiscent of fictional lodger Moll Flanders's wry comment 'as for Household stuff I had little or none' (Chapter 2). Other single women, on the other hand, appear to have been comfortably off: Mrs Parsons who lodged on Batchellor's most prestigious first floor had her own servant, and Elizabeth M'Donald was a ward of court at Michael Bourke's, her father's executor. Bourke valued M'Donald's lost possessions at £200, the second-highest lodger claim after the Wiffens' £410 3s. 6d. There were, however, thirteen single women for whom no occupation was given. They may have constituted Earle's 'women without gainful employment', maintaining a degree of shabby gentility in a respectable area.[180] That might be a reasonable assumption for the three garreteers or for widowed Ann Baker who shared a less-favoured room, Batchellor's second-floor back, with another single woman, Mary Ledger.

Although there is certainly an occasional frisson of the erotic, there is almost no evidence in the sources that these female lodgers were the professional sex workers found in literature. Pilkington, sitting in her window opposite gentlemen's clubs, was at worst a 'demirep' who earned respectable money by her pen. Her friend Swift in his diary for 12 October 1711 alleged his friend Mrs Vanhomrigh moved lodgings because 'She found she had got with a bawd … '. Some years later Curwen wrote in his journal that 'A young woman lodger whom I strongly suspect to be a whore was delivered of a child in the lodgings over my head', which may be true, but may also be the angry reaction of a grumpy snob to a poor night's sleep. As an apprentice, Place remarked that his master's seventeen-year-old daughter 'had genteel lodgings where she was visited by gentlemen', but again this was gossip rather than hard fact.[181] Venetian libertine and adventurer Giacomo Casanova (1725–98) claimed to have become a London landlord in 1763 when he advertised rooms on the upper floor of his rented house in Pall Mall with the express intention of recruiting a mistress, but this must surely be read as an exception and indeed as a form of masculine, boastful story-telling.[182] Instead the evidence from respectable lodgers like Boswell, Curwen, and Inchbald is that it was perfectly acceptable to live over milliners' shops, the classic lodgings of sex workers in novels.

Lodging did not, therefore, in itself undermine the respectability of the single female. The obsession in fiction and images with their virtue, or rather lack of it, is instead a reflection of the cultural dominance of the male gaze combined with the rise of sensibility narratives of seduction. *Chronicle* advertisements tend to confirm a lack of anxiety over the female lodger. Landlords/ladies hardly ever specified whether they preferred to accommodate men or women and in the forty-seven cases where they did the tally was almost exactly equal: twenty-three specified men and twenty-four women. In real life, many women seem to have exhibited a marked preference for the independence of life in lodgings – Mary Hays' 'idea of being free'[183] – and landlords/ladies to have been willing to meet this demand. Their overall choices were more limited than those open to men, but their priorities seem to have been broadly the same.

The locations where lodgings were found both matched quite closely the locations of fiction and images and remained constant over the period, although there was more choice towards the end of the eighteenth century as the newly-built Westminster suburbs gradually gained ground at the expense of the City of London. The lack of census series makes comparison tricky, but the scale of lodgings also seems fairly constant between the late-seventeenth century (King, Spence) and the 1851 census. In the eighteenth century the suspicion of lodgers as a group that had existed since the late-sixteenth century subsided. Private lodgings in a family home were increasingly marketed to the respectable and genteel as a socially acceptable and enjoyable way to live. Such lodgings were, however, always explicitly distinguished from the cheap, crowded common lodging-houses and tenements of London's poor met with in crime reports.

There was also both continuity and homogeneity in the sort of households that opened their spare rooms to private lodgers. The majority were, like their fictional counterparts, from the middling sort, especially shopkeepers and those in clean artisanal occupations such as the manufacture of clothing and dress accessories. It is not always clear which of the 'headline' occupation or the taking of lodgers was the subsidiary business, but in any case, the decision to take lodgers was a rational, entrepreneurial one, which fitted with concepts of thrift, saving, and prudent use of assets. Married couples without small children at home were well-placed to service lodgers, but it was also a useful means of earning extra income for single women, including widows. It provided a financial safety-net, and the prospect of interesting encounters.

Their lodgers, by contrast, came from across the social spectrum (apart of course from the underclass). Most were single, although there were married couples. Their immediate reasons for lodging were diverse. The impoverished 'garret-poet' of fiction and art had parallels in real life (Johnson and Chatterton, for example). Lodging was also a regular choice of accommodation for creatives with a reasonable, but unpredictable, income – writers, actors, artists. Lodging-rooms could be found quickly and changed easily as life circumstances demanded.

It was not unusual for the lodger to be of a higher social status than the landlord/lady (examples covered are Boswell, Hickey, and diplomat Thomas Wiffen in Compton Street). 'Prince Giustiniani may happen to be as much surprised as we are at his lodging in a butcher's shop,' exclaimed author and patron of the arts Horace Walpole (1717–97) in 1771.[184] We do not know whether Giustiniani was indeed surprised, but in 1769 the Duchess of Northumberland was unperturbed by her lodging at a Basingstoke apothecary's when attending a masked ball at the Duke of Bolton's Hackwood Park country house, all other accommodation being taken. She seems to have been satisfied, describing it as 'private' and 'very neat'.[185]

However, one of the most noticeable aspects of lodging and class is the presence within a single home of lodgers of different social standing: New England merchant Samuel Curwen and the 'whore' giving birth, or, at the time of the Compton Street fire, Hannah Barker's five lodger households: on the ground floor her sister, an 'upper servant' out of place, on the first floor a tailor, and on the second floor a single-parent milliner and child, a clergyman's daughter out of place and a servant with an Irish surname also out of place. This was most definitely reminiscent of *Olla Podrida*'s 'distinctions of Altitude' and of 'forward and backward'.

While some of these lodgers saw their accommodation as a temporary expedient driven either by their life-cycle stage or by financial necessity, for many it was a more positive choice that both made economic sense and freed their time from housekeeping and its burdens. There was no general fetishizing of home ownership. London was a city of strangers and new arrivals. In an age that increasingly idealized domesticity yet created commercial pressures that demanded risk-taking and mobility, living in someone else's spare rooms made social sense too. It could provide comfort, respectability, a surrogate family for both landlord/lady and lodger, and the community of 'friends' that Naomi Tadmor identifies as crucial in eighteenth-century society.[186]

4

Matchmaking

Chapter 3 established that there were thousands of eighteenth-century London householders eager to make money from their spare rooms and enjoy the company that this could bring. Similarly, there were thousands of men and women for whom lodging was an ideal solution to their accommodation needs: affordable, flexible and with all the comforts of home and domesticity. There was, however, a confusing array of possibilities in a competitive marketplace:

> There seems nothing in London so much wanted as room; no, not money, or even health; for there is money to buy, but no space to be bought. And if one in forty wants health, thirty-nine want room,

commented Birmingham autodidact, historian, and keen traveller William Hutton (1723–1815) after a visit in late 1784.[1] At the humbler end of society, David Love (1750–1827), Scottish pedlar and poet, cannot have been the only person to find it overwhelming. On arrival, probably in the late 1780s, he was 'so bewildered' that he did not know where to turn. He ended up taking a room south of the river in the Borough.[2] Higher up the social scale, in 1831, Carlyle, also newly-arrived from Scotland, had to draw himself a 'chart' of the route from his Woburn Buildings lodgings to publisher John Murray's in Albemarle Street.[3] In Europe's largest city, there was also a terrifying array of risks, as the guides to London and to the business of letting warned.

Chapter 4 now considers how the two parties, landlords/ladies and lodgers, first made contact with one another across the great span of this city, how they decided whether they were compatible and how they came to terms over the details of their lodging arrangement. The chief source for this is accounts, some of them very detailed, in life-writing, with occasional recourse to crime reporting and back to fictional representations in novels, plays, and images.

———————————

As we have seen, advertising in a newspaper such as the *Morning Chronicle* was one means of communication between two parties who were still strangers. It had been used since the late-seventeenth century:

> If any *Merchant* wants a Lodging at a *Packer's* House, and a little distance from the *Exchange*, with or without Diet, having all other conveniencies: I can help him,

ran an early example from 1694.[4] The number of newspaper advertisements, including those for lodging, increased in the eighteenth century with the expansion in the number of newspapers and periodicals. An advertisement was, as James Raven points out, 'regular, of the instant and relatively cheap to advertisers'. Both advertiser and reader knew in advance the publication dates, costs, and expected format. An advertisement was guaranteed to reach a large audience both in the capital and beyond.[5] The *Chronicle*, for example, was selling around 2,000 copies a day in the 1790s and 4,000 in the first decade of the nineteenth century.[6] Readership was, of course, higher. However, advertisements for lodgings were never a mainstay of the *Chronicle*'s or other newspapers' advertising pages. There were far more for new publications, theatrical productions, servants, auctions, whole houses to let, and lost horses. A deterrent factor may have been the cost of advertising – Raven finds that in the mid-century a short advertisement cost the advertiser around 1s. 6d., although there is evidence too of discounts and of advertisements being placed *gratis*.[7]

Another deterrent to the use of newspaper advertising must have been uncertainty over what exactly was on offer, given the reluctance of landlords/ladies to provide an address or much other detail. A meeting between advertiser and respondent had to be arranged. This was a time-consuming process as many advertisers used an intermediary, often a named shop, inn, or coffeehouse, as the place to which those interested should reply:

> A Single Gentleman or Lady may be accommodated with BOARD and LODGING, at the house of a Single Lady, at Thirty Guineas per annum. Enquire at Mr. Hale's, Shoemaker, No. 11 Peter's Street Bloomsbury; or at Mitchell's Circulating Library, Islington … Letters, post paid, addressed to B. at the above-mentioned places, will be attended to.[8]

While some of these intermediaries may in fact have been the landlord/lady themselves, many were acting as a *poste restante* and local information centre, maybe in return for cash, maybe for the prospect of additional footfall in the shop. Printmaker and draughtsman J. T. Smith (1766–1833) was in his youth assistant to the sculptor Joseph Nollekens (1737–1823). He helped Nollekens's wife, Mary, by writing out a notice of a house she was letting. This was then pasted with a wafer in the window of Mrs Bland's turner's shop, seven doors down the street.[9] A 1782 advertisement in the *Morning Herald* shows Gibbon's Pall Mall landlord Mr Taylor, a grocer, acting in this way for 'F.F.' who wanted a place as a servant or butler.[10] Anyone enquiring after F.F. would have either to write and await a reply, or to attend the shop to find out what the position was, whether F.F. was still available, and whether the parties were suited. It was the same with lodging advertisements.

Shops, inns, coffeehouses and similar businesses were widely understood as informal repositories of information on lodgings available in an area. Bee advised:

> let the stranger make inquiries of tradespeople in the neighbourhood … of the butcher, baker, greengrocer, perhaps at some evening assembly of smoke-a-pipe citizens … the barbers' shops.[11]

It was from his shoemaker that in January 1780 Curwen learnt 'of a convenient lodging without interruption of children'.[12] A 1787 trade card 'LODGINGS to be Lett Furnished' printed for Mr Angell of 22 Brompton Row and collected by Sarah Sophia Banks (1744–1818) implies that the more 'professional' landlords and ladies used printed cards to advertise their rooms in either their own or other shops and business places, though to date a search of digital resources has not produced any other printed London examples.[13] Networks of landlords/ladies were also willing to make a recommendation to an enquirer when they had no vacancies or a lodger needed a new place, much as Burney's Mrs Voluble in *The Witlings* did. Curwen's Exeter landlady Sally Bretlands, for example, recommended him to Mrs Froade in Bristol. The two women were cousins.[14]

From the mid-seventeenth century attempts were made to commercialize this informal knowledge system by establishing formal exchange offices with registers of lodgings available and wanted, often alongside businesses that held registers of servants for hire and placements wanted, houses to let, and so forth. The advertiser paid a modest sum to enter their details in the register and the enquirer a smaller one to access them. In theory the enquirer then needed only to attend one office, check the list for what was available and set off in hot pursuit. The Exchange-Keeper's Office of General Enquiry opposite the Royal Exchange, itself a key node for City lodgings, advertised services which included lodgings in 1738.[15] The best-known, however, is the Universal

Register Office, established in 1750 by author Henry Fielding (1707–54), his blind magistrate brother John (1721–80) and grocer, Bloomsbury vestryman, and father to Mary Nollekens, Saunders Welch (1711–84). This office was also located in a major lodging node: the Strand. Henry's pamphlet of 1751 and press advertisements promoted the idea that the Office could 'bring the World as it were into one Place': matching buyers and sellers, teachers and scholars, masters and apprentices, masters and servants. A landlord/lady paid 6d. to be entered in the books and a lodger-to-be 3d. to read them. The register of lodgings (and houses and estates to let) detailed 'whether furnished or unfurnished, and Number of Rooms. If in Town, the Street in which the House stands, with all its Conveniencies'.[16] The Office achieved some early success and spawned competitors with confusingly similar names.[17] The Universal Agency Office, 130 Pall Mall, advertised its wide range of services, which included dealing in army commissions and church preferments, in the *Chronicle*. The Agency charged a hefty 5s. to register board and lodgings, and 2s. 6d. for 'weekly or monthly lodgings' but exempted 'persons taking lodgings' and other purchasers from paying commission.[18] It was clearly used by some landlords. In the July 1794 *Chronicle* a 'Medical Gentleman' advertised for an invalid, elderly (and rich) lodger for his town and country house, with a spa break included as part of the 'system', giving this office as the contact point.[19]

Like newspaper advertisements, using a register had a cost to the landlord/ lady, with no guarantee of success. There was also the risk that the register office might fill its books and windows with fictitious opportunities 'in order to make a parade of business', thereby wasting enquirers' time and money.[20] The most popular method of advertising a spare room, one that lasted well into the twentieth century, remained the bill in the window, mentioned by, among others Pilkington, Boswell, Inchbald, and Shelley's biographer Hogg. It was typically handwritten, was free and could be put up or removed instantaneously. Examples are included in two of the 'let me alone' prints discussed in Chapter 2 (see Figure 5).[21] If we are to believe actor and sex worker Poll House, aka Mrs Mary Dacres, bills might be found even in the rough streets of St Giles: 'A Garrit to lit for a yung Gentilwomun' – a reflection of the spread of literacy.[22] The bill was small and so relatively discreet, whereas prints imply that at the lower end of the market, the common lodging house or quasi-brothel might have a permanent sign.[23] For the landlord/lady the chief drawback of the bill was, despite its small size, the publicity, and the potential stream of time-wasting or scamming knocks at the door. For the lodger it was the prospect of a weary tramp round likely districts in search of a bill. Boswell looked at some fifty rooms before settling on the Terries in Downing Street.[24] Avoiding the tramp was the main selling-point of the Universal Register Office. It saved 'Gentlemen and Ladies the Trouble of Walking, and the Expence [*sic*] of riding about Town in search of such Conveniencies'.[25] The long-term survival of the bill in the window indicates, however, that this was not perhaps of such great concern to those who would lodge. After all, they would need to visit and examine any rooms offered in the register offices before striking a deal.

The bill and the tramp were sufficiently recognizable to the audience that they featured in novels and plays. In *The Provok'd Husband*, a play of 1728, it is a servant who has been:

> gaping and stumping about the Streets, in his dirty Boots, and asking every one he meets, if they can tell him, where he may have a good Lodging for a Parliament-man.[26]

In a comic short story in the *Lady's Magazine*, heavily indebted to an earlier *Idler* article by Johnson, a newly-wed couple and the husband's friend hunt for lodgings for the couple who are visiting London, using a coach to reduce the time spent.[27] Henry Fielding employed the conceit of the bill and its lack of discretion in his farce *Miss Lucy in Town* (1742). Her woman Tawdry asks Mrs Haycock, 'Have you put a bill on your door, ma'am, as you said you would?' Haycock is clearly a little ashamed (as well she might be, the lodgings are the scene of attempted seduction):

> It is up, it is up. *O Tawdry!* that a woman who hath been bred and lived like a gentlewoman, and followed a polite way of business, should be reduced to let lodgings.[28]

Many life-writers recorded their walk (or ride) around London in search of somewhere suitable. Savile and her mother had looked in the villages west and south of London in 1727. Later that year she also hunted over two days for central London lodgings for her brother and his family who planned to attend the coronation of George II. Savile's account illustrates how exhausting an experience this was: 'Mrs. Stewkly's in Lisle Street, Degar's in Leicester Fields and another in the same place. Degar's the best', then the following Tuesday more in Dover Street, Lincoln's Inn Fields, Queen Square, St Martin's Lane, Suffolk Street, and Pall Mall.[29] During his nine years in England Curwen 'Took rounds to enquire for new lodgings' many times.[30] In September 1782 Inchbald went looking for lodgings on a fine day. She was successful, striking a deal the next day and moving in four days later. In April 1788, several lodgings having intervened, she 'walked and saw many Lodgings wore my Hat' on two consecutive days. By 1807 (now aged fifty-four) she found the process more tiresome:

> 23rd March ... at three I went and saw Lodgings and board in the Edgware Road, Lodgings in Leicester Place &c _ _ at Dusk bought my dinner Cooked & dined at seven. Looked at many Lodgings.
>
> Tue 24 March Read & Low about the Prospect of new Lodgings
>
> Wed 25 March Gloomy and so cold I did not go after Lodgings as I proposed.

She eventually decided to stay on with Miss Baillie the milliner, even agreeing to pay her two guineas a year more.[31] After their expulsion in 1811 from Oxford University for atheism, Shelley and his friend and biographer Thomas Jefferson Hogg (1792–1862) travelled to London by coach, stayed in a coffeehouse, and started their search for lodgings straight after breakfast. Shelley was fussy and dismissed many on slight, snobbish grounds. They eventually settled on two bedrooms and a sitting room at 15 Poland Street where 'A paper in the window announced lodgings'.[32]

The search for the paper in the window was all very well, but how did lodgers decide where to start their tramp? Inns were often the place at which out-of-town visitors were set down from their coaches (Chapter 3). Many new arrivals therefore followed the advice in *The Thorough-bred Poor Gentleman's Book* and stayed a night or so at an inn, coffeehouse, or hotel as Curwen and Shelley and Hogg had done, and perhaps picked the proprietor's and staff's brains before conducting their search from this base. Others relied on their network of friends and family as proxies to help them in their search. This was sometimes pursued in advance by letter, facilitated by the nationwide and well-understood postal service. It worked especially well if the would-be lodger could not come to London immediately, as in the case of Savile's brother.[33] Horace Walpole helped friends on several occasions. In October 1744 his cousin Henry Seymour Conway (1721–95) could not stay in his accustomed London lodgings as they were let until Christmas, so wrote from the Netherlands, where he was stationed with the British troops:

> I had thoughts of troubling you to find me out a convenient lodging or rather a little snug and very cheap house if one could find such a thing about Pall Mall or towards you in St James's Street.

In 1761 George Montagu (1710–80), formerly MP for Northampton and now living as a country squire, enclosed in a letter to Walpole one for a Mrs Morland asking her to look for a lodging for him for the following February. In 1767 Montagu identified good lodgings at Morgan's china shop on the corner of Arlington Street (Walpole's address) and Piccadilly and in November 1768 had established that they were available, but he still wrote to Walpole asking him to pass by to see whether building works next door would prove a disturbance. Walpole felt that they would: 'I fear nothing for you but the noise of workmen' – quite apart from the general noise of a great thoroughfare like Piccadilly.[34] The chief disadvantage of making arrangements by letter was that by the time a letter had been sent to the landlord/lady, a reply received, and a booking letter sent, the opportunity might well have been lost to the bird-in-the-hand of a caller-in-person.

An experienced out-of-towner could write in advance to a previous landlord/lady or one known to the family. In 1758 the young Gibbon 'got our old lodgings in Charles Street' (by St James's Square), where his family had stayed the previous May.[35] Haydon arranged his lodgings at 342 Strand (on the corner with Catherine Street) before leaving Devon in 1804.[36] Beattie, Courtney, Curwen, and Sterne were among those who returned to or attempted to re-book past lodgings. The network of family and friends was another source not only of information, but also of support in the form of 'guaranteed' accommodation as part of the reciprocal obligations of kinship.[37] The Blakes lodged in two first-floor rooms at 3 Fountain Court, Strand, from 1821 until his death in 1827. It was the home of Catherine's sister Sarah and her husband, wine cooper Henry Banes.[38] Sterne almost certainly found his Bond-Street landlady Mrs Fourmantel through his pursuit of the singer Catherine 'Kitty' Fourmantel whom he had met in York in 1759. Kitty lodged in Meard's Court, Soho, in 1760, while Sterne at the time lodged in Pall Mall. By the time he moved to Bond Street the relationship with Kitty had cooled.[39] Some seekers after rooms stayed only initially with family or friends, probably finding the arrangement awkwardly lacking in the true independence that lodgings could provide. In 1770, on arriving in London from Bristol aged eighteen, Chatterton at first lived in unfashionable Shoreditch at plasterer Mr Walmsley's where his aunt, Mrs Ballance, lodged. The Lambs had good reason to look to an old schoolfriend, John Gutch, as landlord given Mary's well-known history of violence and mental ill-health, for 'Gutch knew all our story'. In 1831 Carlyle came from Scotland alone. He relied on family in the first instance, lodging in Woburn Buildings alongside his brother Jack, a struggling physician, in the house of Jack's fellow Scots medic, George Irving.[40]

Word-of-mouth of available rooms from fellow lodgers, a network formed once lodging, certainly informed the many moves made by Curwen, who often chose to lodge near American friends, and by Inchbald.

The search was most difficult for those who came to London from farther afield. On landing at Dover in 1764, the Mozarts sent ahead Porta, an Italian manservant who had made eight previous journeys to London, to look for lodgings, and stayed their first night in the capital at the White Bear Inn, Piccadilly, the terminus for the Kent coaches. It was a satisfactory arrangement: 'It was a very good thing too, for he [i.e. Porta] arranged everything well and did all the bargaining,' wrote Mozart *père* to a friend back home.[41] Ukawsaw Gronniosaw (1710/14–75), an African prince released from enslavement in New York, came to England two years before the Mozarts. He sought out the only Englishman he knew, Methodist preacher George Whitefield (1714–70), whom he had encountered in America. Whitfield helped him find lodgings.[42] Foreigners, including the Scottish and Irish, often found it particularly comforting to take advice and support from and live with fellow countrymen, as Boswell, Beattie, and Carlyle all did. Boswell's Mr Terrie was a fellow Scot married to an Englishwoman, and Downing Street was 'a whole row of lodging houses, chiefly for Scotch and Irish members'.[43] Beattie turned to Anne Hunter (1742/3–1821), wife of Scottish surgeon John (1728–93), when struggling to find lodgings in 1773. She directed him to her father's house in Suffolk Street. He was also a Scottish physician. In 1788, Dublin-born Martin Archer Shee was secured lodgings by Irish friends (many of them law students) already in London. Although himself studying art, he lived very much amongst them, often relying upon them for financial assistance.[44] For some this co-operation helped bridge the language barrier. Until he had the confidence to branch out for himself Emin relied upon an Armenian merchant, Stephenus Cogigian, for employment and accommodation.[45] Grosley's landlord Mr Martin was, like Grosley, French. A chef in the royal kitchens, Martin, his wife, and children spoke fluent English as well as their native French, and could act as interpreters.[46] By clinging together with fellow countrymen and women, overseas lodgers found a buffer against danger in an almost unknowable city, and could access the emotional comfort of being among people with whom there could be mutual understanding.[47]

There had always been significant numbers of Frenchmen and women travelling to London, as Grosley did, or living and working there more permanently, like Martin, many of them clustered in the parish of St Anne Soho as lodgers (see Chapter 3). They therefore developed, like the Scots and Irish, especially strong networks. In the late 1690s François Misson (*c.* 1650–1722) wrote a French guide to London for newcomers (translated into English in 1719). He advised anyone planning to visit London to use existing networks, letting a friend know and asking him to 'hire him a Lodging, or a Bed, otherwise he may be very much at a Loss'.[48] In 1800, when the chaos of the French Revolution and Terror led to a spike in the number of French refugees seeking accommodation, émigré priest and lexicographer Abbé Tardy (*fl.* 1799) wrote another guide specifically aimed at this new, more urgent, market: *Manuel du Voyageur à Londres.*[49] He counselled finding an interpreter before launching into the street-by-street search for doors and windows sporting the words '*Furnished Lodgings, Lodgings for Single Gentlemen*, etc.' The actual choice of rooms should, however, be made by the lodger him- or herself. An alternative was to head for help at Guéudon's or Saulieu's, French restaurants in Leicester Square and Gerrard Street respectively, where they could rely upon more experienced compatriots.[50] Another source of assistance to these émigrés was more personal. The exiled Bishop of Léon, Jean-François de la Marche, dispensed aid from his 'small chamber' at the Queen Street, Bloomsbury, home of his sympathetic and motherly landlady Dorothy Silburn, a Catholic widow whose house 'was filled from morn to night ... more like a hospital than a decent lodging'.[51]

Whatever means were used to find a potential lodger or lodging, for each party there remained the hurdles of the initial face-to-face encounter, viewing of the room(s) and negotiations over the exact terms of any deal. 'I thought my seeking a lodging was like seeking a wife,' mused Boswell – who had yet to enter the marriage market.[52] In reality each party to lodging had rather less time for courtship, generally making a snap decision in the hallway: was the other to be trusted? In an age when most purchases were made on credit, shopkeeper landlords/ladies had the advantage of a great deal of practice at using their instinct based on appearances. Boswell was highly pleased that his powers of gentlemanly persuasion convinced sword-cutler to His Majesty, Mr Jefferys, to grant him credit when they were not already acquainted, acknowledging that his gentlemanliness was a performance of 'external appearance and address'.[53] The performance swayed Jefferys. In the same way a potential lodger's performance might influence a landlord/lady positively or negatively. Where there was lingering doubt, a landlord/lady asked for a reference (a 'character') and/or a deposit, which carried the risk that those who considered themselves socially superior might take it as an insult. According to one biographer, towards the end of his life Turner was asked for one when taking lodgings (probably here used in the sense of the whole cottage) near Cremorne Pier, Chelsea. He was now famous as an artist but:

> The landlady, seeing a little, thick-set, shabby man, asked him for reference; which demand provoked the angry retort, 'My good woman, I'll buy the house outright.' She proposed a written agreement in return to which he proffered advance payment showing a wad of notes.[54]

Some lodgers came from groups where there was popular prejudice against them. On the one hand, there is no surviving hard evidence that racial prejudice, the eighteenth-century equivalent of the notorious notices 'No dogs, no blacks, no Irish' found in the windows of London lodgings in the 1950s and 1960s, was a part of the decision-making. Chinese artist Chitqua, or Tan-Che-Qua (*c.* 1728–96), for example, was an unusual visitor to London in 1769. He lodged with Charles Marr, hatter, on the corner of Strand and Norfolk Street, a typical landlord and a classic lodging location. Chitqua was visited by, among others, Boswell, and antiquary Richard Gough (1735–1809). The latter airily claimed that Chitqua, despite wearing traditional Chinese clothing, met 'with no insults in the streets'. Though he appears to have had no prior London patron who helped him find his accommodation, Chitqua probably derived some protection from his reasonable language skills and association while in London with leading artistic and literary figures. Maybe too Marr was fascinated by this 'exotic' lodger and excited by the stream of celebrity visitors – after all, he had personally shown Boswell into the back parlour and introduced the two men.[55]

On the other hand, lack of tangible evidence of prejudice is not the same as a lack of prejudice. Linda Colley has detected a rising sense of Britishness in the eighteenth century, and there are plenty of examples of John-Bullish patriotism leading to the ill use of foreigners in the streets.[56] Gough's remark about Chitqua escaping insults implies that an obvious foreigner might generally expect such treatment, and indeed on his homewards journey the British sailors abused Chitqua as a 'Chinese dog'.[57] Overseas lodgers like Emin were therefore probably more likely to need a 'character' and probably found it harder to obtain one until they had an established employment, a classic conundrum.[58] In consequence the busy free market in lodgings was not equally open to all.

Ignatius Sancho (?1729–80) was an African who had lived in England from the age of two. From 1774 he owned and ran a grocer's shop in Charles Street, Westminster. He had direct experience of racism when out in public. In Vauxhall

Gardens in 1777 he, his wife and children 'were gazed at – followed, &c. &c. – but not much abused'. Despite his status as a propertied man and correspondent with the famous, it seems he felt his position was precarious and contingent since he compared himself to a lodger: 'I am only a lodger – and hardly that'.[59] Sancho owed his position to natural intelligence but also to the patronage of the Duke of Montagu. It certainly seems the case that less confident black lodgers relied on a version of patronage by respectable white protectors to assist them into work and accommodation, as Gronniosaw had done. When freed slave Jonathan Strong (*c.* 1747–73) left hospital, where slavery abolitionist Granville Sharp (1735–1813) had sent him for treatment for terrible injuries from a beating, he recalled that Sharp had 'paid for my lodging'.[60] Mary Prince (b. *c.* 1788), also a freed slave, used the Moravian church network to find rooms and work.[61] As former slaves these were humble people in Georgian London and unsurprisingly their lodgings, even those of Gronniosaw, were to the east of the City, where, as we have seen, black residents were not uncommon, rather than the smarter West End, where white Europeans and American visitors, and Chitqua too, were often welcomed. They were excluded by race as well as income from the more respectable sectors of the lodging market.

White foreigners also came under suspicion. An article published in the *Gentleman's Magazine* in 1751, but first written in 1708/9, argued against the naturalization of foreign Protestants (i.e. the Huguenot French) who:

> generally living in lodgings, and at little charge, frequently escaping public taxation and parish duties, would be able to undersell [*sic*] and undermine the native merchants.[62]

Whiteness and loyalism did not always help Curwen. In 1778 the younger daughter of his Exeter landlady interpreted his constant writing as a sign that he was ministerial spy operating for Lord North.[63] Ireland remained part of Britain in the Georgian period, and the Irish were one of the largest migrant groups in London. Many of our middling-sort lodgers were Irish: Swift, Pilkington, Goldsmith, Sterne, Curran, and Shee, for example. Nevertheless, the Irish were often associated in the popular mind with the poorer labouring classes around St Giles and the docks.[64] The Ratcliffe Highway murderer and Burke and Hare were all Irish. Goldsmith identified a general anti-Irish feeling in England, 'where being born an Irishman was sufficient to keep me unemployed'.[65] Irishmen and women were immediately recognizable not by their appearance so much as by their accents, which were a source of comedy in novels and plays and even in

Old Bailey reports. James Fitzgerald's 1725 account of the theft of his watch and money was rendered thus:

> O' my Shoul, I wash got pretty drunk, and wash going very shoberly along the Old-Baily, and there I met the Preeshoner.[66]

There is evidence in life-writing sources that finding rooms was often harder for the identifiably Irish. Was it accent that led a landlord to demand an 'earnest' (deposit) from Swift and his servant Patrick? An indignant Swift refused and the 'dog' let the room to another before he could move in.[67] Apothecary Simon Mason let rooms at his shop in Hatton Garden in the early 1740s and without a second thought recorded his anti-Irish sentiment as far as lodgers were concerned:

> Another set [of rogues] are upon the Hibernian Establishment of Fortune hunting; one of these Gentlemen came to me with a purse of twenty Guineas, to let him lodge at my House for a Fortnight, and give him a Character, being about to marry a Lady of Fortune, which I absolutely refused with disdain.[68]

It was on account of his accent that actor Charles Macklin (?1699–1797), who had already anglicized his name from MacLoughlin to make it easier for the English to pronounce, found it difficult to secure accommodation in the London of the 1730s. He recounted a misunderstanding over his old and new name between his landlady (a glover in the Strand) and a visiting relative. Like Mason, she immediately jumped to the conclusion that, as an Irishman, he must be a rogue and swindler, and gave him notice to quit:

> *Landlady.* 'Sir, I'd have you to know, that I have kept this house these five-and-thirty years, and have always maintained an honest character. I also have had very respectable lodgers in my house; but I never had any person that assumed two names before!
>
> … I am too experienced to be imposed upon, and I must request, that you will quit my house directly; for I cannot suffer any one to remain in it who has two different names!'

Macklin was only able to calm her down and remain by insisting that he had *'friends in this town'*, that is, he had a network of support in London from which he could provide a 'character'.[69]

Chronicle advertisements were, as we have seen, dominated by notions of respectability and gentility, concepts which probably made it hard, though not impossible, for some other groups to find a host household that would accept them as lodgers. Young single women are one likely category, given the common conceit of the lodging-house as brothel (Chapter 2). The potential reputational damage to a landlord/lady is demonstrated in an 1809 libel case. In August 1808 one Jefferies, a carpenter who let rooms in his house in Artillery Street (now Lane), off Bishopsgate in the City, successfully sued Duncombe, a neighbour who had suspended a lit lamp in front of Jefferies's house to imply that it was a 'bawdy house', with the result that Jefferies's lodgers decamped.[70] Knowingly letting a room to a sex worker might also be a bar to legal action by a landlord/lady, as an immoral purpose rendered a contract null and void, although courts could be sympathetic to the lodger on the grounds that accommodation was, as the political economists maintained, a necessity. In *Crisp v. Churchill* (1794) Chief Justice Eyre held that landlord Crisp's action to regain occupation of a lodging-room was not maintainable as the defendant, Churchill, 'an infant and a prostitute', 'must have a lodging'.[71] Pilkington's Green Street, Mayfair, landlady (a 'top' laundress married to Lord Stair's *valet de chambre*) was especially careful when a 'very genteel pretty Woman', who was pregnant with no sign of a husband in tow, took lodgings in the house, as they, the hosts, had 'very good furniture'. She clearly feared the 'Lodging-Slum' to which Bynon and Elizabeth Wilkinson were prey in 1806.[72]

Cruden encountered prejudice from landlords/ladies not because he was Scottish, but because his bouts of mental ill-health and committal to mad-houses were public knowledge. He had to both pay a deposit and provide proof of his (relative) sanity. In October 1753, a few months after his release from a Chelsea asylum, he took rooms with Mrs Stephens at the Dial above the Flying-Horse in Upper Moorfields. Before Cruden could move in, she heard rumours that that he was 'not in the exercise of his reason'. She therefore told him, 'something had happened, and he could not have the lodging'. Cruden had paid a deposit and so campaigned to change her mind, first through a friend and then by threatening her with going before a justice. Finally, he went over his landlady's head to the house-owner, watchmaker Mr Smith, and was at last admitted. Cruden felt that 'he and the [Stephens] family live[d] in peace and harmony', though he may have been deluded – self-knowledge was not his strong point, and it is hard to picture Mrs Stephens as entirely happy about the matter. After four months, she served him notice to quit (see Chapter 6) and Cruden moved on.[73]

Lodgers in their turn were also cautioned to assess carefully the character of a prospective landlord/lady, especially if the rooms were unfurnished, because of the risk of distraint mentioned by most guides. Trusler even advised obtaining a written undertaking.[74] If they had their doubts, they could of course take the room for a week or two and extend the stay if it worked out.[75] Lodgers could display prejudice too. Shelley ruled out one lodging because 'he took umbrage at the voice of the mistress', and Carlyle disliked the appearance of one he dubbed 'the scratch-wig landlady' who 'had a look of second table knavery' (perhaps serving family left-overs to boarders).[76] Unsurprisingly, what lodgers wanted was an open, yet obliging, patient and respectful manner, and first impressions counted for much in this regard. Curwen was especially demanding in this respect. At the Folletts' in Sidmouth in 1777, he was pleased to be 'welcomed in a friendly manner by the family'. He described Mistress Stockdale, a prospective landlady in Bristol in 1780, as 'of an agreeable aspect, and manners mild'. Back in London in the same year, the elderly Mrs Longbottom in Furnival's Inn Court was a positive paragon of landlady virtues: 'excellent tempered, humorous, of a social and generous disposition, free from Knavish and dishonest craft that too justly characterizes people of lodging and boarding house professions'.[77]

It was, however, a delicate balancing act, because of at least equal importance was the location of the house and the material ambience of the room(s). Walpole had worried that George Montagu would find Piccadilly too traffic-ridden. A noisy situation was off-putting, but this had to be squared with the convenience of being 'centrical', as Carlyle recognized. The worst lodging he viewed in 1831 was 'in the nastiest, noisiest, but then a fashionable street!'[78] Then there was the interior, the room itself. Johnson's and the *Ladies Magazine's* fictional newlywed 'Peggy Heartless' lamented the time taken to find lodgings because of the fussiness of the naïve couple's friend Mr Quick, who accompanied them on their search. Rooms had too much afternoon sun, were dirty, crowded, had poor furniture.[79] In real life, Pilkington was thrilled by a first floor where 'the furniture was not only new but rich' and the price amazingly cheap (5s. a week). She agreed to take it but never moved in, claiming that when she called round the following day she found the landlady in the room in bed with a man.[80] It was clearly not a respectable house. Boswell used the word 'pretty' of apartments he considered good, implying the light, tasteful, and neat appearance that Vickery identifies as a generally 'recognised manner of decoration'.[81] Curwen took an instant liking to Furnival's Inn Court because the second-floor room's window looked south over the garden.[82] It was probably 'airy', that much-favoured adjective in *Chronicle* advertisements. Charles Lamb jokingly remarked of his Temple garret which looked over the Thames and the Surrey Hills, 'I shall be as airy, up four pair of stairs, as in the country'.[83] Shelley had taken against the exterior of 15 Poland Street at first, but once inside fell in love with the décor:

> The walls of the room had lately been covered with trellised paper; in those days it was not common. There were trellises, vine-leaves with their tendrils, and huge clusters of grapes, green and purple, all represented in lively colours. This was delightful; he went close up to the wall, and touched it: 'We must stay here; stay for ever!'[84]

Shelley was probably right to be delighted. Wallpaper was an increasingly popular and quick way of decorating a room. It appears in French artist Louis-Philippe Boitard's (*fl.* 1733–67) self-portrait of the 1730s set in his London lodgings (Figure 10). By the end of the century there is evidence of wallpaper in richer students' college rooms (including Shelley's in University College, Oxford), but it was probably relatively rare in private lodgings.[85] Only one *Chronicle* advertisement promised wallpaper, and this was in Lincoln's Inn

Figure 10 Louis-Philippe Boitard, *Self-Portrait with Two Young Men*, 1730–40. A painting of a multipurpose lodging-room: bedroom, parlour, and studio. It is hung with wallpaper, a curtain screens the bed and pictures adorn the walls. Yale Center for British Art, Paul Mellon Collection: B1975.4.1027.

chambers rather than a private house.[86] From a landlord's/lady's point of view paint, rather than the more 'modern' paper, was in all likelihood the preferred and more practical decorative finish as damage would have been easier to touch up between tenancies. This is probably the reason that Gibbon, on leaving lodgings and moving into his own house in 1772, wrote so delightedly of the blue shag flock wallpaper with a light blue and gold border that he was having installed.[87]

As ever in London, space was at a premium and, apart from noise, a common issue with lodging-rooms was the lack of the proverbial room to swing a cat. Swift, a veteran of London lodgings, suggested in *Gulliver's Travels* (1726) that a room 'of sixteen foot square, and twelve high [*c.* 4.9 metres square by 3.7 metres high], with sash-windows, a door, and two closets' was 'like a *London bed-chamber*'.[88] Curwen almost had second thoughts over Mrs Smithson's: 'Seeing the doors of my intended new lodgings open I entered and found the rooms so inconveniently small that I fear my abode will be short there.'[89] In Ampton Street the Carlyles suffered from 'hamperedness' but then, as Carlyle pointed out, 'one needs but little room to work profitably in; *my* craft [writing] especially requires nothing but a chair, a table, and a piece of paper'.[90]

Many of our lodgers – Inchbald, Haydon, Place, the Blakes – had to consider when viewing a room its suitability not just for sleeping but as a multipurpose space for cooking, eating, and working. The Places' and Blakes' circumstances (Figure 11) had something in common with the imagined room in *The Lottery Ticket*, where the husband is working at his carpenter's bench, his wife has an apron full of food she has just bought along with the ticket of the title,

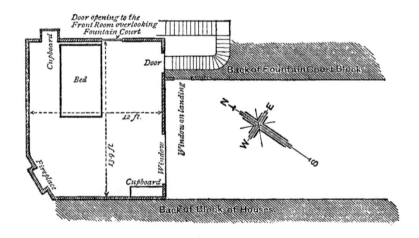

Figure 11 *Plan of Blake's Room in Fountain Court* and *Blake's Work-Room and Death-Room: 3, Fountain Court, Strand, c.* 1880. Floorplan: (p.102) and sketch (above) of William's and Catherine's first-floor rear living accommodation at 3 Fountain Court, where they lodged from 1821 to 1827. This room, which appears to be wainscoted and perhaps painted, served as kitchen, dining-room, parlour, and bedroom and also accommodated an engraving table. It was accessed via the slightly larger front room which opened off the landing. Alexander and Anne Gilchrist, *Life of William Blake …*, 2 vols (2nd edn, London: Macmillan, 1880), I, 322 and 348.

cupboards, and shelves groan with household crockery, pots and pans and provisions, washing hangs on a line, and two children tug at their mother's skirts.[91] It was presented as a crowded but happy scene. The reality of life was often less attractive, like the room of artist Mauritius Lowe as reported to Frances Burney:

> all dirt and filth, brats squalling and wrangling, up two pair of stairs, and a closet, of which the door was open, that Seward well said was quite Pandora's box – it was the repository of all the nastiness, and stench, and filth, and food, and drink, and – oh, it was too bad to be borne![92]

The better-off could of course negotiate for more space, either a larger and better room, a suite, or a whole floor, as Gansel occupied in Craven Street. Boswell had three rooms at the Terries' and, when viewing Poland Street, Shelley and Hogg were shown the papered sitting room and a bedroom adjoining on the first floor. There was then:

> some debate about a second bedroom, and the authorities were consulted below. We might have another bedroom; it was upstairs. That room, of course, was to be mine [i.e. Hogg's].[93]

It was with relief that twenty-five-year-old Place wrote of his family's move in 1796 to lodgings over a baker's shop of a room with a closet in which he could work:

> It was a great accommodation to us; it enabled my wife to keep the room in better order. It was advantageous too in its moral effects. Attendance on the child was not as it had been always, in my presence. I was shut out from seeing the fire lighted the room washed and cleaned, and the cloaths washed and ironed, as well as the cooking.

Place was clear about the moral as well as physical benefits of these two rooms. It was not only less 'hampered', but presented a more respectable, gendered front to the world, separating the woman's housework from male, breadwinning labour.[94] It was more domestic, more of a home.

Maximizing the size of rooms or the status of an address was not always a priority, however. The young Franklin, Inchbald, and Place all chose and changed their lodgings with a view to putting by some savings, something Boswell was not troubled to do, though he often felt himself short of money.[95] As Johnson had explained to Boswell in 1763, an address could remain secret since one could readily socialize in coffeehouses. Boswell had already come to a similar conclusion:

Sometimes I considered that a fine lodging denoted a man of great fashion, but then I thought that few people would see it and therefore the expense would be hid, whereas my business was to make as much show as I could with my small allowance. I thought that an elegant place to come home to was very agreeable and would inspire me with ideas of my own dignity; but then I thought it would be hard if I had not a proportionable show in other things, and that it was better to come gradually to a fine place than from a fine to a worse.[96]

Making a show in Georgian London was about these 'other things', the personal appearance and manners of the sort that allowed Boswell to buy his sword on credit. For Goldsmith it was clothing rather than accommodation that indicated his standing. Cutting down on basic living costs – rent, food, and heating – allowed him to spend more at his tailor's and on entertaining. He regularly recorded sums for teas, wine, and suppers and in 1762 spent four and a half guineas on a wig, cane, purple silk 'smallclothes' (underwear, small linen items such as handkerchiefs, sometimes also close-fitting breeches), and a scarlet roquelaure (a short cape).[97] Place was of the same mind:

when out of the house we always made a respectable appearance and were generally considered by those who knew us; as flourishing people, who wanted for nothing.[98]

For many lodgers their rooms could be modest provided their self-presentation indicated creditworthiness.

————————————

This discussion of the size and number of rooms leads naturally to the issue of price and other terms. Once an acceptable match of room and lodger was made, there began the hard negotiating before an agreement was reached. Despite the advice in legal guides there is little evidence in life-writing that the agreements were written, rather than oral, contracts. Savile was a notable exception when taking rooms for her brother for the coronation: 'Oblig'd to set my hand to a paper of the agreement and Mrs. D'Agar did the same.'[99] 'Oblig'd' suggests a degree of annoyance on Savile's part, as though she had not expected this. The coronation would have been a busy time for landlords/ladies and Mrs D'Agar probably wished to bind the Saviles to prevent them continuing their search, potentially leaving her with a vacancy at short notice. At a time when demand was high and supply short the Saviles' elevated social status seems to have counted for little.

Rents varied hugely, depending upon the location, the position within the house and the season. London was busiest and rooms most in demand in the Season, the winter months when Parliament sat, and the nobility and gentry were in town. There were also special occasions, such as coronations, when demand increased as Savile had discovered in 1727, and the German Count Kielmansegge in 1761: 'The arrival of so many foreigners, as well as people from all parts of England, had raised the price of lodgings a little.' He had to pay 35s. a week (£91 annualized) for a bedroom/dressing room and servant's room, and friends paid three guineas (£163 16s. annualized), albeit for 'a somewhat bigger' room.[100]

Guidebooks offered only very broad advice on what one might typically expect to pay. Usually the range they suggested was so broad as to be of little help at all.

> Furnished lodgings, that is the first floor with a servant's room, &c. in such a house, will let for from two guineas a-week to three and a half, in proportion to the goodness of the furniture, the conveniencies wanted, the trouble given, the time they are engaged for, and the season of the year,

advised Trusler. Trusler linked lodging rentals to the price of a whole house. A house twenty-one-feet wide (6.4 metres) wide might let for four to eight guineas a week outside the Season. In the Season the lowest prices would rise to seven guineas and a landlord/lady could demand a four- to five-month commitment (making Kielmansegge's rent in fact a bargain). As a rule of thumb, a house rented at fifty guineas a year would let furnished for two to five guineas a week. As lodgings, the first floor commanded one to two guineas a week, and the parlour and second floors two thirds of that. Given the large number of variables introduced, Trusler could only set out some guidelines for negotiation.[101] According to Leigh, in 1822 furnished first-floor rooms were 'from two to three, four, or six guineas per week; and on the second floor, they are about two thirds of those prices'. Leigh too advised of the variables: 'it is necessary to be very particular about the articles which are to be furnished, and the attendance which is expected.'[102] Tardy gave a wider range: between four and five shillings to two or three guineas a week.[103] Though the authors of these guides did not aim to find a readership among potential landlords/ladies, their figures again make it clear that that letting out rooms was a sound financing strategy that might comfortably cover the rent of well-located premises.

Price was rarely addressed directly in *Chronicle* advertisements. The commercial nature of the lodging transaction was more often concealed behind euphemistic terms such as 'moderate', 'liberal', or 'reasonable', a reticence that alongside 'respectable', 'genteel', and 'airy' preserved the gentility of the parties in this section of the accommodation market, and left scope for negotiation. Where a price was given in the *Chronicle*, the parameters across the thirty years surveyed started somewhat lower than Trusler at around £30 per year stretching to four guineas a week (£218 8s. per year). The upper end, exceeding even that paid by Kielmansegge's friends in 1761, is not represented in any of the life-writing studied and, if achievable, can surely only have been intended for the very wealthy staying for a short period.

In winter 1710 Swift's rent was below the lower end of the *Chronicle* market in the late century: 8s. a week (£20 16s. a year) in both Bury Street and St Alban Street, but only 5s. a week (£13 a year) in Pall Mall.[104] The *Chronicle's* base level of £30 was the sort of price point at which Boswell searched for rooms in 1762, and towards the maximum that Curwen (who struck a hard bargain, being conscious that he had to live off a 'pittance' of cash brought from America and a sum borrowed from a friend) was prepared to pay in the 1770s and 1780s.[105] In 1769 the more mature Boswell paid more: one and a half guineas a week for rooms in Bond Street (£81 18s. a year). He understood that this was something of a bargain as it was autumn. Apparently they fetched twice this sum in the Season.[106] Even these rents were out of reach of those seeking to live on the £30 a year that Johnson claimed was sufficient to avoid appearing 'contemptible'.[107] In arriving at this figure, Johnson had in mind living in a garret at 1s. 6d. a week (under £4 a year). In the 1720s Franklin found rooms at this sort of price level, paying between 1s. 6d. and 3s. 6d. a week (£9 2s. a year) in the Little Britain and Lincoln's Inn Fields areas.[108] Inchbald, who was careful with money and often moved for reasons of economy, still paid only 7s. to 15s. a week in the 1780s (£18 4s. to £39 a year).[109] In 1790s Holborn, Place paid between 2s. and 4s. out of a weekly income of around 14s., later struggling to afford sixteen guineas a year, a big increase for what was, however, a 'light airy and comfortable' address.[110] While it is impossible to pin down precisely or tabulate the cost of a room in Georgian London, what is clear is that the market provided variety and catered for every depth of pocket.

These figures vary enormously but even so do not tell the full story, since it was only by detailed 'discourse' (MP Roger Whitley's expression) that landlords/ladies and lodgers agreed what was covered by the rent and what would be billed separately as 'extras'. The major 'extra' item was food and drink, and some landlords/ladies were undoubtedly scrupulous in billing for everything beyond what had been contracted. In 1831 the Lambs queried an unexpected 6d. on their bill and were told that it was because a visitor had taken a large amount of sugar in his tea (which was also billed). Incidentally, the visitor was William Wordsworth (1770–1850), and the retail price of sugar was approximately 6d. per pound.[111] Clearly lodgers had to be on their guard when negotiating the extras.

Some lodgers were also boarders; that is, they ate with the household and any other lodgers. This avoided the bother of shopping and catering for oneself and provided a convivial experience at mealtimes. Even a light snack could be a sociable occasion. Franklin's pleasurable evening chats with his Lincoln's Inn Fields landlady of the 1720s were accompanied by food and drink: 'Our supper was only half an Anchovy each, on a very little Strip of Bread & Butter, and half a Pint of Ale between us.'[112] For landlords/ladies boarding also added an extra income stream to the rental and left them in charge in their own kitchen. On the negative side for lodgers, boarding tied them to the landlord's/lady's daily timetable and might entail paying over the odds for the sort of 'second table knavery' that Carlyle feared.

There were many options between full board and no meal service at all, and many ways in which lodgers mixed a degree of boarding with catering for themselves. Misson described well the possible meal arrangements:

> As to Eating, there are many Ways for that, as any Body may easily imagine: You board at some House, you have Victuals brought to your Lodgings, you take a Cook if you please, &c. There are Cooks Shops enough in all Parts of the Town, where it is very common to go and chuse upon the Spit the part you like, and to eat it there.[113]

In her youth Inchbald often provided and prepared her own food and drink, carefully noting the amounts spent in her diaries (around 4s. to 5s. a week in 1780 on top of her 9s. rent), which indicates that controlling her costs was paramount.[114] In older age, when living at the Salterellis' for example, communal meals were both more convenient and more sociable, and Inchbald was of course more financially secure. Cold food, bread toasted on the fire and simple dishes could be prepared and eaten in one's room, at the expense of working and sleeping with the lingering smell. Among the possessions lost in the 1707 Charles Street fire by lodger Ann Smith were a frying pan, gridiron, saltbox, and dredging box, implying such basic cookery probably over the fire in her own room.[115] Images and life-writing reveal the range of diets supplied in this way. In Plate 4 of Hogarth's *Harlot's Progress* the table holds the remains of bread, cheese, and tea. Moritz ate alone in his room, as fictional Moll Hackabout did, typically 'some pickled salmon, which you eat in the liquor in which it is pickled, along with some oil and vinegar'. Boitard's self-portrait depicted himself with two friends taking tea and what looks like bread or cake at a folding table (Figure 10).[116] A century later at both South Molton Street and Fountain Court Catherine Blake cooked and the couple ate in the same room in which they worked and slept (Figure 11).[117] In around 1813 Shelley lived off 'panada', a dish easily prepared in his room: bread soaked in boiling water, squeezed dry, chopped up with a spoon, and topped with pounded sugar and nutmeg. He and Hogg also 'meekly sought relief in buttered toast', supplemented by the occasional penny bun.[118] Such frugality sometimes came, however, at the price of loneliness, as Dickens's memories suggest. When he was twelve his father was a prisoner for debt in the Marshalsea. Although only a child, he lived apart from his family in Camden lodgings and worked in the infamous shoe-blacking factory. Despite his tender age he had to find his own solitary breakfast of a penny cottage loaf and pennyworth of milk. He recalled, 'I kept another small loaf, and a quarter of a pound of cheese, on a particular shelf of a particular cupboard; to make my supper on when I came home at night.' A benefit of moving to Lant Street in the Borough was breakfasting with the rest of his family in the Marshalsea.[119]

Other lodgers chose to take only breakfast at the house (tea, coffee, or chocolate, and bread and butter or rolls) and made other catering arrangements for the rest of the day, which might include purchasing some meals and refreshments in the house as they required. Even here there were possible variations. Emin recalled a 'system' organized by Mr Philpot, his Strand grocer landlord. Emin bought his own sugar and tea, and each morning ate a pennyworth of buttered roll for breakfast:

> The kettle on the fire in the small room below stairs near the shop, was boiling gratis; each person put a spoonful of tea in the joint-pot; and each had his cup and saucer, in which he took care to put sparingly a certain quantity of sugar. If he dined with them on common days, he paid three pence for his dinner; and if on Sunday, a groat.[120]

Purchasing one's own supplies avoided the high markup applied by the Lambs' landlady, but if storage was accessible to others there was the risk of theft familiar to anyone who has shared accommodation. Servants were thought to be light-fingered, and Smith recorded Mrs Nollekens's belief that landlords/ladies were not above suspicion: 'the lower class of people in general, who let lodgings, were much addicted to pilfer from every article of consumption.'[121] Lodgers therefore often kept these private food supplies under lock and key. Moritz had a locking cupboard for his tea, coffee, bread, and butter and the Carlyles kept their special butter, sent from the Scottish farm, in a can with a padlock.[122]

Dining out was another option. Sara Pennell has drawn attention to the 'ready availability of victuals around the clock' in eighteenth-century London.[123] It was an option that did not suit everyone's taste or pocket, however. Eating-houses were crowded, noisy, and generally masculine spaces (Figure 12). It could also prove expensive. Moritz had begun on this basis and then switched to the pickled fish suppers, a frugality that pleased him. Tardy suggested that a tavern meal cost a steep three guineas, although there were cheaper alternatives. In the 1760s Johnson told Boswell that it was possible to dine (the midday meal) for 6d., and the impecunious young Wilkie wrote in a letter to his brother in 1805 that he generally breakfasted in his lodgings and dined at around two o'clock in the afternoon in a Poland Street ordinary ('a place of eating established at a certain price' according to Johnson's *Dictionary*) with friends at 13d. a head: 'as cheap as any person can have such a dinner.'[124] Ordinaries and cookshops could

Figure 12 Thomas Rowlandson, *An Eating House*, ?1815. A busy eating-house. Note that all the customers are men. Metropolitan Museum, NY: The Elisha Whittelsey Collection: 59.533.254.

also supply hot takeaway meals to eat at home. 'Porridge Island' was an alley of takeaways near St Martin-in-the-Fields, convenient for many lodgers, and of which it was said 'fine gentlemen' availed themselves in order to spend more on outward appearances.[125] As a young journeyman apothecary in a three-shilling room at his master's in Fish Street Hill in the City, Goldsmith was accustomed to eat in this way: 'a lukewarm dinner served up between two pewter plates from a cook's shop'.[126] The Mozarts, on the other hand, found eating-house takeaways so nasty (and maybe, to foreigners, unfamiliar) that Mrs Mozart switched at Chelsea and then in Frith Street to catering personally for her family.[127] Sharing the hosts' kitchen was, however, a matter that needed negotiation and was, as Chapter 5 will reveal, an area where conflict could arise.

Much the cheapest way of eating was, however, to scrounge free dinners from friends, Swift's preferred method. His lofty 'I don't dine with boarders' was in part an expression of snobbery but perhaps was also aimed at concealing the extent of his freeloading: in 1712 he lived at Kensington for two weeks 'partly for the air and Exercise' but 'partly to be near the Court, where dinners are to be found'.[128] Elizabeth Carter also 'kept no table in London' but went by chair to dinners at friends'.[129] Thomas Lawrence was only seventeen when he moved to London in 1787. He persuaded his mother to come up to London to cook for him to save him from eating out. When he moved to 41 Jermyn Street (see Chapter 3) his adoring parents took lodgings close by where Thomas continued to take his (free) meals.[130] Scrounging required an intimate London network of family and friends bound by kinship and affect (Lawrence's parents and Carter's friends) or by patronage, where something was expected in return for the meals (Swift). Most lodgers were not so fortunate.

Food and drink were not the only potential extras. Lodgers also had to bargain with landlords/ladies over heating and lighting, room use, linen and laundry, and 'attendance' – the level of service that would be provided by the host and his/her servants. Coals and wood were needed for fires in lodging–rooms, and candles for light. Most lodgers at all levels of the market paid extra for these expensive consumables. At the poorer end, Love reckoned on 6d. a peck (equivalent to about nine litres) per week for coals in the winter months on top of his 3s. weekly rent.[131] In December 1779 Curwen agreed a shilling a week for coal with Mrs Froade of Bristol, but generally bought his own coals, firing (wood), and candles.[132] Inchbald also bought them herself and had her own coalman (who had to run the gauntlet of Miss Baillie's dog Pickle when delivering).[133] Some template lodging agreements in legal guides included the use of cellar-space for storage of the lodger's fuel.[134]

Lodgers could attempt to economize on these extra items but at the risk of discomfort in a century when thermal comfort was increasingly valued.[135] As with food and drink, lodgers devised strategies to reduce expense. Swift, who used two bushels (four pecks) of coal a week in winter 1712, added loose bricks to the back of the grate to retain the heat and was accustomed to pick off some of the coals Patrick put on the fire.[136] In 1757 Franklin narrowed the Craven Street fireplace and invented an iron frame with a sliding plate in order to burn less fuel. His quasi-marital relationship with his landlady presumably enabled these alterations.[137] Another way of avoiding either expense or a cold room was going out or its opposite: staying in wrapped up, or even in bed, to put off the need for a fire. Swift, who had a fire only in his sitting-room, often wrote in bed in the morning for ' 'tis very warm weather when one's in bed'.[138] Inchbald practised her lines in bed.[139] And who could not pity Samuel Boyse (?1702/3–1749), a poet so destitute in 1740 that, his clothes pawned, he wrote to pay for food sitting in his lodging-room bed stripped of sheets, covered in a blanket with a hole cut for his writing hand?[140]

Using the landlord's/lady's parlour was another way of sitting somewhere warm and comfortable without using one's own coal supply. At Star Court, Place sat in his landlady's room of an evening when it was wet and cold to save on the cost of a fire.[141] The parlour fire provided not only heat but the cosy domestic experience of being a part of a household rather than a houseful, Schopenhauer's 'own hearthside' (Chapter 3). It was a place to socialize with others including visitors, and especially relative strangers, without revealing to them one's bedroom and the sort of untidiness evident in Boitard's self-portrait. Swift had the use of the parlour in St Alban Street where he received 'persons of quality'.[142] It was in his parlour that landlord Mr Marr introduced Chitqua to Boswell. Boswell agreed the use of 'a handsome parlour all the forenoon' with the Terries. It eventually allowed him to dispense with a second room upstairs (with a consequent saving on rent) and made a break from sitting in one room: 'I come always down to my [*sic*] parlour, which is more cheerful for me; and I have my hair dressed every day'.[143] Goldsmith entertained in the parlour at Edgeware – tea, a dinner, even a dance.[144] At some of his lodgings Curwen enjoyed tea, cards, and conversation in the parlour with hosts, their families, and other lodgers. In Southampton Buildings Hazlitt used the parlour to read the newspaper.[145] The parlour was, however, part of the private accommodation of the host family and, like the Terries, some landlords/ladies were reluctant to give unlimited access. After Star Court, Holborn, at his sixteen-guinea lodgings at the Ashleys', Place and his children used the parlour with the family when

Ashley, a London Corresponding Society colleague, was at home. When he was not, Mrs Ashley would shoo them out.[146] Parlour use was, therefore, like kitchen-sharing, a further subject for negotiation.

Finally, there were the servicing arrangements to sort out before the deal was struck. The room would need tidying and cleaning. Bedlinen had to be changed. Lodgers might bring their own sheets or these could be provided as part of the contract. Laundry was organized in-house or put out by the lodger. The same went for shoe-cleaning. Medical student Hampton Weekes and his fellow lodgers were annoyed when the servants refused to shine their boots and shoes unless they each advanced them 5s. a quarter. They had little choice but to agree.[147] Inchbald seems to have enjoyed cleaning her own room (or at least to have enjoyed the cash saving).[148] Sometimes it was the landlady and her family who performed these chores. Sometimes they had help, as Tim Meldrum describes, from poorer female lodgers (such as, maybe, the servants out of place lodging at Hannah Barker's the time of the Compton Street fire). More often, however, it was the household servant, typically a maid, who did the hard work.[149]

We have seen that Paul's legal handbook provided a template agreement for a landlord letting a furnished room 'together with the use of his maid-servant, in common with other lodgers, at such times when he himself can spare her' (Chapter 2).[150] Several *Chronicle* advertisements mentioned the availability of servants as part of the general agreement: 'The Servant of the House will attend', for example.[151] However, servants could be averse to working in a house with multiple lodgers where they had to respond to the calls of their employer, prioritize the needs of demanding lodgers, and sit up until all hours to let them back into the house, as this advertisement implied:

> WANTED a stout active Boy, about 16, as a yearly Servant, to wait and do other usual services in a house where there are no lodgers.[152]

Maid servants faced additional issues of sexual harassment. Author Eliza Haywood (?1693–1756) warned them to be on their guard against gentleman lodgers who 'when they stay out till after the Family are gone to Bed, come home in Liquor … [and] take this Opportunity of making Offers to you.' Nor should they accept any presents from lodgers.[153] Casanova was necessarily more than averagely generous, given the sexual role she was to play, with regard to the lodger-mistress (Pauline) he recruited in Pall Mall. His maid would do Pauline's laundry, buy her food and run her errands. His cook's wife would on consultation prepare her dinner and supper.[154] This again seems to be in the realm of erotic quasi-fiction, however, with its queasy suggestion that Pauline is to be held captive in a luxury prison.

Just as in fiction, servants could alternatively be brought in by the lodger. They would have been more loyal and not waylaid by the calls of others. On the other hand, the lodger had to pay for their accommodation, often in the garret of the same house with the household servants, though sometimes elsewhere. Maid Kitty Hamilton, who featured in John Macdonald's (b. 1741) account of his life as a footman, did not live with her mistress but lodged out, for example.[155] In Anne King's Leicester Fields home her murderer Gardelle was not the only lodger. There was a gentleman called Wright whose servant slept in the garret.[156] Four lodger's servants were claimants after the Compton Street fire of 1785. All were women and two of them, one a wet-nurse, were employed by one lodger, Mr Davis.[157] Jonathan Swift had his Patrick, the Mozarts brought another servant besides the Italian Porta, and Franklin arrived at Craven Street in 1757 with two 'servants'. In truth, they were two enslaved black men: Peter and King.[158] These servant-lodgers acquired accommodation and the opportunity to enjoy something of London, but it was not of their own choosing and was constrained by the needs of their lodger-employer. Another option was for the lodger to have a maid who came in by the day, as the older, ailing Inchbald did at the Salterellis'. She too was of colour, and never named by Inchbald other than as 'the black'.[159]

The 5s. weekly rent of the room where Pilkington caught her landlady *in flagrante* included linen, plate, and china.[160] Bringing one's own linen and so forth avoided the bedding equivalent of nasty meals – rough sheets complained of by Swift in Chelsea, and thin blankets that Wilkie found of little use in keeping him warm.[161] Thomas Wale included in a trunk for travelling (to Moscow rather than specifically to a lodging) table- and bedlinen and cutlery in a case.[162] Visitors to London from afar, such as Curwen (who did bring at least one blanket from America, together with a 'fine linen pillow' and a pair of sheets) usually relied on linen and other extras being provided by the landlord/lady, though Schopenhauer indicated that, at Bath at least, this and a range of other household items could also be hired 'splendid or prettily simple'.[163]

This overview of what was involved in finding and choosing a lodger or a room indicates just how well-understood and flexible, yet at the same time complicated, any lodging arrangement was, and why it is so difficult to put a price on this accommodation in the period. For this reason, the rents of rooms have been included in the text of this study wherever possible. Some lodgers had a significant advantage in being able to use existing networks of family and friends to find their accommodation, but many had no contacts in London and were obliged to search from scratch. This search was more than usually difficult where a lodger had to overcome prejudice based on race, nationality or, for young women, marital status.

The large and active market in rooms meant that it was possible to find respectable accommodation fairly instantly and at almost any price point upwards of a few shillings a week, but where a lodger was more demanding it could be a time-consuming process as convenience, space, comfort, value, and the congeniality of the landlord/lady had to be weighed in the balance. Despite the attempts to monetize it, finding a room or a lodger and coming to a deal remained a process that generally took place face-to-face and so retained an element of the serendipitous. In negotiations the hosts usually had the upper hand. It was, after all, their home and so their choice to make and, as many were retailers, they also had extensive prior experience of assessing the character and creditworthiness of customers.

Having met and agreed terms the two parties would now have to manage the move and learn to live alongside one another in a busy household within the confines of a family home. It was not always easy, and the arrangements made in the parlour or on the doorstep did not always last. A key area of conflict was around those nebulous extras – nebulous because it seems most contracts were oral rather than written. How a *modus vivendi* was achieved – or not – is the subject of the next two chapters.

Moving in and rubbing along

Let us assume that the landlord or lady and the lodger have come to terms and a date – quite often the same or the next day – has been set for moving in. Chapter 5 considers the process of moving possessions and arranging the room or rooms to the lodger's satisfaction. To what extent did the lodgers surveyed here feel that they could make their accommodation in someone else's house – the householder's personal, private, and domestic space – their own 'home within a home'? *Chronicle* advertisements insisted on the society and company that lodging might afford but how far was this afforded in reality? What were the ongoing small issues of living cheek-by-jowl with members of the host household and with other lodgers under the same roof? Could these be resolved?

———————————

As Swift learned when he refused to pay a deposit, speed was of the essence. It was still the same in the 1830s. The *Through-bred Poor Gentleman's Book* advised the reader to 'Say you send your things at once, *sleep there*'. This saved on money spent on a hotel but also secured the room.[1] Whether or not in London for the first time, most lodgers would have luggage in the form of at least one trunk or box. In 1712, when books took up all the space in the 'great Box' he had bought, Swift had to purchase another for 'Cloathes & Luggage'.[2] If moving from one lodging to another, at least half a day or so was spent packing up possessions. 'Pack up all morning,' wrote author Mary Godwin (1797–1851) in her diary entry for 9 November 1814. As she and her lover Percy Shelley were almost constantly on the run from bailiffs it was a process she knew well from regular repetition.[3] In 1782 Inchbald started packing as early as 9 May for a move on 4 June, when a cousin 'came and took all my things to my new Lodgings'.[4] Sometimes the landlord's/lady's family or a servant helped. In Hazlitt's case this was landlady Mrs Walker's youngest daughter Betsey.[5]

The packed trunk(s) then had to be transported to the new accommodation. Swift used a stagecoach to move to Chelsea in 1711.[6] Goldsmith sent his books to Edgeware Road in two 'returned postchaises'.[7] At the poorer end of lodgers, Suffolk 'workhouse poet' Ann Candler (1740–1814) sent in 1779 'the best of my goods, which were very decent' to London by the Ipswich hoy (a hoy was a small, coasting ship), while she and her children travelled by land. Presumably she then had to collect their boxes from the docks.[8] Disgraced Oxonians Shelley and Hogg hired a hackney coach (available from stands at published, fixed rates) for the move to Poland Street as soon as they agreed terms.[9] An alternative was a hired porter with or without a cart (a 'carman') or handcart (Figure 13). Porters waited for custom at some 100 official stands or worked casually, and charged up to 5s. a day.[10] Crossing the Thames, as the Saviles and Curwen did to Wandsworth and Battersea respectively, might require a boat.[11] These costs were high for the

Figure 13 George Cruikshank, *The Piccadilly Nuisance*, 1835 (orig. pub. 1818). On the left of Cruikshank's etching of busy Piccadilly in the heart of London's West End is a porter with a customer's trunk on his back. In the background is Hatchett's, a hotel and coffeehouse incorporating the White Horse Cellar: the arrival point in London for coaches from the West country. This is where some new lodgers would have stayed for their first night before striking out to find rooms. Courtesy of the Lewis Walpole Library, Yale University: 835.08.01.50+.

more cash-strapped of our lodgers. In 1801 Lamb told his friend, the traveller and scholar of China, Thomas Manning (1772–1840), that he had sold the spare bed to pay for removals.[12]

It was an exhausting process too, especially when it came hot on the heels of the tramp around town, as diarists noted. 'How little do these persons, possessed of *houses* and *servants*, know of the difficulties and dangers we poor lodgers experience every time we remove to a new lodging!' lamented Inchbald.[13] 'May I never MOVE again, but may my next Lodgings be my COFFIN,' wrote Lamb to another friend, Robert Lloyd, in 1810. He could not know that several further moves still lay ahead of him.[14] How much worse it must have been when the move was unplanned because a lodger had been summarily evicted. D. T. Egerton's (1797–1842) print *The Unfortunate Discovery* shows a young couple standing on the doorstep of a genteel house (Figure 14). In the doorway glowers

Figure 14 D. T. Egerton, *The Unfortunate Discovery*, 1824. Egerton's image shows a young couple who have just been summarily evicted. At their feet are the customary boxes and trunks. There are also the small items that would have made their lodging-room a home: pot-plants, a lap-dog and a caged song-bird. Yale Center for British Art, Paul Mellon Collection: B1985.36.1338.

their hatchet-faced landlady who has just found out that they are not married. The young woman weeps, he is hands-in-pockets and embarrassed, and at their feet tumble their household goods including the ubiquitous trunk and boxes. There is no hired carriage or porter to take them away.[15]

————————————

Once moved, there was the equally tiresome business of unpacking. Again writing to Manning, Lamb summed up the chaos of the move and transition:

> Such a heap of little nasty things, after you think all is got into the cart: old dredging-boxes, worn-out brushes, gallipots, vials, things that it is impossible the most necessitous person can ever want … Then you can find nothing you want for many days after you get into your new lodgings.[16]

The lodger and host then had to adjust to their new circumstances, learning to live together and with other members of both household and houseful. After only a relatively brief encounter when viewing and negotiating, it was hard for either party to tell whether the arrangement was going to be a success. On her first day in Wandsworth, Savile went to bed at eleven after unpacking and settling in. She was deeply anxious, describing herself as 'Very peevish. Fretted at everything, dreded the Lodgings, expected everything disagreable in them'.[17] Strange rooms could feel empty and bleak, especially for a lodger far from home, family, and friends. Irish law student Curran admitted that he was initially holed up in his room: 'For the first five months I was almost totally a recluse'.[18] American artist Charles Robert Leslie (1794–1859) agreed. He arrived in London in 1811 aged just seventeen, his knowledge of the city formed only by the sources discussed in Chapter 2: Burney's novels, Hogarth's prints and the *Picture of London* guide. This was not enough to feel at home even though he had an American friend in the lodgings with him:

> I was solitary, and began to feel that even in London it was possible to be unhappy. I did not feel this in its full force until I was settled in lodgings, consisting of two desolate-looking rooms up two pair of stairs in Warren Street, Fitzroy Square.[19]

It was not only sheets and blankets that on closer acquaintance seemed a little inadequate. The furniture could also disappoint. It had of course been chosen by someone else, the landlord/lady. Not only was it in accordance with that someone else's taste and pocket, but it had to make a good enough impression at first viewing while avoiding any unnecessary capital expenditure that ate into the profitability of the letting exercise. At the same time, however, there was that rising expectation of material comfort in the home which, as Styles has shown, was not restricted to middling-sort homeowners, but penetrated the lower end of the lodging market too.[20] On reflection some rooms were, to lodgers' eyes at least, 'very slightly furnished'.[21] Haydon's second-floor room had a mirror, but it was 'half-rubbed, broken-down' and had only one pivot-pin left, 'and that excessively loose'.[22] At Furnival's Inn Court, Curwen's landlady Mrs Longbottom provided 'no closet, nor case of drawers, nor any convenience for holding'. One of his first actions on moving in was therefore to buy at a Snow Hill auction a bureau table.[23] Carlyle put up with a bed six inches narrower than he was used to while his landladies were in the process of moving.[24] These lodging-rooms offered the opposite of comfort. They were reminiscent of the sixteenth-century poets' garrets.

Unpacking possessions might leave the room seeming pokier than expected, and to excess belongings being stored elsewhere. Both Swift and Curwen left filled trunks at friends' houses, for example.[25] In 1805 Inchbald wrote with wry humour of her tiny room at Miss Baillie's:

> My present apartment is so small, that I am all over black and blue with thumping my body and limbs against my furniture on every side: but then I have not far to *walk* to reach any thing I want; for I can kindle my fire as I lie in bed; and put my cap on as I dine; for the looking-glass is obliged to stand on the same table with my dinner.[26]

Her words also echo the old cliché of the poet's shabby garret, as do those of Charke and Goldsmith, each of whom penned rhymes about their rooms. Hers contained a chest of drawers, old bed, and single chair. In his, the window-glass was broken and 'five crack'd tea cups dres'd the chimney board'.[27] What might be lacking even in a lodging-room better-furnished than these is indicated by Gibbon's enthusiasm for doing up his Bentinck Street house. For his first 'proper' home, he acquired not just the flock wallpaper but also mahogany furniture, and bookcases painted white with 'a light frize'.[28] In an interval of relative affluence in 1768 Goldsmith moved to barrister's chambers in Brick Court and similarly bought the luxury furnishings of which, as a lodger, he had been deprived: Wilton carpets, mahogany sofas with blue upholstery and matching curtains and chairs, chimney glasses, Pembroke and card tables, and book shelves.[29]

———————————

After unpacking, the trunk often remained an important part of the room's furnishings. In common with the boxes and trunks of servants, it provided a degree of 'material continuity' between life in lodgings and the owner's personal history, a place where possessions could be 'sedimented'.[30] It was a deeply personal and personalized (with initials, for example) object. It offered comfort to the lonely and, as lockable storage for things they did not want the landlord/lady, their family and servants to see, an important private storage space.[31] Abigail Gouring, like Ann Smith a lodger caught up in the 1707 Charles Street fire, claimed £7 for one trunk in which she stored linen and woollen clothing.[32] Clothing and linen, most probably kept in trunks, also dominated the items for which lodgers claimed in the aftermath of the Compton Street fire, though some had also lost books, furniture, plate, and the materials and tools of their trade.[33]

Curwen had two trunks with him and treated the items they stored with care, regularly unpacking, checking over and airing their contents.[34] In December 1780, two days after coming to Furnival's Inn Court, and again in July 1782, four days into his time in Battersea, he made inventories. He had a large number of books and other reading materials, and also clothing and accessories, wigs, toiletry and medicinal items (including 'ointment for piles'), writing materials and tools, playing cards and cribbage and backgammon sets, and souvenirs of the British towns he had visited. His portable possessions were considerable and largely practical. The cards, cribbage, and backgammon sets anticipated sociability. Some, however, probably held a greater meaning. It was not only his pillowcase and sheets that were 'brought from home' (Chapter 4): there were too some smallclothes, a pair of gold sleeve buttons that belonged to his wife, and a razor inscribed 'W.L. Salem'. The buttons may or may not have been reminders of a loving relationship (he and his wife were not on good terms). They may also have represented a portable reservoir of value brought in case he needed to access extra cash (though in 1782 he did add that that they were 'to be restored to her or her heirs'). The razor was perhaps a link, now lost to us, to the home and friends he had fled.[35] Here a lodger's trunks were a repository of both material and emotional continuity.

'Home' was the word used by most of the lodger-diarists of their rooms – when they returned after an outing for instance. In most respects they were right. As John Hollander points out 'home' encompasses many concepts. It is where 'They have to take you in', where a court says you live, where you lay your head, eat, work, make love, experience being greeted, keep your possessions, feel safe.[36] Domestic touches helped to achieve a fuller sense of home. To be sure, some lodgers were not concerned to make their room homely, a personal, private, and comfortable space. They perhaps followed Johnson's advice that no one would ask where you lived. Although Swift's London lodging addresses were 'good' by the standard of lodgings, they were far inferior to the townhouses of many of those with whom he associated. He was, therefore, sometimes cagey about revealing his circumstances. After a dinner, the politician and Swift's patron, Robert Lord Harley (1661–1724), left with Swift in a hackney carriage. Swift insisted on stopping at St James's coffeehouse rather than at his Bury Street lodgings.[37] In 1710 an Irish friend Dr Raymond was to come to London and hoped to lodge in the same house as Swift. Swift was horrified: 'that must not be' he confided, later noting that he had 'slipt' Raymond off to someone else. He preferred to receive 'persons of quality' in a parlour and was mortified when Patrick sent a visitor upstairs in error and he was obliged to make someone already there – 'a hang-dog instrument of mine' – hide in his bedroom for an hour.[38]

Swift was probably, therefore, one of those not especially concerned to make his rooms a haven of snug domesticity. As he joked to Esther Johnson and Rebecca Dingley when they complained to him about their somewhat bleak lodgings in Wexford: 'clean sheets, but bare walls; I suppose then you lay upon the walls.' However, even he had some items that provided emotional comfort: his books and proper coffee. When lodging in Dublin in 1702 he had purchased his own coffee roaster, and his London accounts show regular expenditure on coffee beans. He started his book collection anew in each fresh lodging:

> when I leave a Lodging, I box up the Books I get (for I always get some) and come naked into a new Lodging; and so on.[39]

'Books do furnish a room.'[40] They featured among the possessions lost by Mary Orton, another lodger in the 1707 Charles Street fire, who claimed for a trunkful, by three victims of the 1785 Compton Street fire, and in many lodger-diarist accounts of their rooms, in part because as diarists they were by definition writers engaged with the republic of letters in their various ways.[41] Books were of course highly portable, easy to pack up and move, and reading was a pastime that could easily be enjoyed in the limited space of a lodging-room, maybe under the bedcovers to save on those expensive coals. Bringing and buying one's own books also allowed a lodger to maintain and exhibit their sense of identity and taste both to themselves, to the landlord/lady, and to any who visited their room. Congreve had a library of thirty-three shelves of books in Arundel Street.[42] Chatterton, Curwen, Lamb, and Hazlitt all referred to their books. Hazlitt used them as improving parting gifts to his landlady's daughter Sarah. She replied they were of no use to her, a rejection of Hazlitt himself and a reflection on the class difference between many lodgers and their hosts that has already been noted.[43] Some landlords/ladies supplied books for lodgers to read. Playwrights Charles Dibdin (1745–1814) and Richard Cumberland (1732–1811), and Francis Place all referred to books made available to them. In the Radical Place's case these included the works of Paine (as featured on the wall of the *Gentleman of Moderate Fortune* (Chapter 2 and Figure 3).[44] Shared and gifted books were another form of sociability within a shared house.

Nor was Swift the only lodger to use drink and foodstuffs to foster a sense of linkage to their origins through their taste, smell, and nostalgic associations with a past home. Curwen sometimes bought 'Indian corn' (maize) and, close to Christmas 1782 while the host family (the Poyntons of Orange Court, Leicester Fields) was out, used it to make himself a plate of hasty pudding, which he ate alone in his room.[45] Carlyle's precious butter came from home. Before she joined him in London, he also asked Jane to send oatmeal and ham. He and Jane later taught their English landladies in Ampton Street to make the Scottish 'national dish', porridge.[46]

If a room was taken unfurnished the lodger was responsible for selecting all the contents. This avoided suffering the poor taste of the hosts and might be a positive pleasure as one *Chronicle* advertiser looking for a room implied in her afterthought: 'N.B. The Lady chooses to furnish her own bed-chamber.' It could prove a potentially expensive and drawn-out task, however. It took Inchbald two weeks of 'frugal researches' to equip a second-floor room in 1792, though by 1810 she was clearly fond of her furniture which gave her a sense of place throughout subsequent changes of address: 'I am *attached* to my old furniture, – I have known it so long ... '. However, not all landlords and ladies with furnished rooms were tolerant of larger items like Curwen's bureau, as Inchbald discovered. Mrs D__ of Kensington Gore had 'crazy' furniture but 'would not suffer one bit of mine to come in'. Too many possessions forced a lodger to look in the more limited unfurnished market where (see Chapter 6) Inchbald experienced in 1810 the fear of losing her furniture to pay the debts of her landlord, as all the legal guides warned could happen.[47]

Inchbald probably chose unfurnished lodgings for reasons of economy. The Places were sometimes compelled so to do in the early years of their marriage and, in contrast to the more middling-sort and established Inchbald, Francis chronicled their ups and downs through items they were gradually able to buy for their rooms, or were forced to sell. For this couple, the presence of certain material possessions in their rooms signified success as well as comfort and respectability. For example, they set up a second-floor back room in Wych Street with:

> a bedstead, a table three or four chairs and some bedding … and a few utensils … and began to congratulate ourselves on the improvement of our circumstances and the prospect before us.

As we have seen, it was particularly important for this aspirant man that his male work be separated from female domestic activities. Before he was able to move to the room and closet in 1796, this had been by the expedient of putting up 'an iron Rod close up the cieling [*sic*], on which ran a couple of curtains', by which means they could make some of their space more private.[48]

For most lodgers, however, their sense of home was created by small, portable possessions, knick-knacks. These too were often replete with meaning. In 1725 Muilman insisted her estranged husband collect and hand over her tea-kettle, lamp, and standish (ink and pen-holder).[49] Pilkington had some of her furniture, plates, and dishes with her in St James's and watered pot-plants on the leads under the dining-room window. Inchbald had ornaments and pictures which she recalled rehanging, and Hazlitt treasured a bronze bust of his hero Napoleon, which he displayed on his Southampton Buildings mantelpiece.[50] As well as the Scottish foodstuffs, Carlyle asked Jane to send him little things that were not, in a lodging, 'come-at-able, and yet were good to have', such as jelly-glasses and a butter-knife.[51] Pets occasionally created a sense of home and, as a living presence, eased loneliness. In 1711 Swift discovered that his servant Patrick was keeping a tame linnet in a closet, and in 1828 the naturalist Charles Darwin (1809–82), then an undergraduate at Christ's College, had a dog in his Cambridge lodging over a tobacconist's in Sidney Street.[52] Music also helped to make a room a home. Goldsmith, Curran, and Dr John Wolcot (1738–1819, clergyman and, as 'Peter Pindar', a satirical poet) all relaxed by playing musical instruments, having with them in their lodgings respectively a flute, a fiddle, and a piano and violin.[53] The fiddle was important in rescuing Curran from his early homesickness and loneliness; maybe Wolcot could still take pleasure in his Cremona violin when blind in his old age. Like food, a tune could remind lodgers like the Irish Goldsmith and Curran, and the Devonian Wolcot of their origins. Playing filled a room with sound when a fellow human presence was lacking.

Inchbald was not the only owner of pictures. Wolcot's Somers Town sitting-room was furnished with books and paintings – some were copies of Reynolds, some his own work.[54] Despite their slender means and Charles's distaste for their possessions when seen piled in a hand-cart, the Lambs spent a considerable time making their Temple rooms cosy, putting up shelves, cutting up books to paste prints on the wall and adding rugs and chairs. They loved to entertain, and visitors found their rooms 'tidy and comfortable, if their furniture was on the shabby side'.[55] Towards the end of her time in London (and towards the end of her life) Pilkington was down on her luck, living alongside her long-time friend, artist James Worsdale (*c*. 1692–1767) in his lodgings in a large old house in Cornhill in the City. Pilkington described their mock-genteel, make-do living conditions:

> We had four play-bills laid for a Table-cloth, Knives Forks, or Plates, we had none ... The Butter, when we had any, was deposited in the cool and fragrant recess of an old Shoe, a Coffee-pot of mine served for as many Uses as Scrub ever had, for sometimes it boil'd Coffee, sometimes Tea, it brought small Beer, and I am more than half afraid if has been applied to less noble Uses.

Even in this ramshackle lodging they had, as her biographer Norma Clarke remarks, 'a domestic life of sorts'.[56]

Domesticity was not all about material comforts, however. It was also strongly associated with the concept of a shared life within the home, Stobart's 'relationship with people'.[57] We have seen how *Chronicle* advertisements placed by both landlords/ladies and lodgers offered 'company' and 'society' as a motive for and a benefit of a lodging arrangement. These words promised a harmonious household bound by ties more emotional than financial. Yet rent was at the heart of lodging. It was only in return for the rent that the lodger had licence to occupy space in someone else's home. This was potentially an awkward situation. As householder, the host held, whatever their relative social status, ultimate control, making the 'house rules' (meal-times, locking up for the night, guests), managing their servants' time, and monitoring general comings and goings. This was especially true of landlords, for as Karen Harvey shows, domesticity for eighteenth-century men was closely tied to concepts of housekeeping as management, what contemporaries understood by 'oeconomy'.[58] Nevertheless, the lodger had to be accommodated metaphorically as well as literally if the cash was to continue to flow.

We have evidence that landlords/ladies made a special effort when welcoming new lodgers. Despite her misgivings on moving in with the Wandsworth Quakeress, by day two Savile and her mother were jaunting to Wimbledon races with the landlady's grandchild, and dining and conversing with the family. Gertrude decided that she was 'a very good sort of Woman, very oblidging to us, and better than her word in helping us to several things she woud not undertake for', that is, throwing in a few extras without charge.[59] When Curwen moved to Mrs Wilson's in Islington in October 1775 he appreciated a sociable first night:

> there found my fellow Lodger B.P. [American friend Colonel Benjamin Pickman, also from Salem] and the three Ladies before a good Coal fire in the great parlour with whom after a dinner and tea I passed an agreeable enough Evening at Quadrille.[60]

Inchbald had a similarly pleasant reception when returning to London in 1780 after her husband Joseph's sudden death:

> unpackd – then Dresst and dined below with my Landlady … at Dark walked with my Landlady to many shops … supped with her and read the Paper.[61]

Such generosity on the part of landlords/ladies could not always last beyond the first few days, however. Where misinterpreted as permanent by a lodger, its loss led to disappointment. Closer acquaintance might even render the parties mutually annoying, such that the hoped-for company became irksome. Margaret Nicholson (?1750–1828), in 1786 the would-be assassin by dessert knife of George III, left service and took lodgings first in Oxford Street and then in 1783 with Jonathan Fiske, stationer, in Wigmore Street. In her new life she enjoyed the independence that we have seen was a motive for lodging, making her living 'as her own mistress' by her needle. Neither landlord foresaw her attempted violence. At worst she was merely irritating: 'she frequently wearied her landlords with importunities to present a petition to his Majesty on her behalf.'[62] Lodgers were also irked by their landlords and ladies. Curran's first London landlord exposed his lodger to 'the conversation of a man no ways agreeable to me, a dull, good-natured, generous, unexperienced, opinionated, deep-read, unlearned, disputative sort of a character'. Curwen often went through an initial surge of excitement at finding 'the one', only to decide on closer acquaintance that the landlord/lady was variously 'unpleasing … both selfish and unobliging', 'clownish [and] unobliging', 'a very disagreeable family', and 'piggish'.[63]

Curwen's use of the term 'unobliging' on three occasions indicates a potential source of difficulty that was in large part gendered.[64] Female lodgers such as Pilkington and Inchbald seem to have expected to look after themselves to a considerable extent: boiling their own kettle, assembling simple meals, tending to houseplants, and cleaning the room.[65] The male lodger, however, could be inclined, especially where he felt socially superior to the host family, to treat them as little more than servants, forgetting that he, the lodger, was merely a paying customer in their house. High-handedness on Curwen's part may well account for the frequent change in atmosphere as a tenancy progressed. In February 1782, for instance, he 'Supt on boiled eggs of my own designing, Landlady [Mrs Atwood] not having taken her tea refused to do so for me'. Pilkington, who was generally understanding as a lodger (readily bed-sharing with one landlady when her son-in-law came to stay), found that her demand to have the floorboards of her room lifted so that she could recover two lost guineas was a bridge too far. It met a blank refusal.[66] Lodgers were often at a loss to understand that while their room was in one sense their home, it remained under the control of another, the landlord/lady. Despite paying rent, they were often astonished by any evidence that their hosts were running a commercial business, especially when that host was a woman and so lacking in societal authority. 'Her Custom was to live upon her Lodgers,' complained Pilkington.[67] When Curwen bought his bureau, he acknowledged Mrs Longbottom's financial motives but did not sympathize with them:

> landlady to take it off hand at departure if she should prove true to her word, but chance is against me. People in this line, here, have no other motive, consideration or rule of conduct but interest.[68]

However, there were sociable lodgers who hit it off with their landlords/ladies, integrated with the household, and developed lasting friendships, Franklin for example. This required co-operation and adjustments on both sides, together with a willingness on the lodger's part to be appreciative of (and probably pay for) those little extras. Inchbald's first London landlady, who took her shopping, was Mrs Barwell. The pair remained in contact until Barwell died in 1813. They called on one another, and Inchbald helped her with a gift of one pound in 1808. In addition to helping wean George 'Pretty' Brooks, Inchbald kept in touch with him and his family too, in 1805 visiting with two alarming presents for the five-year-old: a gun (a toy, one hopes) and a hammer. When Inchbald died she left a bequest of £50, equivalent to a year's modest income, to Miss Baillie, her Strand milliner landlady.[69] Like Addison's alter-ego lodger in the *Spectator* (Chapter 3), Moritz was close to his landlady's two young sons, Jacky and Jerry:

> The eldest Jacky, about twelve years old, is a very lively boy, and often entertains me in the most pleasing manner, by relating to me his different employments at school; and afterwards desiring me, in my turn, to relate to him all manner of things about Germany.[70]

Thomas Carter, the Essex tailor and a self-educated man, moved to London at some time after the Battle of Waterloo. Carter had been in London before and pre-arranged his lodgings with a fellow-tailor he knew. They were in the 'rude, noisy, and dirty locality' of Seven Dials, but away from the street, the house and the family's circle were respectable and welcoming: 'I regularly took my place with him [the landlord] and his family.' In 1816 the landlord and his family moved to more up-market Bedford Court, Covent Garden, and Carter went with them. Carter joined the landlord's book club, and on Sundays took his meals with them and enjoyed 'a commodious seat at the family hearth', paying nothing for the fire and only a 'very modest price' for the food'.[71] This was surely a companionable arrangement. The genteel might expect to sit in the parlour, but a kitchen could also be a warm, shared space. A convivial moment by an autumn kitchen fire in East Smithfield is captured in an Old Bailey trial of 1785. Widow Esther Casson, her maid, and two lodgers were all conversing into the late evening over a bought-in pot of beer when burglar Charles Kinross broke into the house.[72] Even Curwen, not easy to please (and very much a parlour rather than a kitchen man), remained on good terms with Mrs Bretland of Exeter after he had moved. They took tea together, on one occasion he stayed there until one in the morning, and she came over to nurse him when he was ill with chest pains at a rival Exeter lodging.[73] In these examples landlords/ladies and their lodgers really did experience the promised benefits of company and remained linked in a new network of support. This was the comfort that Richardson's Clarissa finally found at the Smiths'.

Where a relationship was good enough male lodgers might prevail upon the women of the host family to undertake small, intimate tasks for them, especially sewing. It was just one example of a gendered attitude to landladies, positioning them as substitute wives and mothers, reflected in the hypothesis (Chapter 3) that deep down the lodger often wished to be the pampered only child of the house. 'Mother', in particular, was used by several lodgers of their landladies. Far from home, Emin described his first London landlady, Mrs Newman, Dowgate Hill, as 'motherlike' and, later, the Philpots as 'he ... a father, and his wife a mother'.[74] Poet William Cowper (1731–1800) had lost his 'real' mother when he was six years old, and in 1765 was recovering from depression when he lodged at Revd Unwin's in Huntingdon. He much appreciated the kindness of Mrs Unwin 'whose behaviour to me has always been that of a mother to her son'.[75] Haydon regarded Mrs Coppard as providing 'motherly care' for his friend Wilkie.[76]

Sometimes a task was undertaken for money. Congreve's landlady Mrs Porter sewed shirts for his friend Joseph Keally to earn a little extra cash.[77] Others seem, surprisingly, to have been obtained free of charge, indicating that landladies perhaps also saw themselves as mothers to their lodgers, or felt unable to shrug off their female responsibility for these tasks. In Downing Street 'Mrs. Terrie gets all things that I want bought for me, and Miss sews the laced ruffles on my shirts, and does anything of that kind', remarked Boswell with satisfaction.[78] There could be an element of mutuality to these small tasks. Sarah Walker agreed to add frills to Hazlitt's shirts, and he gave her a length of plaid silk for a gown.[79] Another homely provision was the warmed bed. Boswell noted with pleasure both this and having his feet bathed in milk.[80] Curwen too appreciated the comfort and forethought of a warmed bed. At the very edge of our period, in Henry Heath's (*fl.* 1822–42) *Notions of the Agreeable* no. 35, an attentive, motherly landlady is warming her lodger's bed (unaware that he is already in it asleep) because 'it'll make him so comfortable, and cure his cold!'[81] She is therefore at one and the same time maternally caring and yet, in line with the stereotype landlady of Chapter 2, an intrusive busybody. Being 'mothered' was probably not available to women lodgers like Inchbald. Her diaries frequently recorded 'working' (as opposed to being 'at her part' or writing), that is, mending and sewing her own clothes (and sometimes costumes). She never mentioned the warmed bed. As a woman it was up to her, the lodger, to create the sense of family with the Barwells and the Brooks by showing affection towards them and, especially, their children.

It was not only in Exeter that Curwen received help from a landlady when ill. He experienced frequent anxiety over his health, often disguising the unpleasant outcome by writing backwards: 'small egrahcsid, leaving a aesuan', for example.[82] Others also received this sort of care from their hosts. Swift contracted shingles in 1712 at Mrs Crane's.[83] Exciseman John Cannon (1684–1743) had smallpox at Mrs Winch's in Newbury, Berkshire. He entrusted her with his possessions should he die.[84] Sterne died at Mrs Fourmantel's after a lingering illness. Wilkie's Mrs Coppard supervised his move to Hampstead for his health and visited him there regularly.[85] Tending a sick lodger, like mending his clothes, also positioned a landlady in a familiar gendered role: here as a nurse. All three female relationships – wife, mother, nurse – were conveniently easier for male lodgers to understand than a business one with a woman.

The care and consideration provided by landladies did of course lend the human touch to their relationships with their lodgers that Mrs Isam had shown Robert Greene back in the 1590s. Nevertheless, the commercial relationship was at bottom always there. Expenses on medical care – medicines, a physician's or nurse's attendance – were generally billed as extras by prudent hosts. Swift paid Mrs Crane £1 12s. 2½d. for his treatment for shingles.[86] Beattie paid a landlord for lodgings and separately for drugs.[87] There were also limits to this care. Curwen was confined to bed for several days at Mrs Atwood's with bowel trouble. She organized an apothecary and then went out on a social visit with her children. She clearly felt that dealing personally with the egrahcsid and aesuan was not something for which she was contractually bound. Curwen, a businessman himself, felt palpable rage at this overtly business-like attitude on Atwood's part: 'Sympathy in people of her rank and occupation is a needless unprofitable sensation, gain engrosses all feeling.'[88] Motherly Mrs Unwin was providing Cowper with emotional support, but she was still charging rent (albeit reduced when he faced financial hardship).[89]

There were three further good tests of a successful relationship between a landlord/lady and lodger: a long stay, moving house with the landlord/lady, as Franklin and Thomas Carter did, and the lodger becoming sufficiently embedded, respected and trusted to earn his or her name on the door. Congreve, as we have seen, spent twenty-three years at the Porters' in Arundel Street. Sterne lived with Mrs Fourmantel for three years, terminated only by his death. Gansel, despite his feckless and reckless way of life, had been lodging for sixteen years with the Mayos in Craven Street and for a similar length of time with their predecessors. He was almost a permanent fixture. Similarly, Inchbald lodged with the Shakespears in Leicester Fields for seven years in the 1790s and stayed on for a further four when they sold up to her fellow-lodgers the Brooks, Pretty's parents. After one year in Turnham Green she then lasted around five years with Miss Baillie.[90] Wilkie took his two sitting-rooms and two bedrooms with Mrs Coppard in late 1808. After his bout of ill-health he could no longer afford the rent. She excused him the notice period, allowing him to stay on as a 'visiter' until he found a new lodging. In 1811 he rejoined her as a lodger in 29 Phillimore Place, Kensington, and when his father died two years later bought his own house just five doors away. The relationship seems to have been one of mutual dependence.[91] The Carlyles followed their Ampton Street landladies when they moved a stone's throw away to 47 Frederick Street, as did Mary Hays. Hays lodged for four years with Ann Cole, who ran her recently-deceased father's bookselling and printing business in Kirby Street, Hatton Garden, and then, after a break living with her own family, lodged for a further three years at Ann's new home, 22 Hatton Garden itself.[92] These examples show how the relationship between landlords, ladies, and lodgers could develop into something more enduring than the briskly commercial exchange of cash for accommodation – a co-dependence and a friendship in both the practical and emotional sense of the word.

The name on the door is more archivally elusive. Moritz was impressed by the Strand with its 'constant succession of shop after shop', and acknowledged the multiple occupations (as found in Compton and Greek Streets in 1785): 'not unfrequently, people of different trades inhabit the same house'. What surprised him was:

> to see their doors, or the tops of their windows, or boards expressly for the purpose, all written over from top to bottom, with large painted letters. Every person, every trade or occupation, who owns ever so small a portion of a house, makes a parade with a sign at his door.[93]

A *Chronicle* advertisement of 1796 offered three parlours and a second-floor bedroom 'on of the Capital Streets out of Oxford-street'. The landlord or lady preferred 'a Professional Man or Artist', throwing in 'N.B. May have their name on the door, if of any use'.

'Use' for the lodger would include helping callers find the right house, and advertising their professional or other services. For the landlord/lady, however, it was a concession that undermined the householder's sense of property. In all probability it was not lightly granted. Macklin appears to have availed himself of this possibility. He was a litigious man and in 1774 pursued through the courts some of his critics who had been heckling and disrupting his *Shylock* at Covent Garden. One of the defendants having been hit by a lady sitting near him in the two-shilling gallery, and believing her to be Mrs Macklin, had followed her home to an address in James Street, Covent Garden. This had 'the name of "Macklin" upon the door'. The court heard that the house was 'a Lodging-house, where there are several families'.[94] Lodging-house it may have been but the lodger's name on the door indicated a degree of permanence and importance, of home.

The defendant in Macklin's suit, a Mr James, was an unwelcome caller. Landlords/ladies and their servants were the gatekeepers of the house. When the household included lodgers the admission, or not, of callers was one of the many complications introduced. The parties had to come to terms with how to handle them. Macklin was one of the era's celebrities whose fame depended upon an apparent intimacy created by a blurring of the line between their public and private identity, and facilitated by the development of a popular print culture.[95] In common with other artistes, Macklin received, even encouraged, many callers. Press advertisements for theatrical benefits routinely gave the actors' lodging addresses. Tickets for James Quin's (1693–1766) 1739 benefit performance (*King Lear* at the Theatre Royal, Drury Lane) could be obtained at his lodging, the sign of The Sun, a druggist's in Bedford Court, Covent Garden, for example.[96] Devotees could visit the Mozarts' rooms over the Frith Street stay-maker's each day from noon until three in the afternoon to hear the prodigies perform, test them, and buy concert tickets and the child genius's compositions.[97] Artists' patrons and clients called at their rooms, as did the associates of those, like Swift, in town for business and, like Boswell, in pursuit of pleasure.

Fame of any sort increasingly drew attention from the public. After the success in 1785 of Inchbald's comedy, *I'll Tell You What*, the door at Mrs Hall's in Great Russell Street, where she then lodged, was 'eternally besieged, and a large majority of her callers determined to see her, if she was within.'[98] If the landlords/ ladies concerned experienced this as invasive, there was the compensating benefit of being at the centre of glamorous worlds not otherwise readily open to the middling-sort shopkeeper: theatre, art, literature, politics, and the nobility. 'My lodgings is [*sic*] every hour full of your Great People of the first Rank, who strive who shall most honor me', gloated Sterne, thinking with pride of his elevated callers: Lords Chesterfield and Rockingham, Ladies of the Bedchamber, the bishops.[99] Well-known artists such as Lawrence and John Opie (1761–1807) attracted crowds of fashionable sitters and admirers.[100] Sometimes there was the opportunity to play an active role in their lodgers' high-profile lives. In 1808, when Wilkie was lodging in Solls Row, a friend of his landlord and lady was the model for the old woman's hands in *The Cut Finger*. Two years later when a young woman modelling for Wilkie was timorous, Mrs Coppard sat in the room 'to give her confidence'.[101]

Even infamy or a bad turn of events could be turned to financial benefit by the landlord/lady. The low-life Burke and Hare murders were not the only crimes that excited tourist interest. After Margaret Nicholson launched her dessert-knife attack on George III, her landlord Fiske was taken up and questioned and his house twice searched. Undaunted, he monetized his relationship with his now notorious lodger. Within a few days he was entertaining 'all ranks of curious people' at his home such that the Home Secretary impounded the key to Nicholson's room. Fiske was also was one of several to rush out a pamphlet, *The Life and Transactions of Margaret Nicholson*, capitalizing on his first-hand knowledge of the irritating lodger he now styled 'our heroine'.[102] Incidentally Nicholson remained a lodger, albeit involuntarily, first at the Half Moon Street house of Mr Coates, King's messenger, and his wife and, after she was declared insane by the Privy Council, in Bethlehem Hospital, where she remained a subject of continued touristic curiosity until her death.

However most lodgers and their visitors were neither famous nor notorious, and all callers were in addition to the host householders' own visitors. Danish entomologist Johann Fabricius (1745–1808) stayed in London in the summers of 1772–75, 1782 and 1787. He described a standard 'code' of knocking or ringing at the street door which identified the caller:

> A servant, a porter and the like knocks just once; if he brings a delivery for the kitchen, he pulls the bell without knocking. The postman always knocks twice … Those belonging to the better classes knock three times, and women knock six or eight times, of which the knocks in the middle are slower and more distinct. The lady of the house or her servant not only knocks most persistently but simultaneously rings the bell too, so that everyone inside the house may know she is home again.[103]

Lodgers may also have developed their own knocking styles, and sometimes had their own street doorbell. An Old Bailey case from 1758 implies that a silversmith's house which had been burgled was fitted with a doorbell for those calling on the first-floor lodger. Householder John M'Farlan testified:

> I heard the bell of the door of my one pair of stairs floor tinkle, the girl came down stairs and went to the door, I says to my wife, it is nobody wants us, it is somebody wants the lodgers up stairs.[104]

Generally, however, lodgers added to the work of policing the door against unsuitable visitors: practitioners of the 'dining room post', bailiffs, and those whom the lodger was reluctant to see admitted. There could be confusion and misunderstanding too, as Macklin had discovered. Curwen was annoyed enough to complain to his diary when he missed a visit from Captain Carpenter inviting him out to a mutual friend's. His 'blundering careless landlady' passed on the wrong name – 'Hayns' instead of the totally different 'Mather' – and it took two days of enquiry to resolve the mystery.[105] In a house with several lodgers the problems multiplied and etiquette was needed to avoid all the callers becoming a nuisance to others in the hall, stairs and rooms themselves, as Erasmus Jones warned in his 1737 conduct guide for the upwardly mobile:

'Tis very rude and indiscreet for any one coming to a Lodger, to proclaim his Business up and down the Stairs to all the People in the House.[106]

Visitors from the *beau monde*, however, were unlikely to think such advice applied to them. In Bury Street, St James's, Pilkington had two gentlemen callers at nine o'clock at night who were heard shouting on the stairs 'Poke after me, my Lord, poke after me', and demanding the maid light them to her room. They were Colonel D–nc–be (Duncombe, 'the most lewd, debauch'd, gaming, swearing, blasphemous Wretch that lived') and the Duke of Marlborough.[107] In another example of the interplay between cultural representations of lodging and the social reality, this arrogant disregard by elite men for the house rules of those lower in the social pyramid was celebrated in sporting journalist Pierce Egan's (1772–1849) wildly popular *Tom and Jerry* series. George Cruikshank illustrated the eponymous Tom and Jerry making a noisy night-time call at the house (in the shadow of St Paul's, another lodging node) where their friend Bob Logic roomed.[108]

Equally important for harmonious relationships was respect for the diurnal and nocturnal rhythm of the host household. Lodgers had to learn to fit in with this. Failure to do so spelt trouble. Chapter 3 showed how, when advertising, lodgers promised they kept regular hours and were no trouble. Curwen did the same in a note written to a friend, describing himself as 'scarce ever out in the evening'. He claimed to be in bed by ten o'clock and up between eight and nine in the morning.[109] When lodgers, especially the young and creative, moved in they could find their own concept of 'acceptable hours' clashed with the generally early hours kept by the trading middling sort who were the typical hosts. Antiquary and draughtsman James Peller Malcolm (1767–1815), writing in 1808, thought that a tradesman 'and his lodgers' generally rose at between six and nine in the morning.[110] Johnson described his friend Savage as so inured to a vagrant way of life as to be unaware of the need for sleep of those with regular work. Savage was:

a very inconvenient Inmate; for being always accustomed to an irregular Manner of Life, he could not confine himself to any stated Hours, or pay any Regard to the Rules of a Family, but would prolong his Conversation till Midnight, without considering that Business might require his Friend's Application in the Morning.[111]

Even the cheerful Inchbald was vexed by the early rising of her Frith Street landlady Mrs Grist: 'Her landlady was sometimes out of favour with the Muse for ringing her bell in the morning to get the servant up', though as Mrs Grist showed 'general kindness' the easy-going Inchbald was 'soon appeased'.[112]

Early starts were irritating, but late nights caused greater problems. Boswell epitomized this clash of cultures across a social divide:

> whenever I have been a little too late abroad at night, I cannot help being apprehensive that Terrie my landlord will reprove me for it next morning. Such is the force of custom.[113]

Tradesmen and women not only rose early but went early to bed. Hickey commented that the Maltons, his Chelsea landlord and lady and their family, were in bed by ten as though this were surprising.[114] Georgian householders were fearful of intruder crime, and securing the house for the night was an important routine marking the end of the day.[115] Boswell's Mr Terrie even kept a pair of loaded pistols by his bed. The landlord/lady or a trusted servant held the master house-key and copies of room-keys were a vital element of domestic control and so security.[116] Few lodgers mentioned their own key to the street door, and where they did this seems to have been a temporary arrangement. J. T. Smith related an incident before his lifetime in which:

> A gentleman who had stayed one night at Slaughters' Coffee-house until past twelve o'clock, discovered that he had forgotten the street-door key of the house where he lodged; and as he had agreed with his landlady not to disturb her other inmates beyond that hour, was prevailed upon by Roubiliac [the sculptor, 1702–62] to take the other rubber, and sleep in a spare bed much at his service.[117]

Swift described looking around for 'the woman that keeps the key of the house'. She told him that his own servant Patrick, a man hardly likely to be allowed possession for long, had it.[118] Curwen recalled being locked out until nine in the evening because the maid had just gone out, invited by 'an opposite neighbour' to sit in her parlour.[119] Keys to their own rooms were, on the other hand, standard. Gansel was locked and bolted in his room in Craven Street when the bailiffs called. After it became apparent he was having some sort of mental breakdown, Cruden locked himself in his room at the Grants' in White's Alley, Chancery Lane. There was clearly no duplicate key in this case. The Grants had to break the door down to extract him and expedite him to the Chelsea mad-house.[120]

A lodger who remained out on the town after hours was a nuisance as it required someone reliable from the household, usually a maid, sitting up to unlock and relock the street door. There were plenty of night-time diversions in

London and waiting up for the lodger was a wearisome chore. Medical student Hampton Weekes and his fellow student lodgers were told by their landlord Whitfield that he was no longer prepared to sit up two nights a week waiting for their return from the play.[121] If the maid fell asleep or the household had given up the wait, there might be a general Tom-and-Jerry-style disturbance on the street that woke the entire household, even neighbourhood. Inchbald recorded of one of her fellow-lodgers at Miss Baillie's: 'Mr. Hood alarmed me at Midnight coming home Tipsy & I in Bed.' Curwen, despite his insistence on his regularity, returned late to his lodgings on several occasions. At his more institutional lodgings at the Herald's Office, taken after he left Mrs Wilson's in Islington, he was caught out by a 6d. fine for returning after midnight.[122] In Exeter in 1779 when out at Mrs Bretland's until one in the morning he was 'Shut out nor could gain admittance till by a sad racket at door disturbed them.' Unaware of the trouble he had caused in the small hours, he added, 'This determines my removal.' At the Councels' in 1783 he was back at about eleven o'clock 'family being just retired to bed'. Yet the previous year he had complained about a friend of his landlady knocking on the door in the night on returning from the theatre.[123] As a last resort the locked-out lodger had to pass the night elsewhere, Beresford's 'Sleeping, on a sudden and desperate emergency, at a low lodging-house.'[124] J. T. Smith reminisced about his younger self in lodgings in Gerrard Street, Soho where he:

> acquiesced in the regulation of my landlady; one of the principal of which was, that I never was to expect to be let in after twelve o'clock, unless the servant was apprized of my staying out later, and then she was permitted to sit up for me. Being in my twenty-first year, of a lively disposition, and moreover fond of theatrical representations, I did not at all times 'remember twelve'.

Unable to afford night lodgings and afraid to walk the street as poet Savage had done, he used to go the watch-house, either at St Paul's or at St Anne Soho, where in return for a couple of pints of porter for the keeper, he could sit by the fire and watch human life go by.[125] Curwen's double standards and the many clashes over late nights are yet another example of lodgers' inability to see themselves as subject to the authority of their landlord or lady.

———————————

Learning to live alongside one another also involved coming to terms with individuals' quirks and habits, and dealing with them with discretion, as Inchbald and Mrs Grist did. Unsurprisingly, many of the small conflicts that arose took place in the communal spaces of the house: the hall, stairs, kitchen and parlour, as Malcolm recognized:

> discontent and altercation exist but too frequently between the landlord's family and the lodger. Kitchens used in common by both parties are sources of discord; the cleansing of stairs ascended by all the inhabitants of the house is another.

In *Underwood v. Burrows* (Chapter 2) it was access to the stairs, water closet and doorbell that the landlord had denied. At Mrs Longbottom's Curwen entered into a dispute over a Silesia lettuce (now an heirloom variety) he had purchased and left in the kitchen which had gone missing. He accused the maid of theft.[126] It was no wonder Carlyle kept his butter under lock and key. In Nicholson Street, Edinburgh, Sylas Neville and his servant-cum-mistress Sally had the whole use of the kitchen but found the landlady Mrs Wright 'a prying Devil'. Within a month there was a falling out between Wright and Sally, probably stoked by the latter's ambiguous position and presence in the kitchen.[127] It was in the kitchen too that Hazlitt overheard a conversation between landlady Mrs Walker and her three children. They were speculating about the size of their Welsh lodger Griffiths's penis, comparing it favourably to that of a third lodger, Mr Follett.[128]

Hazlitt's anxiety over the incident underlines the lack of privacy for all parties in houses with lodgers. 'The chambers are all so close together that what we say or do is liable to be overheard,' said Neville of Mrs Wright's house.[129] Peering through keyholes or gaps in flimsy wainscot partitions, even party walls, was a feature of narratives of adultery and crime. 'Curiosity, my lord, led me two or three times to look through the key-hole of the chamber-door, in which I knew Captain Gambier and my mistress [Lady Knowles] lay,' said a maidservant in *Admiral Knowles v. Gambier*, a criminal conversation suit of 1757.[130] And counsel for the prosecution explained in the 1796 trial of Eleanor Hughes, a landlady who had murdered one of her lodgers:

> The persons who had inhabited that house before them had bored holes with a gimblet, in the wainscoat [*sic*], by which their house is separated from the house of Hughes which holes were imperfectly stopped up with paper, and through which they could see what was passing in every part of Hughes's house.[131]

Even landladies who were not nosy and their servants necessarily entered rooms as a matter of routine to introduce guests, bring meals, lay fires, and draw curtains. They must sometimes have been surprised at what they saw. Franklin was accustomed to rise early then sat in his bedroom naked for half an hour to an hour reading or writing, calling this his 'tonic bath'.[132] According to Lamb, Samuel Taylor Coleridge (1772–1834) received visitors while seated on his close-stool (commode).[133] When actor John Bannister (1760–1836) was shown into Wilkie's lodging-room the artist was discovered 'sitting on a low seat, dressed as a woman, with a looking-glass before him, performing the part of model for himself'.[134] On another occasion Haydon also found Wilkie drawing himself in the mirror, this time as a nude.[135] The important thing was that, unlike Hazlitt's hosts the Walkers, landlords/ladies should maintain a sense of discretion and resist broadcasting these encounters as a joke.

Lodgers were mildly eccentric in other ways, had their habits and hobbies, or were careless with their hosts' possessions, but they were often inconsiderate and rarely the ones who had to clear up any mess. Boyse ate and Swift customarily wrote in bed. Crumbs are always a nuisance and attract pests, and writing was also a messy business in the era of quill pens and dipping ink. Swift mentioned an incident when ink was spilt on the floor, blaming Patrick (of course) for over-filling the standish. There must too have been blots on the bedlinen. In 1711 he 'borrowed', as an improvised swimming cap, and lost, his Chelsea landlady's napkin when bathing in the Thames.[136] Johnson had 'apparatus for chymical experiments' which on one occasion left him 'covered with soot like a chimney-sweeper, in a little room, with an intolerable heat and strange smell'.[137] Curran, an extremely diligent law-student, rigged up his own 'alarm' to wake him at half past four in the morning. It consisted of two tin vessels suspended over his bed. On retiring he poured water into the topmost tin which slowly dripped through into the lower one which then overflowed onto his head. The daily process and the 'no small trouble' he had getting the quantity of water right must have dampened his bed and room somewhat.[138] At bedtime, Goldsmith, rather than emerge from the warmth of the bedcovers, threw his slipper at the candle to extinguish it, splattering grease around the room. At Edgware Road he made notes for his work and drew on his lodging-room walls.[139] The ailing and elderly Joseph Simons, a jeweller and engraver lodging on the second floor of Mr Scheiffer's in Compton Street, had apparently twice set fire to his room, though he was blameless on the occasion of the 1785 fire, and Thomas Carter set fire to his pillow when reading in bed. Both these instances confirm an element of truth in the trope of the lodger careless around fire (Chapter 2).[140] Carlyle liked his pipe. In Ampton Street he obeyed the rules and so was 'sadly at a loss for a smoking place'. He climbed out of the window and stood 'like "a sign of the times" on the top of a lead cistern', used the balcony, or walked the streets.[141] One of the delights he anticipated on moving to his own house was the avoidance of these house rules of another: 'I can wander about in dressing-gown and straw-hat in it, as of old, and take my pipe in peace.'[142]

Even without holes, flimsy partition walls in London, Edinburgh, and elsewhere made for little privacy. It was all too easy to know other residents' business. Where noise was concerned, the fiction of sociability often collapsed. Family relationships within the host household were often, like their lodgers' bodies, laid bare and not all lodgers were sufficiently restrained to pretend nothing had happened. Disputes arose and escalated precisely because landlord/lady and lodgers were not bound to one another by ties of affection. Foote's Zachary Fungus should perhaps have read Erasmus Jones's advice on the need to be aware of the noise and disruption one caused as a lodger:

> In a House of Lodgers, it is the highest Degree of Rudeness to stalk up and down the Stairs, like the People to the Long-Room at the Custom-House; modest and well-bred Persons suffer great inconveniences, when they are thus jumbl'd among the rude Vulgar; I have known a Philosopher study under a Fencing-School; and Country-Dances had over the Head of a Parson in a high Fever.[143]

As Jones implied, lodgers did not necessarily respect each other any more than they did their landlords/ladies. The cover image of this book shows a landlord more concerned that his lodger's cough is disturbing the other lodgers in the house than for the man's health. Inchbald recorded arguments from the lodging-room above her and from next door.[144] For the same reason, music and general carousing by lodgers was a major source of disputes (see Figure 15). Boswell was rebuked for holding a noisy 'party' in the Terries' parlour outside the permitted hours.[145] Singing was a problem once Weekes's landlord Whitfield had numerous student lodgers.[146] We never learn whether Curran's fiddling, a comfort to himself, annoyed other inhabitants of the Orange Street house, but Curwen (inevitably) objected to two fellow lodgers who 'diverted themselves and family and disturbed me with German flutes'.[147]

For landlords and ladies and their families the possibility of being overheard was worse. It represented a considerable diminution of the privacy that was essential to the domestic ideal. Boswell, Cruden, and Cannon all complained of overhearing quarrels within the host family and with other members of the household. Some lodgers actually meddled in family affairs. Boswell told Mrs Terrie that she should make her husband 'give over letting lodgings, as he was very unfit for it'.[148] Curwen doled out advice to the Poyntons when their daughter ran off abandoning her husband and child, offering to intervene with the mother-in-law.[149] At his Gloucester Street lodgings in Bloomsbury in 1769, Neville (Sally

Figure 15 Henry Heath, *Comfortable Lodgings*, 1829. Landlords/ladies of houses with multiple lodgers had to balance competing lifestyles. Here it is past three o'clock in the morning and on the ground floor a bachelor party, like that held by James Boswell at the Terries', is in full swing. The first-floor lodger, his wife in the background, and a fellow-lodger in the front garret complain of the lack of sleep. Note the domestic touch of pot-plants on the garret window-sill. Courtesy of the Lewis Walpole Library, Yale University: 829.00.00.51+.

being absent in Eastbourne) insinuated himself as *confidant* to landlady Mrs Willoughby, learned that she was unhappy in her marriage, and then used the knowledge to indulge in a dalliance with her under Mr Willoughby's nose.[150] This gross breach of trust, reminiscent of Chaucer's *Miller's Tale*, is examined further in Chapter 6.

Meals were a further source of discontent. As with rising and retiring to bed, timing was an issue. Mealtimes and menus were, naturally, set by the landlord/lady. In 1776 Curwen's 13s. weekly rent at the Herald's Office included, *inter alia*, breakfast and dinner. After only two weeks he was 'finding an inconvenience in conforming to the family hour, being unfavourably early'. He and the landlady agreed that he would now find his own breakfast and dine 'abroad'. This alteration in their terms suited Curwen rather than the landlady who lost a little income and any company for which she had hoped. Then there was the quality and quantity of the food provided. Landlords/ladies had to be careful not to blow their household budgets by being over-generous with the portions. Emin agreed 1s. a day for lodging, washing and board with Mrs Newman in 1751. After fifty days she had to take him aside and let him know that he was eating too much at this price. He then offered a guinea a month on top of rent, washing and shaving.[151] Sometimes a lodger struck lucky. Curwen's Mrs Longbottom provided 'a table an Epicure wouldn't or couldn't reasonably condemn, she being an excellent cook'.[152] However many lodgers, Curwen included, felt that in their eagerness to extract profit, landlords/ladies were inclined to cut corners. Goldsmith said of his landlady's regime in Edinburgh, where in 1752 he was studying medicine, that a leg of mutton 'served for the better part of dinner during the week', ending as bone broth on the seventh day.[153] In Bishopsgate in 1784 Curwen was lodging with the Robertsons over their apothecary's shop. Although the lodgers were served peas on 19 June for the first time that year, they were 'so far advanced as to have been at almost every poor mans [sic] table in London, so singularly, prudent and unexpensively is our table furnished, the poorest, that for a constancy, I ever dined at'.[154] Shelley's friend Hogg thought this experience of bad food all too common (incidentally implying that in the nineteenth century standards had risen):

The provisions supplied at lodging in London were too frequently in those days detestable, and the service which was rendered abominable and disgusting. Meat was procured wherever meat might be bought most cheaply, in order that, being paid for dearly, a more enormous profit might be realized upon it; and those dishes were selected in which the ignorance in cookery of a servant-of-all-work might be least striking.[155]

Sometimes, as in Curwen's case, these niggling dissatisfactions or budgetary concerns led to a renegotiation of the original agreement between landlord/lady and lodger, much as Burney's fictional lodger in *Evelina*, Mr McCartney, had done. In 1758 Goldsmith, living in Green Arbour Court and already in debt to his landlord, wrote to a cousin that:

> I have already given my Lanlady [*sic*] orders for an entire reform in the state of my finances; I declaim against hot suppers, drink less sugar in my tea, and cheek my grate with brick-bats [as Swift had done].[156]

However, when his landlady's husband was arrested for debt, Goldsmith's conscience clearly pricked, unusual in a lodger. He pawned clothes and borrowed against the security of books he was reviewing for Griffiths's *Monthly Review* to pay what was owed.[157] For Hampton Weekes the boot was on the other foot: household retrenchment meant the loss of what had been a regular two glasses of 'free' wine after dinner, and the gradual introduction of more student lodgers into the household such that one slept in a closet and Weekes ended up sharing his room with two others. They at least had their own beds, but it was not what he had bargained for and must have been less comfortable.[158] Medical students were not in a socially powerful position, unlike Boswell, who was able to demand from Terrie improvements to the comforts of his accommodation: a door to be made between his two rooms, large breakfast cups, a carpet and a bureau then, when he switched rooms to save money, 'a handsome tent-bed with green and white check curtains'.[159] As we have seen, inclusive meals were also renegotiated for the convenience of the lodger and dining arrangements were cancelled at short notice (with the expectation that they would not have to be paid for). Goldsmith apart, there was scant regard for the negative impact on the security and reliability of the landlord's/lady's income.

In conclusion then, the initial welcome was just that: an initial welcome. It was not always sustained as the landlord/lady could not necessarily afford to continue offering services which he or she had not specifically 'undertaken for'. Throwing in some of the extras discussed in this chapter helped retain a lodger, but also meant loss of profit, and landlords and ladies could be firm. Swift regretted that he would probably have to pay for the napkin lost in the Thames and Inchbald's cash account for 25 September 1781 included 2s. for 'a Glass Window breaking' at Mrs Barwell's.[160] More positively, longer-term sociability was possible as the experiences of Franklin, Inchbald, and Wilkie demonstrate, but it was always contingent on the respective personalities of the parties and on their mutual respect for one another.

Once a lodger had moved in, and, as his or her stay extended, the number of social interactions grew exponentially: with one another, with family, with servants, with visitors, with other lodgers. A house with lodgers was necessarily a place where social classes and ages were tumbled together in close and daily proximity. As respectable householders, landlords/ladies used their authority to supervise their multifarious housefuls and maintain good order, but supervision sometimes clashed with their lodgers' desire for privacy and independence. Some interaction became friction, much of it inflected by cultural misunderstandings across a class divide, evidenced by lodgers' readiness when in dispute to describe landlords/ladies as rude or vulgar, as Savile, Boswell, Curwen, and Hazlitt all did.[161] A key misunderstanding on the part of many lodgers was that the landlords/ladies were in some way doing them a favour rather than running a commercial business, albeit sometimes a subsidiary one to the main household occupation. Any hint of their financial motives was therefore time and again dismissed as 'mercenary' by our life-writers, a characteristic that they would also have picked up from the contemporary fiction of Chapter 2.

This misunderstanding was magnified where male lodgers dealt with landladies. Unable to see them as businesswomen seeking to make or supplement a living out of their main asset, the home, these lodgers persisted in imagining their landladies in familiar gendered roles as mothers, wives, nurses, or even servants. When it was plain that the relationship was in reality a commercial one, landladies were criticized for the stereotype meanness, venality, and nosiness seen in representations of lodging arrangements.

Moving out, moving on

Many lodging arrangements came to a natural end. A stay was often for a limited duration: a holiday (John Courtney), a piece of business, or a period of study in London (Nicholas Blundell, Thomas Wale, John Philpot Curran, Hampton Weekes), a temporary situation (Gertrude Savile and her mother). Sometimes bad health attributed to the poor air quality of the capital prompted the moves we have seen to a more peripheral, semi-rural district (the Mozarts, Swift, Wilkie). Then there were the improvements or changes in personal circumstances that permitted moving out of lodgings altogether to a whole (generally leased) house of one's own (Gibbon, the Places). In March 1797 when she discovered that she was pregnant, Mary Wollstonecraft and author William Godwin (1756–1836) married and moved from their respective lodgings to a house in the Polygon, Somers Town.[1] Thomas and Jane Carlyle took the house in Cheyne Row, Chelsea (now a National Trust property) in summer 1834 once they were reunited as a couple in London and had had time to house-hunt together.[2] For these men and women lodging was, as already discussed, an expedient, but a whole house was the aspiration. Sylas Neville sighed in his new home in Norwich after a period passing through lodgings: 'Slept for the first time at my own house ... have never been happy since I left off house-keeping.'[3] In 1823 when the Lambs were enjoying a rare period in a house of their own in Colebrooke Row, Islington, Charles reflected on the sense of authority that he at last felt as a householder at the relatively ripe age of forty-eight: 'I feel like a great Lord ... '.[4] Not all lodgers delighted entirely in the move to a house, however. Some, like Haydon (Chapter 3), felt nostalgia for the freedom of anti-domesticity in bachelor lodgings. After moving to the Polygon and married life, Godwin, for example, kept a small lodging in Chalton Street, where he could be alone to write away from family life.[5]

Less affluent lodgers who achieved a house of their own often became landlords themselves to ease the family budget. In 1798 the Places took fellow

Radical and London Corresponding Society colleague Richard Wild as a lodger while still in lodgings themselves in Holborn. They later helped Wild by allowing him and his wife to lodge with them when they acquired their shop at 29 Charing Cross. Their reluctant gesture was born of understanding: Wild was part of their network and, like the Places before them, the Wilds needed to save up for furniture for a lodging of their own. But as a respectable householder Place turned the policing landlord when he discovered that Mrs Wild had been 'a common prostitute'. By the 1830s Wild in his turn was a landlord in Craven Street.[6] Thomas Carter had been a London lodger but returned to Colchester after his marriage in 1819. As their young family grew, the Carters took lodgers both as a favour and for the supplementary income.[7]

Given the large population of lodgers in the capital, the end was sometimes all-too-natural. As we have seen, Sterne died at Mrs Fourmantel's after a period of illness, and the obituary pages of the *Gentleman's Magazine* included men and women who had died in their lodging-rooms. Here, the record was often brief and matter-of-fact; their being in lodgings was after all nothing out of the ordinary:

> At his lodgings in London, Cha. Earle, esq. late lieutenant-colonel in the army, and major of the 24th foot,

for example.[8] On other occasions, as with Major Baggs and William Elliott (Chapter 3), the death notice contained a note of criticism of the lodger's lifestyle and the implication that living in lodgings represented a low-point which the subject had richly deserved on account of immorality or lack of proper industry. These notices do not mention the responsibility which fell to a landlord or lady on the death of a lodger who might have few or no kin in the capital, but in one 1707 case at the bottom end of the lodging market, a landlord was quite literally left holding the baby. Alice Cook had lodged for two years with Thomas Butcher of Portpool Lane, St Andrew's Holborn (between Gray's Inn Road and Leather Lane). She died in 1707 leaving a three-year-old daughter 'without any manner of subsistence'. The Butcher family cared for her for two weeks 'out of pure commiseration' but Butcher was a 'very poor man' and successfully petitioned the Middlesex justices to have the parish receive her.[9] Thomas Carter and his wife too had a deal of trouble in 1826 when their 'aged and infirm military officer lodger' died. Settling his affairs led to a lengthy bout of stress-induced illness on Carter's part.[10] The transient life of some lodgers meant that the landlord/lady was sometimes not merely a surrogate parent or partner but was in reality the only close contact a lodger had in London. This could prove a heavy responsibility.

There were also tragic fatal endings. Fortunately, no one died in the 1785 Compton Street fire, though many were rendered homeless. By the time the subscription charity was funded and operating, most of the affected lodgers were able to give a new address. They had not moved far, an indication of the ease with which lodging might be found in the city. Mary Benger, who had lodged in Mrs Barrett's Greek Street garret, was now at a greengrocer's in Wardour Street, opposite Hollen (Holland) Street. Gilbert Dring, Hannah Barker's tailor-lodger, gave his address as Mr Maddison's, Francis Street, Golden Square. Genevieve Dumenil, the washer of stockings at McGuire's the greengrocer's, now lived at 5 Falconberg Street (east of Soho Square).[11]

Fatalities in fires and even building collapses were not unheard of, however. As with the Compton Street disaster, these accidents often revealed the presence of lodgers. On Christmas Day 1759 Christian Williamson wrote to her clergyman father Edmund of a major fire in King Street, Covent Garden: 'whole courts are laid flat, whose houses were chiefly wood, and full of lodgers from top to bottom.'[12] Lodgers were at greater risk than their landlords/ladies as they were generally living on upper floors, higher above street level and further from the street door. Andrew Nihell, the surgeon rescued from the rubble of the 1785 Compton Street fire, had lived on a second floor and Curwen recorded another lucky escape from a fire in 1782 at a Snow Hill pastry cook's, though here the householders had perished:

> consuming the house and all within, the family consisting of 7 persons, stock and furniture; one lodger only escaped out of a 2 pair stairs room in front by throwing himself out on a bed put below to receive him.[13]

Elizabeth Adams, who kept an old clothes shop, was a witness in the 1784 trial for theft of Ambrose Cook. She testified that 'The back part of our house fell down, that we had not a bed in the house, and my husband and I was out looking for a house.' Cook was a gardener who lodged with the Adams. When they returned exhausted from house-hunting he allegedly picked her pocket of cash and two nutmeg graters.[14]

Far worse was the house collapse in Houghton Street in 1796. Houghton Street today is a cul-de-sac off Aldwych, part of the estate of the London School of Economics. In the eighteenth century it was one of a maze of older streets of jettied pre-Fire houses around Clare Market, north of the Strand and east of Drury Lane. It was the area where the young Place lived, at the lower end of the lodgings market but not desperately poor. Householders included butchers working in the market and others with more genteel occupations. Richard George was a wine merchant, for example. At half past eight in the morning of 25 June, a Saturday, numbers 7 and 8 collapsed, burying sixteen people under the rubble and killing seven. All but one of the dead were women and children, several of their menfolk having already left for work. The bodies and thirteen survivors were taken in at the St Clement Danes parish workhouse in Portugal Street. The two houses had been densely occupied. Mr Higgins, a smith and bell-hanger, was the tenant of number 7, which was owned by the Duke of Newcastle. Their second-floor front was occupied by Mr and Mrs Gibbon and their two children, the back by Mr and Mrs Brussell (or Bruffell) and Mrs Remmington, the front garret by Mr and Mrs Mills and their three children, and the back garret by Margaret Kirby. Number 8 was the property of Dr Hawse (or Houses) of Jamaica, the householder a Mr Child and his wife. Above them lodged Mr and Mrs Beckford and a child in the first-floor front and Mrs Burrell in the back, Mr and Mrs Deal in the second-floor front and Mr and Mrs Storton and four children in the back, Mr and Mrs Burgess in the front garret and Mr and Mrs French in the back. The Higgins and Child families escaped unhurt (they occupied the lower floors), but the many lodgers above them either met an abrupt end or were rendered traumatized and suddenly homeless.[15]

Death of the landlord/lady or a dramatic downturn in their fortunes could also lead to a sudden parting of the ways that was beyond the control of either party. When the Lamb family – ailing father, paralyzed mother, Charles and Mary, and their paternal aunt Sarah – were compelled to leave their rooms in the Temple in 1792 (Chapter 3), the loss of the father's employment constrained their budget and so accommodation choices dramatically. They were reduced to living 'evidently in uncomfortable circumstances' in lodgings at 7 Little Queen Street, Lincoln's Inn Fields, with Mary working as a mantua-maker to supplement their income.[16] This was the confined and unhappy home where Mary murdered her mother in 1796. Mary became an involuntary lodger at a Hackney madhouse and within the year Charles and his father had moved lodgings to Chapel Street, Islington.[17] Fifty years earlier, Johnson's first London landlord, Richard Norris, staymaker of Exeter Street, seems to have suffered a breakdown when his wife Esther died, forcing Johnson to look for new accommodation. Johnson summarized the clearly chaotic situation in a 1743 diary note: 'Esther died – orderd [sic] to want nothing – house broken up – advertisement – Eldest son – quarrel.'[18] Inchbald started looking for new lodgings in 1788 when her landlady

Mrs Grist fell dangerously ill 'in case of Mrs Grists [*sic*] death &c'. Luckily for both, Grist made a rapid recovery and Inchbald stayed on for almost four years.[19] In 1796 it was the mental ill-health and consequent absence of landlady Mrs Hutchins of 9 Monmouth Court, off the east side of Whitcomb Street, which led to a disastrous loss of control over her houseful of four lodgers: Mr Alexander Webb; Mr James Baker, author of *A Picturesque Guide Through Wales*; Mr Kiplin, an actor at Richmond theatre; and French refugee Count de Gripière de Laval de Moncroe. Mrs Hutchins's mother sometimes stayed the night to oversee the house, but the regular work of cleaning and servicing the lodgers – 'the opening and shutting of the doors and making of the beds and so on' – was undertaken by hired servant, Mary Nott. On 3 June the Count, who had not been seen for six days, was discovered dead from a stab wound on the bed of his locked first-floor room. Despite a suggestion of suicide and her good character references, Mary was found guilty of murder and was hanged on 27 June. We must assume that this household too broke up.[20] These cases reveal the fragility and contingency of living arrangements in lodgings and the importance of having a strong landlord or landlady presence.

The guides discussed in Chapter 2 warned lodgers in unfurnished rooms to research the financial stability of their landlord/lady, for fear their own goods might be seized for distress. The income of tradesmen and women in the eighteenth century could be precarious and even letting rooms was not always an adequate safety net.[21] Inchbald's biographer gives some idea of the problems landlords/ladies faced, remarking of Miss Baillie in 1809 that she had faced in rapid succession 'the departure of one lodger and the death of another, with a bankruptcy in the ground-floor, and the disorder of the times [i.e. the war-time economy]'.[22] Landlords/ladies sometimes borrowed from their lodgers, although indebtedness was usually the other way round (see below). There were the *Chronicle* advertisements proposing a capital sum in return for board and lodging for a term (Chapter 3) and the warning contained in the experience of Mr Kent, the lodger at the centre of the 'Cock Lane Ghost' *cause célèbre* of the 1760s. Kent had lent money to his landlords. One loan resulted in a lawsuit and the other in the 'ghost's' libel.[23] It was not only bookseller Samuel Beacroft (Chapter 3) and William Burrows, the landlord in *Underwood v. Burrows*, who were declared bankrupt. Thomas Lawrence had to leave his lodgings at 24 Old Bond Street (on the corner with Burlington Gardens) when his landlord, engraver William Dickinson (?1746/7–1823), was declared bankrupt in 1794.[24] Wilkie's Mrs Coppard (now living in Kensington and described as a schoolmistress – another possible occupation for a genteel woman of limited means) – and Inchbald's Mrs

Salterelli (described as a boarding-house keeper and now a widow) met a similar
fate some years after their famous lodgers had left, their financial failure another
instance of the difficulty lone women had in earning a sufficient living.[25]

In the 1750s Emin was a servant/student and lodger at Mr Middleton's
Bishopsgate academy, where he also lodged. When Middleton was bankrupted
for £4,000 Emin lost back wages, employment, prospects, and the roof over his
head. He became downwardly mobile, working as a porter, owning just a 'Rag
Fair' (second-hand) coat and waistcoat, and six much-darned sack-cloth shirts.[26]
The final straw between Sylas Neville and the Willoughbys was not the sexual
relationship between lodger and landlady, but Mr Willoughby's arrest for debt
on 18 March 1769. Four days later the family had to leave their house. Neville
was able to access the Willoughbys' professional network of landlords/ladies
and moved to a Mrs Lunn's on their recommendation.[27] Inchbald was finally
pushed into leaving Mrs Grist's in 1792 through fear of the landlady's impending
money problems. Grist informed her on 12 March that she was compelled to
sell all her furniture the next week. This included the 'beautiful bed' in which
Inchbald slept, which was exchanged for 'a little tent one'. By 28 April Inchbald
had taken new rooms with the Shakespears in Cranbourne Passage (connecting
Cranbourne and Newport Streets, demolished 1880), moving there on 18 May.[28]
Eighteen years on, Inchbald faced the same problem with Mr and Mrs Clarke,
her landlord and lady at St Georges Row (on the north side of and overlooking
Hyde Park). Revd Este, who lived next door, was a friend of Inchbald, and
may have been the source of her introduction to the Clarkes. He had not been
entirely honest with her, however. She was unaware when she moved there in
June 1810 that Este also owned the house in which she lodged and that the
Clarkes were in debt to him. By September the situation was desperate. Este
and his son woke the household by banging on the door at night-time to deliver
a writ. A crowd gathered and 'a gun was placed out of the window of the floor
above mine'. Inchbald was both ashamed (Este had been calling her name) and
anxious that were she to leave Clarke might 'stop her furniture for the year's
rent'. Both sides to the dispute appointed lawyers. As a lodger Inchbald was left
powerless, trapped in the middle without any recourse but to start the search
for new accommodation in case Este evicted Clarke. The Clarkes offered her
the chance to go with them to Edgware Road but Inchbald declined: it was too
far from town and she no longer trusted them. Instead she turned again to Miss
Baillie. Her house was full, but landlady networks again came to the fore and
Miss Baillie secured Inchbald a room with her next-door neighbour.[29] As these

examples demonstrate, the precarity of a lodging arrangement was not always due to the moral failures of the lodgers.

Few lodging arrangements ended so dramatically, however, and many lasted for several or even many years (Franklin, Gansel, Inchbald). Nonetheless, lodgers were still thought of as transient. Graglia's guestimate was two moves a year and we have seen from the evidence of life-writers (Curwen, Inchbald, the Lambs) that moves could be far more frequent than this. These frequent, and sometimes impulsive, moves were made possible by the active marketplace in lodgings discussed in Chapter 3. It was relatively easy to change one's abode for something slightly better, slightly cheaper, or slightly more convenient, often inspired by social visits to friends also in lodgings. The grass often seemed greener elsewhere, the classic dissatisfaction of consumerism.[30]

Key grounds for that dissatisfaction included location, noise, and poor quality accommodation. The lodger new to London was of course more prone to make mistakes in these respects. The youthful Franklin left Little Britain for Duke Street, Lincoln's Inn Fields, to be nearer (very near) his work at printer John Watts's in Wild Court.[31] Others, as we have seen, moved away from central locations for cleaner, healthier air (though they were matched by lodgers like Swift and Inchbald who missed the hurly-burly of city life and were moving back). Curran first lodged close to St Martin-in-the-Fields church but discovered it was impossible to study. There was the incessant, inane chatter of his landlord, but above all he hated the constant ringing of 'praying bells, rejoicing bells, and passing bells'. He made a prompt move to Orange Court (just south of Orange Street), still centrical but more secluded.[32] In his first London rooms in Woburn Buildings, Carlyle was irritated by the noise within: 'we have a slamming and a clanking which I "albeit of firmest nerve," sometimes find unpleasant'. Eventually he found the constant din outside from the main road unbearable: 'Hundreds of noisy urchins are sporting on the street; from the New Road comes that old unresting hum of carriage-wheels and quadrupeds and bipeds'. This prompted his move to the relative backwater of Ampton Street.[33]

As Emily Cockayne points out, vermin of all sorts, as well as dirt and noise, were perennially present in homes of every sort and class in eighteenth-century towns and cities.[34] Multiple occupants and a rapid turnover of lodgers exacerbated the problem, as suggested by the poster in *A Gentleman of Moderate Income* (Figure 3). Andrew Cook and Eleanor Brainiff, daughter of the 'bug-doctor' to the king, no less, offered their pest control services in a 1772 *Chronicle* advertisement, listing by name the respectable establishments they had helped, and offering 'reasonable terms' to lodging-houses.[35] Some lodgers endured or found a way round this. Others were not so resigned. In 1715, lodging in Aldgate High Street, Cannon complained that he and his wife had contracted the 'itch' from a damp bed in which a previous occupant had died. The couple resolved to buy their own furniture in future.[36] In 1814 Inchbald had landlord Mr Beale stop up the mouseholes in her room, but kept the house cat in her room overnight eight days later.[37] For Carlyle, however, the ongoing bed bug problem was a second unsurmountable drawback to Woburn Buildings. In Ampton Street, by contrast, 'the people assure us they *very seldom see* a bug'.[38]

If some stays were long, others were very brief, even if that had not been the original plan. Curwen lasted only a week at Orange Court in 1782, but the record must be held by Boswell.[39] Back in London in September 1769, he struggled to find rooms near his surgeon, Mr Forbes (Boswell had for some time been afflicted by what he called 'Signor Gonorrhoea'), eventually finding suitable ones with Mr and Mrs Careless in Carey Street. He slept there only one night, however, before moving to Old Bond Street, a few doors from his new friend General Pasquale Paoli (1725–1807), the exiled Corsican patriot. Boswell was aware that this made him look suspicious, 'somewhat like a highwayman', in the Carelesses' eyes.[40] Maybe he was recalling the life of James Maclaine (1724–50). Before and during his notorious career as a highwayman, Maclaine lived extravagantly in 'handsome Lodgings' in St James's Street, where he 'passed for an Irish gentleman of £700 a year' while fencing the stolen goods.[41]

Before leaving, Boswell paid the Carelesses a full week's rent of 25s., a recognition of the guides' standard 'reasonable notice' for lodging of one week on either side, based on the weekly payment of rent, although some of the template agreements in legal guides suggested a quarter's notice, in line with the notice period for leases.[42] Given the planned brevity of some lodging arrangements, uncertainty over whether the deal would stick, and the difficulty and expense of chasing a vanished lodger for back rent, a quarter was often regarded as inappropriate and impractical. Bird's guidance was more realistic: 'Lodgings taken for a short period' were an exception to the quarter-day rule 'if for less than a year certain, any reasonable notice is held to be sufficient'.[43] Tardy advised his French readers, who were less aware of the English norm, that notice should be one week if lodgings were taken by the week, a fortnight when taken for a month, six weeks when taken for a quarter, and three months if taken for six months to a year. Where adequate notice was not given, the landlord could extract payment for a week, fortnight etc. Tardy explained the justice in this: a landlord/lady was otherwise prevented from re-letting the rooms.[44] On his quitting to move to the Porters' in 1705, Congreve's Norfolk Street landlord, Richard Boddy, refused to hold on to Congreve's possessions for two weeks for this reason.[45] Boddy, like so many landlords and ladies, was firmly in control here as a businessman, offering nothing for free.

Whether notice was always given in writing cannot be known. It certainly was in the case of Alexander Cruden. In 1753, after three months with Mrs Stephens in Moorfields (the landlady who had attempted to withdraw from a lodging agreement when she learned of his insanity), the maid handed him a piece of paper:

> Take notice that I give you warning to quit my lodging one week after the date hereof, according to your own agreement, else you forfeit your note.

Cruden replied with a written note that he would leave and paid a £10 forfeit. Cruden was obviously both a troubled and troublesome man, and it may have been necessary to commit the notice to writing to ensure he took it seriously. Perhaps surprisingly, he found a satisfactory new lodging quite promptly.[46] Sometimes the notice seems to have come rather as a gentle nudge. Charles Lamb noted in a letter in 1801, 'I am going to change my lodging, having received a hint that it would be agreeable at our Lady's next feast.' But then he and the landlord, Gutch, were close friends and a letter would have been excessively hostile on Gutch's part.[47] Some reasons given by landlords/ladies that fell short of formal notice may well have been such hints. In 1817 the Lambs (again) were asked to vacate their rooms in the Temple so that they could be refurbished. This may have been the case, but maybe too Mary's health was again poor, or their active social life was disturbing other tenants.[48] Where a lodger was recalcitrant, there were the more aggressive approaches such as the tactics seen in *Underwood v. Burrows* or the 'Welsh Ejectment'. Falling short of this came raising the rent once the initial agreement period was up, and then evicting for non-payment, or locking the room and withholding the lodger's possessions.[49] As the saying, reported by Curwen, went: 'Better an empty house than a bad tenant'.[50]

Many landlords/ladies and lodgers do seem to have more or less followed the one-week rule even if there is no record of anything in writing passing between them. Pilkington moved from Drury Lane back to a spare room at her old landlady's in St James's only once her week's notice was up.[51] Where he records the process, the punctilious Curwen also seems to have given around a week's notice. He handed in notice to one landlord on 16 October 1775 and moved to Mrs Wilson's in Islington on 24 October. In 1779 he gave a week's notice that he was leaving his Exeter lodgings after the incident in which he was shut out at night. It was the same week's notice at Mrs Froade's, but there were only six days between giving Mrs Atwood notice and shifting to Mrs Smithson's in 1782. He may of course, like Boswell at the Carelesses', have paid for the 'unused' time.[52]

How much leeway a landlord/lady allowed depended not only on the formal notice period but also on the quality of their relationship with their lodger, as we have seen in the case of Wilkie and Mrs Coppard. Emin's first landlady, Mrs Newman, gave him a month's notice, not because he had offended directly but because his patron Cogigian had got wind of the fact that Emin was paying less than he for board. Emin moved three days after the notice period expired and, still without anywhere to go, was compelled to walk the streets before being taken in at Middleton's.[53] Inchbald who, like Wilkie, generally got on well with her landlords/ladies, gave notice in November 1804 that she was leaving Annandale House and moved to Miss Baillie's on 20 December. This may have been a month's notice. She gave notice to Miss Baillie in March 1807. When after an exhaustive search she was unable to find anything 'equally cheap, and equally healthy', Baillie did not hold her to the notice, although she did re-let her room and repaint while Inchbald was holidaying in Norfolk. When she returned Inchbald was, unusually by her standards, annoyed and spent three days at a friend's, but things were patched up between the two (Baillie presumably having an eye to her own weak financial position) and Inchbald returned to a different room, staying until 1810.[54]

Once the final day arrived there was the business of settling up. There might, as Curwen found (below), be disagreements over exactly what was due. Guidebooks generally advised landlords and ladies to agree an inventory, and lodgers on expiry of the notice period to hand back the room and its furnishings in reasonable condition on pain of compensation. Richard Boddy demanded £5 of Congreve for a damaged quilt, for example.[55] There is no evidence of inventories in life-writing, however. It seems to have been a routine courtesy on the host's part to be there, both to collect any outstanding money in person and to bid farewell. It was a small, polite ritual that corresponded to the initial welcome. When Curwen left Mrs Froade's in Bristol in March 1780 they drank tea together and he 'shaking my late landlady by the hand and kissing her a little fondling [*sic*] took a very friendly seeming leave'. It was perhaps a little too familiar, but as Froade had allegedly overcharged him by 14s. and hung on to the money for two days she may have felt obliged to put up with his caresses. By contrast, he was annoyed in January 1784 when neither Mr nor Mrs Councel deigned to appear. There was 'not a soul but the servant to be seen, however left compliments and bid adieu to a very disagreeable family'.[56]

As part of the leaving ritual, lodgers were also expected to tip the landlord/lady and the servants, perhaps in acknowledgement of both the 'little extras' and the disruption any lodger would have caused. Curwen was, unsurprisingly, grudging:

> gave Betty Jones maidservant [to Mrs Froade] customary fee 5/[5s.] to prevent reproaches, her cross unobliging behaviour not deserving a gratuity, but custom must be complied with.[57]

Jefferson 'gave in vales ["vails", or tips] to different servts.' a handsome £4 4s. when he left Mrs Conners's in 1786, and Wilkie gave his landlady Mrs Good a guinea to buy something for her daughter when he left in 1808.[58] Even Coleridge, when living hand-to-mouth in 1810, tipped a maid 5s. 6d. 'for encouragement', though given his endless bowel complaints this may have been conscience money for the chief emptier of chamber pots.[59] However, when Cruden left Mrs Stephens's house (see above) he merely promised her a copy of Dr Watt's *Sermons* in two volumes. His parting 'gift' indicates that he had little idea that he may have been a nuisance in the household, or that cash might have been better-appreciated than an IOU for two weighty tomes.[60]

Chapter 5 looked at some of the common issues that arose between the variety of people in a household with lodgers: the daily 'timetable', food, eccentricity, creating a disturbance after hours in the house or at the street door. Some of these issues were relatively minor and, as we have seen, diplomatically-inclined lodgers overcame them or moved on quietly when the opportunity arose. Sometimes, however, relationships deteriorated to a point where reconciliation was impossible and landlord/lady and lodger parted company on poor terms, though rarely, it seems, as brutally as Egerton depicted in *The Unfortunate*

Discovery (Figure 14). The two key areas of dispute that led to a relationship breakdown were, first, egregiously bad behaviour and, second, money. At the lower end of the lodgings market there was also the issue of theft of the landlord's/lady's furnishings covered by Styles, often accompanied by a vanished lodger owing rent.[61] In these circumstances, legal guides were clear. The proper course was for the landlord/lady to approach a magistrate before entering the room with a witness in tow.[62] This is what Hannah Calverley, of Orange Court, Swallow Street, who let rooms to support her lame husband, did in 1805 when her lodger Elizabeth Crimpshaw alias Jackson and her two children disappeared leaving her three-shillings-a-week room locked. On breaking down the door Calverley found that bedding and household items worth £1 15s. 6d. were missing. She prosecuted Crimpshaw, who was found guilty, fined 1s. and imprisoned for six months.[63]

None of our genteel lodgers were thieves, but some did behave unacceptably. We have seen how Alexander Cruden's mental ill health caused his behaviour to deteriorate to the point that his landlords/ladies felt obliged to have him removed. It included fighting and the unwelcome and obsessive pursuit of women. The composer John Moorehead (d. 1804), when similarly afflicted, 'broke all the glasses and furniture in his lodgings' at Richmond, after which he was committed in a straitjacket to an asylum in Clerkenwell.[64] Coleridge was so impossible that to prevent any disasters or tempestuous scenes even his friends warned others against ever taking him in as a lodger. Coleridge recognized this in himself: 'I am not fit to be in Lodgings, by myself.'[65]

Boswell too provides a strong example of the sort of behaviour well short of madness that could completely destroy a relationship. The morning after his noisy party at the Terries', Boswell left the house early, breakfasted with a friend, and then confronted Terrie again at his office, an aggressively public move by a social superior. He next took legal advice at Sir John Fielding's office, where he was informed that:

> though I had taken my lodgings for a year, I might upon proof of his [i.e. Terrie's] bad behaviour, quit when I pleased, without being under an obligation to pay rent for any longer time than while I possessed them.

The 'bad behaviour' Boswell complained of was merely rudeness, whereas he himself had, of course, both broken the rules about what he once described, proprietorially but wrongly, as 'my' parlour, and disturbed the rest of the host household. However, Boswell was confident of his social superiority to Terrie and so regarded the latter's 'impudence' as intolerable. Later in the day Boswell called on that experienced lodger Johnson, who laughed and told him that the matter would seem trivial in a year's time. Johnson did, however, propose that if Terrie held Boswell to his year's agreement his friend should crank up the dispute, by taking up smelly chemistry – an acknowledgement of the nuisance value of his own scientific experiments – or by subletting the rooms to two Life Guards, presumably deemed even less attractive as lodgers than Boswell. In the event Boswell did the most sensible thing under the circumstances. He quit his lodgings by mutual agreement the following day, dealing with Mrs Terrie and paying 'what little debts I owed her' (no tip is recorded), and moved to the Inner Temple chambers of his best friend, bar-student William Johnson Temple (1739–96), one of the offending parlour party.[66]

Another form of unreasonable behaviour revolved around the ubiquitous and very necessary chamber pot. Although by the mid-century some elite houses had water closets, small rooms for keeping the pot at a remove from the main bedroom or living room, Isaac Ware pronounced these a 'useful addition' rather than a sanitary *sine qua non*.[67] Lodging-rooms were unlikely to be provided with such facilities for most of our period. A *Chronicle* advertisement placed in November 1799 and again in January 1800 for a genteel first floor in Pall Mall offered a water closet, but as a single example this probably implies that thirty years after Ware it remained unusual enough to be worthy of remark.[68] Horribly near the tea-table in Boitard's lodging-room (Figure 10) is a chamber pot, probably full given the dog's interest, and we have already encountered both Curwen's and Coleridge's bowel problems. Someone, usually a maid, had to empty all these pots. In 1784 one East End lodger, the prosecutor in an Old Bailey theft case, referred casually to his 'making water' out of the kitchen door.[69] Malcolm, writing retrospectively of the eighteenth century, thought that uncouth lodgers dispensed with niceties and, like Hogg and boarders' meals, implied that nineteenth-century standards had risen:

> The rentors [*sic*] of single rooms, in first, second and third floors, in mean streets, feel themselves above restraint. Those people empty dirty water mixed with their offal into the gutters, the stench of which is appalling.[70]

In genteel locations such behaviour never did do, however. The lodger was expected at least to facilitate the maid's work in the interest of everyone in the houseful. In late 1782 failure to obey this rule of respectable society in such matters led to a fatal end to a lodging arrangement, and a trial for murder. Dr Daniel Macginniss was an Irish physician just short of sixty years old. He had been lodging for some two months in the second-floor back room of Mr and Mrs

Hardy at 31 Newgate Street. Things had not gone well. Macginniss was a little behind with his rent, and Hardy had apparently indicated that he wanted him to leave. It was five o'clock and already dark on the evening of 28 December 1782. Macginniss had just come in, and the maid, Mary Decrow, lighted him up to his room and took away his breakfast things. Meanwhile, downstairs, the Hardys were taking tea in the parlour in a rear extension to the ground floor. Decrow joined them. This polite scene was almost immediately rudely interrupted by the splashing of the contents of Macginniss's chamber pot onto the parlour skylight. Enraged, Hardy (a hosier and hatter who possibly suffered from the irritability and excitability common among 'mad' hatters as classic symptoms of mercury poisoning) rushed up the stairs to confront his lodger, intending to evict him on the spot. In the course of an angry encounter, Macginniss ran him through the chest with a pistol bayonet, and Hardy bled to death on his first-floor landing. At trial, Macginniss called distinguished character references (including Edmund Burke) and the judge's summing up was helpful to the defendant. However, the jury, in all likelihood middling-sort men who were not unacquainted with lodgers in the household, found him guilty.[71] He was sentenced to hang followed by dissection, though this was later commuted to transportation for life.[72]

The Macginniss case once again underlines the strong class element that came to the fore when lodging relationships soured. Macginniss himself and his supporters clearly thought him a gentleman, whereas Hardy was a mere tradesman. It was an attitude shared by others: the following year Curwen similarly dismissed one landlord as a 'paltry little taylor'.[73] It also reveals the grumbling issues of privacy and key-holding, and some of the tensions and difficulties between servants and lodgers (Chapters 4 and 5) which also lay behind this example of a poor relationship between host and lodger. Macginniss, affronted that his landlord had barged into his private space, pleaded self-defence in the face of provocation. He also blamed the maid for laziness, an accusation which resonated with the court. On the fateful day she had neither emptied the chamber pot, nor removed his breakfast things, nor made the bed. Decrow replied that Macginniss had gone out for the day taking his room-key with him. The court asked her why she did not take the chamber pot when she cleared the breakfast things in the evening. She retorted that her hands were full as she held the candlestick as well. This all rather leads to the conclusion that the middling-sort men comprising 'the court' did not understand the pressures of a servant's life, but probably did understand that Macginniss had deliberately emptied the chamber pot as an act of war.

Inappropriate sexual behaviour within a house that included lodgers was also highly problematic. As the complaint in *Jefferies v. Duncombe* showed, it potentially undermined a householder's reputation for respectability and probity, and risked a misinterpretation of the house as one of ill-repute as seen in novels, plays, and images. Landlords/ladies were therefore often on their guard against anything that smacked of licentiousness. Mr Terrie had in part been furious at Boswell's parlour party because he thought the young men had the maid in the parlour with them.[74]

Young women who were part of the host household, especially servants, were vulnerable to advances from male lodgers taking advantage of the sexual double standard. Indeed, the very density of occupation magnified the opportunity for erotic encounters. The daily routine in households with lodgers entailed regular visiting of their bedrooms by female members of the household: lighting the way on the stairs, bringing hot drinks and rolls in the morning, and warming, or making, the bed, as Mary Decrow should have done, laying fires, and opening and closing window curtains. The bed often dominated a lodger's room (Figures 3, 10, and 11) and the maid's entry offered the chance to pounce, an opportunity both Cannon and footman John Macdonald took.[75] Even a non-predatory lodger might be still in bed or in a state of semi-dress, the reason why the Walker family, Hazlitt's hosts, were able to compare their lodgers' penis sizes. Such tasks placed these women in a vulnerable position faced with John Black's 'gentry, professional, and middling order men' who held 'a strong presumption that these women were sexually available or fair game for seduction'.[76] In the early-eighteenth century William Byrd, on returning to his lodgings in the evening (often aroused by exploits in taverns and bagnios), regularly kissed the maid until he ejaculated.[77] In the mid-century Kitty Hamilton (Chapter 4) told Macdonald that she was offered money for sex by gentlemen lodgers at her mistress's house. He replied she should have complied for free, forcing himself on her as she made his bed until he was disturbed by other lodgers in the house.[78] Parish poor law examinations reveal the outcome of such encounters. Mary Chaddock was a twenty-four-year-old maid working at Mr Henderson's in York Buildings (near Villiers Street, by the Thames) when she fell pregnant by Peter Adams, footman to a Colonel Macdewell, who lodged in the house.[79] Hannah Bradly was twenty-eight and a servant to Mrs Ballester, Warwick Street, near Golden Square, when she became pregnant by Ballester's then lodger, attorney's clerk Thomas Leigh, in 1760.[80]

We have already seen servants warned by Eliza Haywood to be on their guard against male lodgers. She counselled them to get out of the way as long as the approach was only 'Words'. If 'rudeness' ensued, then they should report to their mistress immediately. Haywood optimistically promised that the mistress, 'if a Woman of Reputation', would regard the approach as a personal insult. Haywood believed that a respectable landlady 'would rather lose her Lodger than permit any Indecency in her House'.[81] Sadly for maidservants, Haywood's optimism was misplaced. The double standard prevailed. Landlords/ladies were inclined to protect the reputation of their household by evicting the 'errant' maid rather than the lodger. By the time she appeared before the overseers of St Martin-in-the-Fields in March 1729 Mary Chaddock and her baby girl were lodging elsewhere. Pregnant Hannah Bradly was lodging in Chelsea where she came before the parish authorities. Both had lost their jobs and their accommodation. Other London parish records show that Mary and Hannah were far from alone in this experience.

Male lodgers made sexual advances to members of the host household too: wives and daughters were also vulnerable. Proximity sometimes bred a disruptive intimacy. In 1797 Joseph Farington reminisced about George Cumberland (1754–1848, a writer on painting). In 1787 Cumberland had run off to Europe with Mrs Cooper, the wife of his architect landlord, buying off Cooper with the huge sum of £1,000.[82] Lodgers were also perhaps encouraged by the popular cultural depictions of landladies as bawds presiding over households of sex workers. Three case studies from life-writing by male lodgers demonstrate the power-plays and risks involved.

The first concerns Hickey, who claimed to have been sexually initiated aged seven by a servant, Nancy 'Nanny' Harris, He recounted in jocular tone his attraction for and seduction of Ann Malton, his hosts' sixteen-year-old daughter. He began by walking with her to Ranelagh Gardens (for which he had a season ticket) and playing the harpsichord (badly) to her there. Then it was 'occasionally snatching a kiss', followed by increasingly permitted 'liberties'. Finally, Ann 'proposed ... to admit me to her bed'. Her disapproving parents were aware of the growing relationship and warned Hickey, but to no avail. One night at eleven o'clock, an hour past the Maltons' bedtime, Hickey crept downstairs from his room on the second floor towards the back parlour where Ann slept. But her door-handle creaked, and her father appeared – fully dressed, implying a certain watchfulness on his part – to catch the pair under the bedcovers together. Surprisingly, the outcome was not the eviction of Hickey, though that had been Mr Malton's first thought, but the removal of temptation, in the form of Ann, from the house. There was, however, now a distinct and understandable *froideur* on the part of the Maltons: 'cold and forbidding looks and scarcely ever speaking'. Hickey's stay there did not last much longer.[83]

Secondly, as seen in Chapter 5, Neville's landlord Mr Willoughby suffered as his lodger flirted with his wife, and was compelled to agree with the couple that it was Platonic 'with no harm in it', while being clearly jealous, as Neville happily noted. In March 1769 Willoughby was arrested for debt, held in a sponging-house, and his goods sold. With his rival gone, Neville sat up talking with Mrs Willoughby until half past three in the morning as she declared her love for him. The financial disaster brought some good to Willoughby, however. He used it as an opportunity to separate the lovebirds (Neville to Mrs Lunn's and she to rooms in Wimpole Street and later to an 'apartment' in the debtors' prison), though they continued to correspond and meet for a few weeks.[84] Neville's case demonstrates the contingency that applied to householder control of lodger behaviour. Willoughby had to endure a situation of discomfort, humiliation even, because his finances were shaky, and he could ill-afford to lose the income from his gentleman-lodger.

The final example of sexual impropriety is William Hazlitt's obsession with his Southampton Row landlady's daughter, Sarah Walker, which he unashamedly chronicled in the *Liber Amoris* and in letters to friends. His narrative can be read between the lines to reveal an ongoing battle for control between lodger and householder family. Hazlitt, not the Walkers' only lodger, moved into two rooms on their second floor in August 1820. He was forty-two and recently separated from his wife and child. Sarah was nineteen and, with her sister Betsey and a maidservant, Maria, helped her mother service the lodgers' rooms. An aunt had, in the spirit of Haywood's lecture to servants, advised Sarah to 'keep every lodger at a proper distance', although Sarah's older sister Martha had not obeyed this golden rule. Martha had, in fact, profited from proximity to the lodgers and had married up to one of them, Robert Roscoe, a young lawyer.[85] Hazlitt from the start paid extra to have breakfast delivered to his room on a tray, providing a reason for Sarah to visit him each morning.[86] It was not only coffee and rolls that he received. She sat in his lap with her arms around his neck. She stayed with him longer than with other lodgers – up to an hour at a time. She let him 'enjoy her through her petticoats'. He in his turn offered gifts: the books (refused), the length of plaid silk (accepted), and his bust of Napoleon (accepted, returned, and smashed by Hazlitt in a rage).[87]

One reason for Hazlitt's attraction was the erotic thrill of Sarah's lower class ('I am but a tradesman's daughter,' she said) and semi-servile status. Hazlitt wrote to his friend, journalist Peter Patmore (1786–1855), that 'I like to think of her best in her morning gown, in her dirt and her mob-cap'.[88] There is a touch here of the later-nineteenth-century role-playing master–servant relationship between civil servant and diarist Arthur Munby (1828–1910) and Hannah Cullwick (1833–1909).[89] Hazlitt's and Sarah's relationship was tempestuous, with indications that it was not entirely mutual. Haywood had warned maids about gifts from lodgers. Those made by Hazlitt to Sarah were, in effect, an attempt by a well-established older man to buy the attention of a poorer and much younger woman who could not avoid contact with him. Sarah's correspondence with Hazlitt when he was away certainly betrays no affection on her part. Her letters were curt: no, the first floor was let and, no, there were no letters for him.[90] When all was said and done, Sarah's job was to keep the lodgers satisfied. She was in no position to undermine the family economy by being rude to the lodgers, but she was not required to submit entirely to their unsought sexual advances.

Hazlitt nonetheless wanted exclusive rights over Sarah and was angry at the time she spent with other lodgers, especially trainee lawyer John Tomkins, who arrived in 1821 and was close to Sarah in age. At one point Hazlitt went as far as to take 'nearly the whole of the lodgings at a hundred guineas a year' so that she would have 'a little leisure' – or, rather, more undiluted time for him.[91] On the other hand, he openly flouted any notion of his own fidelity, expressing surprise that the Walkers had never objected to 'girls of the town' coming up to him 'continually'. Sarah had even shown some of them up herself.[92] Hazlitt moved out to Chapel Street, Mayfair, in October 1822. But he did not let the matter rest. He commissioned a friend to lodge with the Walkers, spy on Sarah and attempt sex with her. She did indeed flirt, as she had with other lodgers. She kissed him on the stairs and let him rest his hand on her thigh. But she drew the line when he 'put his hands between her legs without ceremony' as she was closing the curtains one evening: 'Let me go, Sir, and returning to the door, asked if he would have the fire lighted. She did not come up again'.[93]

In 1824 Sarah set up house with Hazlitt's rival Tomkins and the couple had a child, though they may never have married. The 'I am to be let alone' prints (Chapter 2) assumed that an attractive young woman of the household might be part of the lodging package, but Sarah did not see herself in this way. She quite possibly did regard her parents' young gentlemen-lodgers as a potential route to a more secure middling status, a route her sister Martha had trodden before her. An eye for a good catch did not make her person available to all, however. The double standard meant that Hazlitt paid no particular price for his poor behaviour in the Walkers' house, other than their reluctance to have him back again and slight, temporary loss of face with his circle. Haydon (by now a married man and father) thought his conduct folly, that Hazlitt was 'in love, to a pitch of insanity'.[94] Hazlitt had not achieved his aim with Sarah and, as other lodgers did when thwarted by the host household, lashed out on a class basis. Sarah was 'a common lodging house decoy, a kissing convenience', Mrs Walker 'the most disgusting, vulgar, old wretch'. Haydon, who in his bachelor days had commented on a fellow lodger that 'An attractive girl on the second floor of a house full of young men is in a rather dangerous position', agreed: Sarah was 'a lodging-house hussy'.[95] The two friends stood shoulder-to-shoulder in their sense of sexual entitlement.

———————

If male lodgers were able to shrug off sexual misconduct, the same could not be said of disputes over money. For landlords/ladies money was, despite all the protestations about company, family, and society, absolutely fundamental to a lodging arrangement. In the absence of exceptional and personal reasons (such as Mrs Coppard's evident fondness and concern for David Wilkie), when they were unsure that the rent would ever be forthcoming, they had little reason to keep a lodger on. At the time of the hatter Hardy's murder, Macginniss was behind in his rent and already risking being given notice. One shrewd move when a lodger did not pay was to clear the room, call on the justices and bailiffs if necessary, as the guides advised, and find a more financially sound replacement. Better an empty room than a bad tenant!

Lodgers knew this, and those whose income was precarious were at pains to avoid their lack of funds becoming apparent to the landlord/lady. This is a possible reason for Shelley preferring hotels for financial negotiations with his father – it avoided being overheard and so exposing his indigence to a landlord/lady. Good quality clothes, as enjoyed by Goldsmith, and a string of well-connected visitors helped to keep up appearances, but lodgers went to greater lengths than this to conceal the state of their affairs. When Pilkington lodged with Mrs Trifoli (or Thiffola, wife of an absent German physician, or 'quack' as Pilkington put it) in Duke Street, St James's, in 1742, she recalled how 'I concealed my Distress with the utmost Care from my Landlady; called every Morning for the Teakettle, though I had no Tea'. She also pretended she was dining out then walked alone to Westminster Abbey until the dinner hour could be considered over. Her tactics failed to convince Trifoli, however, who had her arrested for debt. On release from the Marshalsea prison Pilkington had nowhere else to go and so reappeared at Trifoli's, where her papers remained. Unsurprisingly the rapprochement did not last. Pilkington was turned out and had to be helped into new lodgings by actor-manager Colley Cibber (1671–1757).[96] Still in the 1740s, bailiffs also visited the lodgings of Teresia Muilman 'while she and her Sister, with other Company, were at Dinner in the Parlour; and, having knocked at the Door, rushed into the House, and ran up Stairs, expecting to find her above'. The sisters double-locked the parlour door and, while this was being broken down, Teresia made her escape by the kitchen window. Following this incident, she moved lodgings to Whitehall.[97]

There is too the well-worn anecdote of the time when, living at Wine Office Court in 1763, Goldsmith faced the predicament of arrest for debt by his landlady. He was saved by his friend Johnson, who allegedly headed over and, seeing the manuscript of the *Vicar of Wakefield*, staved off disaster by rushing it to a publisher and selling it for £60 cash.[98] It made a scene in the garret-poet tradition and was indeed captured almost a century later by historical genre painter Edward Ward (1816–79).[99] Several decades later in the 1790s things were no different for young artist Shee:

> for one whole winter, during the time he occupied apartments in Craven Street, he rarely, if ever, *dined*, except when enjoying the hospitality of friends. His daily practice was to walk, after his labours in the painting room were over, from Craven Street to St. Paul's Church-yard, and back again; this expedition occupying about the time which a man might be reasonably supposed to devote to the business of a solitary dinner, at a tavern or eating-house, within some moderate distance of his lodgings. On his return, he of course lost no time in calling for tea; and it is highly probable that the inordinate consumption of bread-and-butter with which he accompanied his liberal potations of that cheering and soothing beverage, betrayed the secret of his abstemiousness, which his daily pilgrimage to St. Paul's was expressly devised to conceal, as a humiliating fact, from the notice of his landlady and her household.

Shee's poverty-induced strategy was recalled by his son, who felt that the landlord or lady were aware of the ruse and resented his father's overconsumption of bread and butter at their expense.[100] The anecdote reminds us of Emin, forty years before.

For some lodgers, rapid moves out of one lodging and into another prompted by money problems were a feature of life. This was true even at the respectable end of the market. 'Kept' women were especially at risk as Egerton's print (Figure 14) and the 'whore biographies' discussed in Chapter 2 made clear. If abandoned by a lover their income generally dried up and they were often obliged to move. Irish gentlewoman 'Coquetilla', for example, ran away with her father's coachman to live in rooms in Gerrard Street, Soho. She was forced into an alternative form of keeping, by bawd Mrs Hall, when he left her heavily pregnant. After various escapades in the world of sex work and a stable period in the country living with 'Colonel D', whose children she bore, Coquetilla returned to London and again lived kept, by 'Saxillus', in London lodgings.[101] The well-known courtesan (the *ODNB* again) Kitty Fisher (?1741–67), of the lost pocket in the nursery rhyme, began her working life as a milliner. Seduced from this, real-life imitating the trope of the eighteenth-century sex worker, she next went into keeping in lodgings until, deserted and penniless, she sought a place as an upper maid. Later she lived again as a kept woman in the Haymarket on a generous five guineas a week (£273 a year). She eventually married well (John Norris, 1740–1811, MP for Rye) in 1766 but died only a few months later.[102] While these narratives may contain a degree of fiction, both point to the precarity of life in London for single women, reflected in their restricted employment and so accommodation options.

Young men from relatively prosperous backgrounds were not prey to sexual exploitation but were inclined casually to owe back rent, effectively borrowing from their landlords/ladies. They generally felt confident in their ability to talk themselves out of eviction in a situation where they were usually the social superiors, gentlemen whose word was supposed to be their bond. However, debt, unlike sexual misbehaviour, did generally force a lodger to leave. Shelley, stripped of his allowance (£200 a year paid quarterly) by his father after his 1811 marriage to Harriet Westbrook, signally failed to reduce his spending. Not only did he live in hotels, but in 1812 when he owed £30 to Mrs Hooper, a landlady in Lynmouth, he sent her only £20, yet in 1813 treated himself to a carriage, an expensive luxury item.[103] Once his marriage had collapsed and he was living with Mary Godwin, the couple was surviving on £4 a week raised by obit bonds (borrowings against a future inheritance), and faced a near-permanent threat of arrest for debt. The couple lived in a constant 'bustle of moving', flitting from lodging to lodging across the capital to escape their creditors.[104] Shelley's letters between September 1814 and May 1816 were sent from nine different London addresses: Margaret Street (north of and parallel to Oxford Street), Somers Town, Nelson Square (Southwark), two addresses in Hans Place (Kensington), Arabella Road (Pimlico), Marchmont Street (Bloomsbury), and 13 and 32 Norfolk Street (Strand).[105]

In 1801 Coleridge, who lamented the receipt of 'Dunning Letters etc. etc. – all the hell of an author', borrowed £25 from his landlord, tailor Mr Howell of King Street, Covent Garden, but on going away for a few weeks had the cheek to leave with them a cheque for the same amount for Daniel Stuart (1766–1846), editor of the *Morning Post* for which Coleridge wrote, on the basis that he did 'not like to leave town so heavily in your [Stuart's] Debt'. A month or so later Coleridge paid Howell by draft for clothes, surely not the method his creditor would have preferred.[106] Mr Howell probably derived some sense of security from the fact that it was the wealthy Stuart through whom the lodging deal had been made. In 1810, on the other hand, back in London after a period in the Lake District and sunk further into opium addiction and financial chaos, Coleridge was unprotected and, like Shelley, had to move rapidly from lodging to lodging in an attempt to escape both debts and demons.[107]

Haydon was also a debtor, owing Mr Perkins, his landlord at 41 Marlborough Street, the huge sum of £200 in 1812. As he had lived there since 1808 it seems likely that Haydon had never paid the rent, even though he had been busy with commissions. In 1812 he had just begun work on his huge (3.9 metres × 3.3 metres) painting *The Judgment of Solomon*, foolishly without a commission from a patron. Amazingly Perkins allowed him two more years until this should be finished.[108] By 1814, the painting complete and exhibited at the Royal Academy, the debt had risen to £400, with money also owed to the John O'Groats (an eating-house on Rupert Street listed in guides to London), his tailor, coal merchant, and baker. The sale of the *chef d'œuvre* to two bankers for 700 guineas allowed Haydon to clear some of this, yet he continued to overspend, scrounging from friends, borrowing, and paying Perkins by bill rather than cash.[109] Perkins may have been somewhat blinded by the glamour of his artist lodger with his visitors 'of rank, beauty and fashion' who called when Haydon's casts of the Elgin Marbles brought fame. Haydon was, after all, able to 'command' that the front door was left open to ease their access to him. However, *Solomon* failed to draw the crowds its purchasers had expected in Haydon's hometown of Plymouth. The painting was sold again and failed again elsewhere in the West Country, and was returned to the artist whereupon economic self-interest held sway and it was seized by Haydon's then landlord. For the rest of his life Haydon spiralled downwards into cheaper and cheaper accommodation and, after a stint as a debtor in King's Bench Prison, ended up in 1823, now with a wife and child, in the 'humble lodgings' outside town in Paddington Green (Chapter 1). When his Paddington landlady disturbed him as he painted in a faun's foot, and requested the £4 he owed her, his reaction remained the class- and gender-infused one of Boswell and Curwen in different confrontational circumstances. She demanded the money, Haydon said, 'with the air of an old demirep duchess' and was a ' ... bullying insolence of a short, wicked-eyed, wrinkled, waddling, gin-drinking, dirty-ruffled landlady – poor old bit of asthmatic humanity!'[110] However low he had sunk, he still felt his landlady was both beneath him and vulgar for seeking payment.

———————

A parting of the ways was, then, most often a natural consequence of the flexibility of lodging. It was expected and anticipated to some degree by the parties. A small percentage of partings was fatally terminal. Sometimes these were also natural. Where tragic and unexpected, they reflected the imperfect nature of London's infrastructure and for the historian offer a rare glimpse of the density of occupation and variety of ways in which its housing stock was used.

For landlords/ladies a constant imperative was avoiding the Scylla and Charybdis of, on the one hand, unpayable rent arrears or, on the other, an extended vacancy period when the room was unlet and rental income dried up. Partings after disputes over money were frequent and laid bare the fundamental business nature of a lodging arrangement. Landlords/ladies were also motivated by the need to protect the good reputation of their household by overseeing the activities taking place within the home. In the sexual arena, this vigilance tended to operate against female lodgers and female servants rather than gentlemen lodgers. The latter indeed often deployed the prevailing gendered class ideology of domesticity to declaim against any surveillance and control, resenting this as an attack on their gentlemanliness. Both male and female lodgers protested that it was landlords/ladies who were at fault, behaving in a vulgar and mercenary manner in the home, a place supposedly a sanctuary from such considerations. At a milliner's in Fleet Street, Pilkington's landlady was 'neither better nor worse than a mercenary Town Jilt ... ' and Curwen, a merchant and man of commerce himself, failed to recognize the same business skills in his hosts, railing against landladies generally: 'People in this line, here, have no other motive, consideration or rule of conduct but interest' (see Chapter 5).[111]

For lodgers, the ability to move on allowed them to adjust their accommodation to the vagaries of their incomes and other needs, such as peace and quiet or convenience. For some (Swift and Curwen for instance) the sheer volume of lodgings on the market across the respectable streets of London fostered a nagging sense of unease, a feeling that they were missing out, that there might always be something better, or better value. For the more demanding lodgers it therefore only took a small difference of opinion with a landlord/lady for offence to be taken and new rooms sought.

7

Conclusion

In following the journey through the world of London's private lodgings from both a lodger's and landlord's/lady's perspective, the immediate impression is one of long-term continuity rather than change. Aspects of lodging found in Chaucer and in the lives of sixteenth- and seventeenth-century lodgers survived into the Georgian period. Many of Davidoff's findings for the later-nineteenth and early-twentieth centuries are equally true of the century before: eating arrangements, sexual risk, the distinction between private lodgings and the common lodging house, lodgers obtaining the comforts of a home without obligation or commitment, landladies entering a world of colourful social contacts.[1] Late-nineteenth-century novelist George Gissing (1857–1903), who both lived in and set his works in lodgings, would have had no difficulty in recognizing the Georgian antecedents.[2] Indeed, there are continuities even to the present day: homeowners are free to take a paying guest into their home without any regulation (other than the need to pay income tax above the tax-free allowance). It is only the bottom end of the market, the common lodging houses, today known as 'houses in multiple occupation' (HMOs), that since the nineteenth century has been subject to statutory sanitary and safety inspection and control.[3] The call for this reform was very much anticipated by eighteenth-century anxieties around cheap lodgings in the allegedly lawless and filthy quarters of the capital, anxieties that played a large part in delineating its slum districts.

The respectable private lodging market – its scale, the districts of London where lodgers were most likely to be found, and the men and women who hosted lodgers – were constant from even earlier than the period discussed in this work, and beyond it into the nineteenth century. Lodging locations were accurately represented in fiction, drama, and images. The City retained its position as a lodging node for merchants and other business-people, but as the built envelope of London sprawled so too did lodging, moving with housing development into Marylebone, Islington, and Kensington, for example. The vast pool of lodgers seeking rooms was at the tail end of the process of funding this physical expansion. Their presence was sometimes anticipated by builders (two street doors, for example) and demonstrates just how removed from reality were the pronouncements of architectural theorists such as Ware on room use. Lodging played a vital part in enabling the expansion of London's commerce and industry by providing almost instant access to accommodation to new workers. It was therefore a neat and mutually satisfactory solution to the pressure on housing in a metropolis of in-migrants from across Britain and overseas. The size of the market and frequent turnover meant that lodging-rooms were easy to find and easy to leave. For middling-sort landlords/ladies taking lodgers was a ready means of maximizing the income from their assets, financing their other business interests and providing an income stream that gave some protection against adversity in pre-welfare-state England.

There were two changes to lodging practices in the period. The first is a minor one: the market became slightly more formalized with the growth of print media, literacy, and the postal service, all of which added new methods for the two parties to come together. Nevertheless, the pedestrian search for 'to let' cards in the window endured until the twentieth century. The second is more significant: the rich variety of London lodgers. It was a variety that fully represented the population of the teeming proto-imperial city. Only members of the nobility were unlikely to be found in someone else's spare room – and even they might be compelled to lodge *in extremis*, as the Duchess of Northumberland discovered. Otherwise, those in private lodgings ran the gamut from the gentry to artisans. There were men and women in equal numbers, singletons, couples and families, the old and the young, and those somewhere in between. There were also those whose origins lay outside London and England. Some were visiting for a relatively brief period on business or pleasure – William Byrd, James Boswell, Count Kielmansegge, Sophie von La Roche. Others made a more permanent move, eager to benefit from the commercial and cultural opportunities London offered, or to escape problems in their home country: Laetitia Pilkington, Joseph Emin, Samuel Curwen, the French émigrés of the late-eighteenth-century. Lodgers also included men and women of colour: the temporary residents of 'sailortown', and those of African descent who had spent some of their life enslaved and found a certain freedom in the metropolis. Such men and women were at an economic and social disadvantage, however, dependent on a white patron to ease them into work and accommodation, and that generally outside the favoured genteel neighbourhoods. For all these individuals and groups, but especially for strangers new to London, lodging offered comfort, not just the new material comfort identified by Stobart but also the older emotional comfort of human contact, in a family setting with the possibility of creating valuable and lasting networks of friends and support.[4] At its best lodging was a home from home.

This rich variety is in contrast to the depiction of lodging in novels, plays and images. The depictions were, like lodging itself, of long-standing and unchanging. There were well-established and often comedic stereotypes of characters and situations before the eighteenth century which persisted through to the twentieth century. Seaside-postcard images of intrusive landladies, terrible cooking and sex-mad honeymoon or unmarried couples are not so far removed from Egerton's *Unfortunate Discovery* or the 'I am to be let alone' prints. These fictional representations suggested that lodging was a dubious and transient affair, the resort of those down on their luck and engaged in immoral activity – from coining to sex work – and that landlords and ladies, but especially ladies, were either complicit in this or were nosy gossips and venal to a fault.

There were very many respectable and long-term lodgers (Swift, Sterne, Inchbald, Wilkie), but the characterization of lodgers as impermanent did have some limited truth. Clearly those in precarious occupations were likely to be living in the most flexible and inexpensive accommodation. The garret-poet had his counterparts in lived experience (Johnson, Goldsmith, Chatterton), and was even exploited by Opie, whose mentor John Wolcot encouraged him to act the part in a top-floor room at Orange Court, Leicester Fields, to encourage public interest in him as an artist.[5] Most singlewoman lodgers, on the other hand, in no way conformed to the sex worker stereotype. The evidence of life-writing shows them to be lodging as much from a desire for independence or for company as their male counterparts. Where they lacked a private income, they used what skills they had to maintain this vital independence: writing, sewing, laundering, small retail businesses (Behn, Pilkington, Margaret Nicholson, the Compton Street fire victims, Mary Lamb). Above all there was no shame involved in being a lodger. It was repeatedly stressed that it was respectable and genteel. For young men in particular, but also for officers on half-pay for example, it could be fun and carefree. These many lodgers from all backgrounds were not necessarily down on their luck. Many freely chose to lodge for the independence, flexibility, and experience it brought. It was no disgrace to be a lodger rather than a householder. On the contrary, it was perfectly possible to maintain one's respectability and gentility while lodging. A great deal of effort was invested by both parties in ensuring that this was the case, that the lodger was less a customer than, as the Victorian euphemism would have it, 'a paying guest'. There is, therefore, little evidence of Davidoff's nineteenth- and twentieth-century generalized 'moral opprobrium' attached to private lodging in itself.[6] Lodging is therefore a salutary reminder that the eighteenth-century political slogan 'Liberty and Property' did not mean that home ownership was a widespread aspiration in this period.

Consideration of lodging practices also opens up to more detailed scrutiny several interconnected historiographical themes of the long eighteenth century: domesticity, class, commerce, and gender. Examining lodging compels us to reconsider eighteenth-century domesticity. Lodging was a domestic compromise for London's thousands of landlords and ladies, as novels and plays suggested (Amelia Booth's Mrs Ellison and Mrs Haycock in *Miss Lucy in Town*). Hosts gave up space and privacy within what was ideally conceived as a family home (not only did Hickey's target Ann Malton sleep in the back parlour, her brothers slept in the kitchen).[7] Hosts also tied themselves to a twenty-four-hour cycle of work for cash within that home, and exposed household members to stranger-danger, whether sexual or, for example, the carelessness around fire exhibited by Oliver Goldsmith and Thomas Carter. On the other hand, they sometimes gained from the cachet of lodgers who were celebrities or in some other way distinguished. A little of their glamour and perhaps their manners may have worn off on them – though where it did it was of course denounced as social-climbing.

Lodgers similarly lacked privacy and were subject to the loss of control over daily life that living in someone else's house entailed. They were independent in that they were not a part of the patriarchal household, yet at the same time dependent – living there only as long as the householder permitted it. Nevertheless, most of them called these rooms 'home', selecting them on the basis of their comfort and amenities. Both men and women lodgers went to some lengths to personalize them with furnishings and objects that carried meaning and brought material and emotional comfort. In this respect lodging-rooms were domestic spaces, albeit cramped and multipurpose ones within another's domestic space. Within these compact spaces some lodgers (Johnson, the Blakes, Wilkie, the Lambs) were able to produce works of enduring beauty. Focussing on the density of house occupation and the smallness of lodging-rooms also gives us a fresh perspective on eighteenth-century motives for associating outside the home in coffeehouses, inns, taverns, and other public spaces. These, rather than their rooms, were the sites where many male lodgers created a social identity for themselves, out of necessity as much as by choice.[8]

The stereotyping and lived experiences of landlords/ladies are more complex. Life-writing and other sources reveal that they were indeed drawn from the middling-sort upper artisan, trading, and retailing backgrounds of stories and dramas. Social class was deeply inscribed in lodging practices. Houses with lodgers contained the middling-sort householders alongside many other people who formed a cross-section of society, all at the same time and in a limited space. Within the house they were physically graded and separated according to the desirability and cost of the rooms, a fact of which they were often acutely aware, as *Olla Podrida* parodied. However, there was inevitable mixing both as rooms were serviced by the landlord/lady or their servants, and in the common parts – hall, kitchen stairs, landing, parlour. This mixing was far more intimate than the superficial social mixing at sites such as Vauxhall pleasure gardens or the theatre. It produced an enhanced knowledge of the way of life of one's social inferiors and superiors, but it was not democratizing, and took no immediate political shape. If anything, it deepened the gulf between the trading middling-sort and their genteel lodgers who often felt socially, even if not financially, more secure. When tensions and disputes arose these lodgers soon descended to high-handed and scornful treatment, and to snobbish insults. Nevertheless, throughout the Georgian period it continued to be a respectable and normal way of living for both parties. Despite what Boswell felt was a bad experience at the Terries' and his more settled, professional status, it is notable that he was not deterred from again lodging in middling-sort households on his next trip to London in 1768.

Density of occupation and social mixing also increased the opportunities for male lodgers to take entitled sexual advantage of servants and other women in the household. Given the importance of respectability to the middling sort it was therefore unsurprising that landlords/ladies took a keen interest in what went on under their roof. However, what for them was reasonable surveillance (the Maltons with Hickey, for example) was to the lodger an insulting intrusion. This surveillance did not operate to protect the women involved. The typical response was to remove the female 'temptress' from the scene and let the lodger relationship wither on the vine.

At the core of both satire and lodgers' snobbery around landlords/ladies was a degree of disdain for the very idea of using spare rooms in the family home to make money, even though lodgers were necessarily the clientele for this practice. The home was an increasingly idealized space, a refuge for the compact nuclear family unit bound together by common aims and affection. Lodging ran counter to this by introducing strangers with no tie to the family other than the weekly handover of cash. It was therefore disruptive of the ideal. A private lodging agreement was legally a contract, typically an oral one. It was enacted in the private space of the home, but it lay outside the three private legal personal relationships considered in Blackstone's *Commentaries* (from which we have seen Gansel quote): master and servant, husband and wife, and parent and child.[9] In an effort to conceal the naked reality that lodging was commercial and thus maintain the ideal of home, landlords/ladies, and lodgers often conspired to locate it somewhere within Blackstone's three relationships. Landladies were reimagined as mothers, potential partners, or skivvies. Advertisements shunned mentioning the exact price and instead focussed on reimagining lodgings as an arrangement made as much for reasons of sociability as for money. Sociability was the fervent hope of lodgers such as Curwen, who entered each new host household full of eager expectation of a surrogate family, of a mother or partner to care for him, or of a servant/nurse at his beck and call. However, in truth money – commerce – always lay at the heart of the deal. When either the money or the extras, services, and attention lodgers expected were not forthcoming they were oblivious of their contracted terms, relationships quickly soured, and the landlord/lady was denounced as mercenary and heartless. Successful relationships were possible (Franklin, Inchbald, Wilkie) but were highly contingent on the personalities of the 'couple', and their willingness to adapt and forgive.

On becoming landladies, women moved into the active lodgings marketplace, although being close to the non-market work of managing and provisioning a household it was often an invisible participation, only coming to the surface after some accident such as the Compton Street fire or the crimes discussed in the forgoing chapters. Life-writing by lodgers is a previously untapped and invaluable source for uncovering these many middling-sort working women. By reading against the grain we can see these women as a skilled and highly professional cohort, often with their own informal networks of other landladies. They had to understand how their rooms fitted into the wider marketplace, promote them at the right price, assess each potential lodger who called, negotiate a profitable rent – what was included and what counted as extras – then supervise the daily routine of the expanded houseful, defuse dissatisfaction, tactfully referee disputes and, finally, know when to issue a notice to quit. When a landlady was unavailable to perform all these complex tasks a lodging household could rapidly disintegrate: on death (Johnson's Mrs Norris) or, more catastrophically, when Mrs Hutchins was removed to a madhouse and Count de Gripière was killed. However, gendered attitudes to work and the home accorded them little recognition for this professionalism. Instead they ran the risk of objectification, of becoming 'public women' in a society in which female engagement in commerce implied that their bodies were also commercialized, what Sophie Carter calls 'packaged commodities competing for the attention of the customer; textually arrayed for the delectation of the male consumer'.[10] The fate of murdered Anne King and the 'I am to be let alone' prints show the harsh treatment that could be expected.

Whether a primary or secondary occupation, then, accommodating lodgers was a common experience in certain parts of London: for landlords/ladies as ordinary an activity as selling bread, books, or breeches, and for lodgers a fully socially-acceptable way of life. The lodging business was therefore no different from the general circulation of business and money hymned in Defoe, or in Mandeville's *Fable of the Bees*, and epitomized in 'It Narratives'. It was an unconstrained capitalist supply-and-demand marketplace. It made sense for the prudent householder and it underpinned with flexible accommodation the choice-driven, consumer-oriented society that was emerging in the eighteenth century. Although they may not have recognized it, when landlords or ladies offered their spare rooms for rent, or lodgers quested the perfect room, all were alike consumers behaving in the new way that Adam Smith identified:

> The great source of both the misery and disorders of human life, seems to arise from over-rating the difference between one permanent situation and another … The person under the influence of any of those extravagant passions, is not only miserable in his actual situation, but is often disposed to disturb the peace of society, in order to arrive at that which he so foolishly admires.[11]

Notes

Chapter 1

1   'The Portland Estate in Soho Fields', in *SofL*, XXXIII and XXXIV, *St Anne Soho*, ed. F. H. W. Sheppard (London, 1966), 37–41, *British History Online*, http://www.british-history.ac.uk/survey-london/vols33-4/pp37-41 (accessed 8 October 2018).

2   Elizabeth McKellar, *The Birth of Modern London: The Development and Design of the City 1660–1720* (Manchester: Manchester University Press, 1999), 2.

3   For the weather in June 1785 see *GM*, 'Meteorological Diaries', May 1786, 358.

4   This is a composite and semi-fictionalized account of the fire based on the papers of the Committee for the Relief of the Sufferers by Fire, CWAC: A2269 and 2270 and contemporary press accounts in the *Morning Post*, 28 June 1785, the *Lady's Magazine*, June 1785, 334, and *St James's Chronicle or the British Evening Post*, 16 June 1785.

5   CWAC: A2269.

6   On fires see E. L. Jones, S. Porter, and M. Turner, *Gazetteer of English Urban Fire Disasters, 1500–1900* (Norwich: Historical Geography Research Series 13, 1984).

7   CWAC: A2269.

8   LMA: WJ/SPD 72–136.

9   Peter Laslett, ed., with Richard Wall, *Household and Family in Past Time: Comparative Studies in the Size and Structure of the Domestic Group over the Last Three Centuries in England, France, Serbia, Japan and Colonial North America, with Further Materials from Western Europe* (Cambridge: CUP, 1972), 24–36.

10 John Tallis, *London Street Views 1838–40* (London: London Topographical Society, 2nd edn, 2002, 1st pub. 1969).

11 The first national census took place in 1801. Lodgers (and their 'households') were first captured as a group in 1851 when the returns included a requirement that heads of households state the relationship to him/her of each resident. Lodgers were found in 12 per cent of households and accounted for 5 per cent of the total population. However, imprecision arises from the different approaches to lodgers taken by different census enumerators. Lodgers may be included within the category 'Visitors', for example (Michael Anderson, 'Households, Families and Individuals: Some Preliminary Results from the National Sample from the 1851 Census of Great Britain', *Continuity & Change* 3.03 (1988), 421–38, 428). For the sixteenth and seventeenth centuries see Vanessa Harding, *People in*

Place: Families, Households and Housing in Early Modern London (London: Centre for Metropolitan History, 2008) and 'Families and Housing in Seventeenth-Century London', *Parergon* 24.2 (2007), 115–38.

12 The slightly awkward 'landlord/lady' has been adopted as a shorthand way of avoiding gendering the hosts.

13 For the everyday as a subject of enquiry see Joanne Hollows, *Domestic Cultures* (Maidenhead: Open University Press, 2008) and Tony Bennett and Diane Watson, eds, *Understanding Everyday Life* (Oxford: Blackwell, 2002).

14 John Summerson, *Georgian London* (New Haven CT: YUP, 2003, 1st pub. 1945); Peter Guillery, *The Small House in Eighteenth-Century London* (New Haven CT: YUP, 2004); Todd Longstaffe-Gowan, *The London Square: Gardens in the Midst of Town* (New Haven CT: YUP, 2012).

15 Amanda Vickery, *Behind Closed Doors: At Home in Georgian England* (New Haven CT: YUP, 2009); Karen Harvey, *The Little Republic: Masculinity and Domestic Authority in Eighteenth-Century Britain* (Oxford: OUP, 2012).

16 http://www.studiesofhome.qmul.ac.uk/.

17 Bridget Hill, *Servants: English Domestics in the Eighteenth Century* (Oxford: Clarendon, 1996); Tim Meldrum, *Domestic Service and Gender: Life and Work in the London Household, 1660–1750* (Harlow: Longman, 2000); Tessa Chynoweth, 'Domestic Service and Domestic Space in London, 1750–1800' (unpublished PhD thesis, Queen Mary University of London, 2016).

18 Jon Stobart, ed., *The Comforts of Home in Western Europe 1700–1900* (London: Bloomsbury Academic, 2020), 2–7.

19 Chiara Briganti and Kathy Mezei, *Living with Strangers: Bedsits and Boarding Houses in Modern English Life, Literature and Film* (London: Bloomsbury, 2018); Frederick A. Pottle, ed., *Boswell's London Journal, 1762–3* (London: Futura, 1982, 1st pub. 1950), 64.

20 Sue Heath and Rachael Scicluna, 'Putting up (with) the Paying Guest: Negotiating Hospitality and the Boundaries of the Commercial Home in Private Lodging Arrangements', *Families, Relationships & Societies* 20.20 (2019), 1–18.

21 Dorothy M. George, *London Life in the Eighteenth Century* (Harmondsworth: Penguin, 1966, 1st pub. 1925); Peter Earle, *A City Full of People: Men and Women of London, 1650–1750* (London: Methuen, 1994); Guillery, *Small House*, 30–1; Jerry White, *London in the Eighteenth Century: A Great and Monstrous Thing* (London: Bodley Head, 2012), 108–13.

22 Joanne McEwan and Pamela Sharpe, '"It Buys Me Freedom": Genteel Lodging in Late-Seventeenth- and Eighteenth-Century London', *Parergon* 24.2 (2007), 139–61.

23 Leonore Davidoff, *Worlds Between: Historical Perspectives on Gender and Class* (Cambridge: Polity, 1995), Ch. 5, 151–79, 'The Separation of Home and Work? Landladies and Lodgers in Nineteenth- and Twentieth-Century England'.

24 See Amanda Vickery, 'An Englishman's Home Is His Castle? Thresholds, Boundaries and Privacies in the Eighteenth-Century London House', *Past & Present* 199 (2008), 147–73 and Hannah Greig and Giorgio Riello, 'Eighteenth-Century Interiors: Redesigning the Georgian', *Journal of Design History* 20.4 (2007), 273–89.

25 Isaac Ware, *A Complete Body of Architecture …*, 2 vols (Farnborough: Gregg, facsimile edn, 1971, 1st pub. 1768), I, 293, 345–7.

26 McKellar, *Birth of Modern London*, 221.

27 Ibid., 158.

28 Sir Josiah Child, *A New Discourse of Trade* … (Glasgow: Foulis, 1751, 1st pub. 1690), 67.

29 Adam Smith, *The Wealth of Nations*, 2 vols (London: Penguin, 1999, 1st pub. 1776), I, 119, 266.

30 John Brown, *An Estimate of the Manners and Principles of the Times* (London: L. Davis & C. Reymers, 1757). On the rise of a consumer society see Neil McKendrick, John Brewer, and J. H. Plumb, *The Birth of a Consumer Society: The Commercialization of Eighteenth-Century England* (London: Hutchinson, 1983). For an overview of the debates about consumption and luxury in the period see Maxine Berg and Elizabeth Eger, eds, *Luxury in the Eighteenth Century: Debates, Desires and Delectable Goods* (Basingstoke: Palgrave, 2003).

31 Ch. 8, 293–343, 'Teresa Cornelys's London – Public Pleasures', in White, *London in the Eighteenth Century*; Phyllis Hembry, *The English Spa, 1560–1815* (London: Athlone, 1990); Benjamin Heller, 'Leisure and the Use of Domestic Space in Georgian London', *Historical Journal* 53.3 (2010), 623–45.

32 Penelope J. Corfield, 'Class by Name and Number in Eighteenth-Century Britain', *History* 72 (1987), 38–61.

33 Samuel Johnson, *A Dictionary of the English Language*, 2 vols (London: Rivington, 6th edn, 1785, 1st pub. 1755).

34 *MC*, 25 May 1772, 27 June 1785.

35 Susan Whyman, *Sociability and Power in Late-Stuart England: The Cultural Worlds of the Verneys, 1660–1720* (Oxford: OUP, 2002), 63.

36 McKellar, *Birth of Modern London*.

37 For late-seventeenth-century population counts and their problems see Kevin Schurer and Tom Arkell, eds, *Surveying the People: The Interpretation and Use of Document Sources for the Study of Population in the Later Seventeenth Century* (Oxford: Leopard's Head, 1992), quotation from 'Introduction', 1; Gregory King, *Natural and Political Observations and Conclusions Upon the State and Condition of England* (mss 1696, 1st pub. George Chalmers, 1802) in George E. Barnett, ed., *Two Tracts by Gregory King* (Baltimore MD: Johns Hopkins Press, 1936), 11–56.

38 Sir John Hawkins, *The Life of Samuel Johnson, LLD* (London: Buckland, Rivington et al., 1787), 207–8 (fn.).

39   John Cary, *General Plan for Explaining the Different Trusts of the Turnpike Gates in the Vicinity of the Metropolis* (London: John Cary, 1790). Note that the map shows Waterloo and Blackfriars bridges and the New (Euston) Road which had not been constructed in the first half of the century.

40   Jonathan Swift, Abigail Williams, ed., *Journal to Stella: Letters to Esther Johnson and Rebecca Dingley, 1710–13* (Cambridge: CUP, 2013), 191–238.

41   Andrew Oliver, ed., *The Journal of Samuel Curwen, Loyalist*, 2 vols (Cambridge MA: HUP, 1972).

42   Alexander P. D. Penrose, ed., *The Autobiography and Memoirs of Benjamin Robert Haydon, 1786–1846* (London: G. Bell, 1927), 286; *ODNB*: entry for Morland.

43   Richard Horwood, *Plan of the Cities of London and Westminster, the Borough of Southwark, and Parts Adjoining (1792–9)*, http://www.romanticlondon.org/explore-horwoods-plan/#20/51.48906/-0.13119.

44   *MC*, 19 April 1780; 17 December 1794; 14 April 1795.

45   For the population and growth of early modern London see Paul Griffiths and Mark S. R. Jenner, eds, *Londinopolis: Essays in the Cultural and Social History of Early Modern London* (Manchester: Manchester University Press, 2000), 2.

46   Faramerz Dabhoiwala, *The Origins of Sex: A History of the First Sexual Revolution* (London: Allen Lane, 2012); Earle, *City Full of People*, 60–2; White, *London in the Eighteenth Century*, 469–509.

47   OBOL, search conducted 19 March 2020.

48   Kevin Schurer, 'Variations in Household Structure in the Late Seventeenth Century: Towards a Regional Analysis', Ch. 12, 253–78 in Schurer and Arkell, *Surveying the People*, 268.

49   S. J. Wright, 'Sojourners and Lodgers in a Provincial Town: The Evidence from Eighteenth-Century Ludlow', *Urban History* 17 (1990), 14–35.

50   Di Cooper and Moira Donald, 'Households and "Hidden" Kin in Early-Nineteenth-Century England: Four Case Studies in Suburban Exeter, 1821–61', *Continuity & Change* 10.2 (1995), 257–78.

51   Hembry, *English Spa*.

52   Using the digitized *17th and 18th Century Burney Newspapers Collection* (https://www.gale.com/intl/c/17th-and-18th-century-burney-newspapers-collection), *Morning Chronicle* advertisements were searched for the term 'lodging'. Obvious repeat advertisements, results for lodgings outside London, or where 'lodging' was used in a more general way (typically as a synonym for 'bedroom' in a sale or long lease advertisement for a whole house) were deleted. The *Burney Collection* does not include every issue of the newspaper and has duplicate copies of some. 'Lodging' (total 1,207 hits) proved much more fruitful than 'lodger'. Other contemporary publications were test-searched in the same way but did not produce anything like the number of hits. The research was undertaken in December 2018.

53 The non-white population was estimated by contemporaries at 15,000, though some historians believe the true figure was up to 10,000 (White, *London in the Eighteenth Century*, 127).

54 For the 'horizons of expectation' paradigm of reader reception theory in which a set of contemporary cultural norms, assumptions and criteria are understood to be brought by a reader to any text, see Hans Robert Jauss, trans. Timothy Bahti, *Toward an Aesthetic of Reception* (Minneapolis MN: University of Minnesota Press, 1982).

55 On 'interpretive communities' see Stanley E. Fish, *Is There a Text in This Class? The Authority of Interpretive Communities* (Cambridge MA: HUP, 1980), 167–73.

56 Examples include Eliza Haywood, *A Present for a Servant Maid* (London: T. Gardner, 1743); the texts discussed in Tabitha Kenlon, *Conduct Books and the History of the Ideal Woman* (London: Anthem Press, 2020) and Erasmus Jones, *The Man of Manners: or, Plebeian Polish'd …* (London: J. Roberts, 1737).

Chapter 2

1 Clara Reeve, *The Progress of Romance …*, 2 vols (Dublin: Price, Exshaw *et al.*, 1785), II, 111.

2 J. Paul Hunter 'The Novel and Social/Cultural History', Ch. 2, 9–40 in John Richetti, ed., *The Cambridge Companion to the Eighteenth-Century Novel* (Cambridge: CUP, 1996), 23.

3 Geoffrey Chaucer, *The Canterbury Tales* (1342–1400), http://www.librarius.com/cantales.htm (accessed 6 March 2019).

4 Griffiths and Jenner, *Londinopolis*, 2.

5 William Baer, 'Planning for Growth and Growth Controls in Early Modern Northern Europe: Part 2: The Evolution of London's Practice 1580–1680', *Town Planning Review* 7.3 (2007), 257–77.

6 For examples of early-modern women lodgers see the token books for St Saviour, Southwark 1571–1643, LMA: P92/SAV/178–321.

7 Revd Alexander B. Grosart, *The Works of Gabriel Harvey …*, 3 vols (London: printed for private circulation, 1884–5), I, *The Second Letter*, 162–76.

8 Thomas Nashe, *Have With You to Saffron Walden* (London: John Danter, 1596), 25.

9 Richard Lichfield, *The Trimming of Thomas Nashe Gentleman* (London: Philip Scarlet, 1597), 19.

10 'Joan Silverpin' was a nickname for a prostitute and a picket hatch was a street door with a grille in its upper half, typical of a brothel. Thomas Middleton, *The Black Book* in Revd Alexander Dyce, ed., *The Works of Thomas Middleton*, 5 vols (London: Edward Lumley, 1840), V, 526–7.

11 John Dryden, *The Wild Gallant: A Comedy* (London: H. Herringman, 1669), 5, 7.

12 Janet Todd, *Sensibility: An Introduction* (London: Methuen, 1986), 65.

13 Daniel Defoe, *The History and Remarkable Life of the Truly Honourable Colonel Jacque ...*, 2 vols (Edinburgh: Ballantyne, 1810, 1st pub. 1722), I, 11, 23, 69, 110.

14 Daniel Defoe, *The Fortunes and Misfortunes of the Famous Moll Flanders, &c.* (London: Penguin, 1989, 1st pub. 1722), 103, 108, 111, 156–70, 206, 223–4, 229, 253.

15 Ibid., 184.

16 Daniel Defoe, *Roxana, or, The Fortunate Mistress* (Oxford: OUP, 1996, 1st pub. 1724).

17 For example, *A Tour Thro' the Whole Island of Great Britain* (1724–7); *The Complete English Tradesman* (1726); *A Plan of the English Commerce* (London: Rivington, 1728).

18 Bernard Mandeville, *The Fable of The Bees: Or, Private Vices, Publick Benefits* (London: Edmund Parker, 1705); Hawkins, *Life of Johnson,* 263 (fn.).

19 Scholarship on definitions and characteristics of the eighteenth-century middling-sort includes Jonathan Barry and Christopher Brooks, eds, *The Middling Sort of People: Culture, Society and Politics in England, 1550–1800* (Basingstoke: Macmillan, 1994); Penelope J. Corfield 'Class by Name and Number'; Peter Earle, *The Making of the English Middle Class: Business, Society and Family Life in London, 1660–1730* (London: Methuen, 1989); Henry R. French, 'The Search for the "Middle Sort of People" in England, 1600–1800', *Historical Journal* 43 (2000), 277–93 and Margaret R. Hunt, *The Middling Sort: Commerce, Gender, and the Family in England, 1680–1780* (Berkeley CA: University of California Press, 1996), quotation 209.

20 *Olla Podrida*, July 1787.

21 See fan in BM collection, 1891,0713.518.

22 Fan: BM, 1891,0713.518; images of crowds at print-shop windows: NPG, D12901 and BM, 1878,0511.654 and J,5.46 and discussion in James Baker, *The Business of Satirical Prints in Late-Georgian England* (Basingstoke: Palgrave Macmillan, 2017), 161.

23 BL: 1848, 0708.19–21.

24 BM: 1868,0822.1541.

25 BM: S,2.87–99.

26 RCT: RCIN 810245.

27 *The Lottery Ticket, or, The Sunshine of Hope* and *The Ticket a Blank, or, The Clouds of Despair* (London: Bowles Carrington, 1792), LWL: 792.09.29.01+ and 792.09.29.02+.

28 LWL: 796.11.28.01.

29 LWL: 777.07.16.01.2+.

30 No. 5, see BM: 1935,0522.10.132.

31 *SofL, South-East Marylebone*, LI and LII, draft Ch. 22, 5–6, https://www.ucl.ac.uk/
    bartlett/architecture/sites/bartlett/files/chapter22_great_portland_street.pdf
    (accessed 20 March 2020).

32 BM: 1866,1114.647 (Anon., 1798), 1935,0522.8.191 (Charles Williams, 1814), and
    1951,0411.4.4 (George Cruikshank, 1814).

33 LWL: 825.00.00.63.

34 Anon, *Low-Life: Or One Half of the World Knows Not How the Other Half Live …*
    (London: John Lever, 3rd edn, 1764, 1st pub. *c*. 1752). See also Carolyn Steedman,
    'Cries Unheard, Sights Unseen: Writing the Eighteenth-Century Metropolis',
    Representations 118.1 (2012), 28–71.

35 Ibid., 2, 5, 10, 19, 21, 24, 31, 33, 44, 55, 80, 102.

36 James Beresford, *The Miseries of Human Life …*, 2 vols (London: W. Miller, 8th edn,
    1807), I, 254–5.

37 Jonathan Lamb, *The Things Things Say* (Woodstock: Princeton University Press,
    2011).

38 BM: 1948,0214.606. On fire more generally see Robin Pearson, 'The Impact of
    Fire and Fire Insurance on Eighteenth-Century English Town Buildings and Their
    Populations', Ch. 3, 67–93 in Carole Shammas, ed., *Investing in the Early Modern
    Built Environment: Europeans, Asians, Settler and Indigenous Societies* (Leiden: Brill,
    2012).

39 Samuel Johnson, *The Rambler* 161 (October 1751).

40 Henry Fielding, ed. David Blewett, *Amelia* (Harmondsworth: Penguin, 1987, 1st
    pub. 1751), 240.

41 John Cleland, *Fanny Hill, or, Memoirs of a Woman of Pleasure* (London: Penguin,
    1985, 1st pub. 1748–9), 70–2, 87, 88, 112–13.

42 G. J. Barker-Benfield, *The Culture of Sensibility: Sex and Society in Eighteenth-
    Century Britain* (Chicago: University of Chicago Press, 1992).

43 Todd, *Sensibility*, 2.

44 Ian Watt, *The Rise of the Novel: Studies in Defoe, Richardson and Fielding*
    (Harmondsworth: Penguin, 1972, 1st pub. 1957), 155.

45 Ibid., 157; Dabhoiwala, *Origins of Sex*, 165–6.

46 Margaret Doody, 'Samuel Richardson: Fiction and Knowledge', Ch. 5, 90–119
    in Richetti ed., *Cambridge Companion to the Eighteenth-Century Novel*, 98;
    Dabhoiwala, *Origins of Sex*, 169–79.

47 Amy Erickson, 'Eleanor Mosley and Other Milliners in the City of London
    Companies 1700–50', *History Workshop Journal* 71.1 (2011), 147–72.

48 Samuel Richardson, *Clarissa, or The History of a Young Lady* (London: Penguin,
    2004, 1st pub. 1748), 469–72 (letter 129).

49 Ibid., 529 (letter 155).

50 Ibid., 756 (letter 230).

51 Jennie Batchelor and Megan Hiatt, eds, *The Histories of some of the Penitents in the Magdalen-House, as Supposed to be Related by Themselves* (London: Pickering & Chatto, 2007).

52 On the Hospital see Miles Ogborn, 'The Magdalen Hospital', Ch. 2, 39–74, *Spaces of Modernity: London's Geographies 1680–1780* (New York: Guilford Press, 1998).

53 Batchelor and Hiatt, *The Histories*, 35, 43, 50.

54 Ibid., 149, 178.

55 Henry Mackenzie, *The Man of Feeling* (London: Strahan & Cadell, 1783), 109, 136–7.

56 On Burney's concern with 'maintaining appearances' see Markman Ellis, *The Politics of Sensibility: Race, Gender and Commerce in the Sentimental Novel* (Cambridge: CUP, 1996), 2.

57 Amy Erickson, 'Esther Sleepe, Fan-Maker and Her Family', *Eighteenth-Century Life* 42.2 (2018), 15–37; Mme D'Arblay (Frances Burney), *Memoirs of Doctor Burney* (Philadelphia PA: Key & Biddle, 1833).

58 Frances Burney, ed. Edward A. Bloom, *Evelina: Or, the History of a Young Lady's Entrance into the World* (Oxford: OUP, 2002, 1st pub. 1778), 176.

59 James Cobb's *The First Floor*, which was performed, is also largely set in a shop, pastrycook Mrs Pattypan's in Piccadilly, and a first-floor lodging-room above (James Cobb, *The First Floor; a Farce in Two Acts* (London: C. Dilly, 2nd edn, 1787)).

60 Frances Burney, *The Witlings*, Act 1, *ll.* 62, 157–8 in Frances Burney, *The Witlings and The Woman Hater*, Peter Sabor and Geoffrey Sill, eds (London: Pickering & Chatto, 1997), 4, 7.

61 Many of these biographies are collected in Julie Peakman, ed., *Whore Biographies, 1700–1825*, 8 vols (London: Pickering & Chatto, 2006).

62 Tobias Smollett, *The Adventures of Peregrine Pickle ...* (London: for the author, 1751).

63 See Anna Clark, *Scandal: The Sexual Politics of the British Constitution* (Princeton NJ: Princeton University Press, 2004) and Gillian Williamson, *British Masculinity in the Gentleman's Magazine, 1731–1815* (Basingstoke: Palgrave Macmillan, 2016), 128–34.

64 Anon., *Memoirs of the Celebrated Miss Fanny Murray ...*, 2 vols (Dublin: S. Smith, 2nd edn,1759).

65 Ibid., I, 91, 93, 101, 198; II, 182.

66 Anon., *Trials for Adultery, or, The History of Divorces ...*, 7 vols (London: S. Bladon, 1779–80); e.g. *Harris's List of Covent Garden Ladies, or, Man of Pleasure's Kalender for the Year 1793* (London: 'H. Ranger', 1793).

67 *Trials for Adultery*, II, 1–24.

68 Francis Grose, *A Classical Dictionary of the Vulgar Tongue* (London: S. Hooper, 1785).

69   Janet Ing Freeman, 'Jack Harris and "Honest Ranger": The Publication and Prosecution of *Harris's List of Covent-Garden Ladies, 1760–95*', *The Library* 13.4 (2012), 423–56.

70   *Murray Memoirs*, I, 100–1.

71   Library of Congress, PC3 – *Harris's List; or, Cupid's London Directory*.

72   See the UCL Bloomsbury Project, Ch. 30 at https://www.ucl.ac.uk/bartlett/ architecture/sites/bartlett/files/chapter30_the_berners_estate.pdf, 5, 6, 10, 11 (accessed 29 May 2019).

73   *Harris's List* (1793), 1–3, 24–5, 85–7; Hallie Rubenhold, *The Covent Garden Ladies: Pimp General Jack and the Extraordinary Story of Harris's List* (Stroud: Tempus, 2005), 158.

74   Rubenhold, *Covent Garden Ladies,* 158.

75   RCT: RCIN 810222.

76   Henry Peacham, ed. Virgil B. Heltzel, *The Complete Gentleman, The Truth of the Times; and The Art of Living in London* (Ithaca NY: Cornell University Press, 1962, 1st pub. 1622), 244, 248.

77   Revd John Trusler, *The London Adviser and Guide …* (London: for the author, 1786), 1–2.

78   Samuel Leigh, *Leigh's New Picture of London …* (London: for the author, 1822).

79   Trusler, *London Adviser*, 5–6, 157.

80   Grose, *Dictionary of the Vulgar Tongue.*

81   OBOL: trial of Henry Watts, t18060219–69.

82   Underwood *v.* Burrows (1835) 7 Carrington and Payne 26; *Morning Post*, 9 October 1835; *The London Gazette* (1841), I, 1566.

83   *Lee v. Gansel*, (1774) 1 Cowper 1; Johann Wilhelm von Archenholz, *A Picture of England …*, trans. from the French (Dublin: P. Byrne, 1791, 1st pub. 1785), 177.

84   William Blackstone, *Commentaries on the Law of England*, 4 vols (London: Strahan & Woodfall, 1795, 1st pub. 1765–70), IV, Ch. 16, 222.

85   https://founders.archives.gov/documents/Franklin/01-14-02-0086#BNFN-01-14-02-0086-fn-0014-ptr (accessed 30 July 2019).

86   OBOL: trial of William Gansel, t17730908–20.

87   *The Newgate Calendar*, 4 vols (London: J. Robins, 1825), II, 483.

88   OBOL: trial of William Gansel.

89   Sir Ambrose Heal, *The London Goldsmiths 1200–1800: A Record of the Names and Addresses of the Craftsmen, Their Shop-Signs and Trade-Cards* (Cambridge: CUP, 1935), 204.

90   John Irving Maxwell, *The Housekeepers' Guide and Lodgers' Adviser …* (London: Cox & Hughes, 1805), 41; William Woodfall, *Law of Landlord and Tenant: To Which Is Added an Appendix of Precedents* (Butterworth, 4th edn, 1814), 178–9.

91   Ibid., Preface.

92   Robert Sutton, *A Complete Guide to Landlords, Tenants, and Lodgers …* (London: Stratford, 1799), title page.

93   James Barry Bird, *The Laws Respecting Landlords, Tenants and Lodgers* …
       (London: W. Clarke, 1794), 80–3.

94   Maxwell, *Housekeepers' Guide*, 41.

95   John Paul, *Every Landlord or Tenant His Own Lawyer* (London: Wm Strahan,
       4th edn,1778), 33. Sutton, *Complete Guide* used the same wording.

96   Woodfall, *Landlord and Tenant*, 179–80.

97   3 & 4 Wm & Mary, ch.9.s.5.

98   John Styles, 'Lodging at the Old Bailey: Lodgings and Their Furnishing in
       Eighteenth-Century London', 61–80 in *Gender, Taste and Material Culture in
       Britain and North America, 1700–1830,* ed. John Styles and Amanda Vickery (New
       Haven CT: YUP, 2006), 61, 66.

99   OBOL: trial of Thomas Saunders, t17231204–32.

100   OBOL: trial of Theodore Gardelle, t17610401–27.

101   *GM*, March 1761, 137; April 1761, 171–8.

102   On disease see Robert Willan, *Reports on the Diseases in London* … (London:
       R. Phillips, 1801).

103   Thomas De Quincy [*sic*], *On Murder Considered as One of the Fine Arts and
       On War: Two Essays* (London: Doppler Press, 1980), 56. *On Murder* was first
       published in *Blackwood's* in 1827 and 1829. This quote is from a 'Postscript'
       written *c.* 1854.

104   Ratcliffe Highway featured in 71 OBOL cases between 1800 and 1811.

105   John Fairburn, *Account of the Life, Death and Interment of John Williamson: The
       Supposed Murderer of the Families of Marr and Williamson; and Self-Destroyer*
       (London: J. Fairburn, 1812), 6.

106   Ibid., 22–3.

107   Ibid., 10.

108   For details of Williams's life see Fairburn, *Account* and *ODNB* entry.

109   Anon., *West Port Murders; or an Authentic Account of the Atrocious Murders
       Committed by Burke and His Associates* … (Edinburgh: Thomas Ireland, junior, 1829),
       121. See also William Roughead, ed., *Burke and Hare* (Edinburgh: Wm Hodge, 1921).

110   *The Times*, 31 January 1829, 4.

111   Ibid., 121–2.

112   Most sources agree that the first sale was of the body of a man who had died of
       natural causes.

113   See https://museum.rcsed.ac.uk/.

Chapter 3

1   Better-off, more permanent lodgers were first enfranchised in 1867 under the
      Representation of the People Act, 30 & 31 Vict. ch.102 of 1867.

2   See for example the late-sixteenth-century surveys 'Views of Inmates' for the parish
     of St Saviour, Southwark, LMA: P92/SAV/1314–17. *Rex v. Whitechapel* (Hilary
     Term, 26 Geo. 3) established that the renting of a furnished lodging at a weekly rent
     was a tenement under the settlement statutes; on lodgers' servants see Joseph Shaw,
     Parish Law ... (London: Henry Lintot, 8th edn, 1753), 260.

3   *SofL*, 'General Introduction', *XXXIII and XXXIV, St Anne Soho*, ed. F. H. W.
     Sheppard, 1–19. *British History Online*, http://www.british-history.ac.uk/survey-
     london/vols33-4/pp1-19 (accessed 20 November 2019).

4   Kirsty Carpenter, 'The Novelty of the French Émigrés in London in the 1790s',
     Ch. 3, 69–90 in *A History of the French in London: Liberty, Equality, Opportunity*,
     eds Debra Kelly and Martyn Cornick (London: University of London, 2013), 79.

5   Craig Spence, *London in the 1690s: A Social Atlas* (London: Centre for Metropolitan
     History, 2000), 90.

6   Derek Keene, Peter Earle, Craig Spence, and Janet Barnes, 'Guide to the Source', in
     *Four Shillings in the Pound Aid 1693/4: The City of London, the City of Westminster,
     Middlesex* (London, 1992), *British History Online*, http://www.british-history.ac.uk/
     no-series/london-4s-pound/1693-4/guide-to-the-source (accessed 14 October 2019).

7   6 & 7 Wm & Mary, ch.6. For information see https://www.british-history.ac.uk/
     london-record-soc/vol2/introduction (accessed 14 October 2019).

8   Supplements part 1 & 2 in *London Inhabitants within the Walls 1695* (London:
     London Record Society, 1966), *British History Online*, http://www.british-history.
     ac.uk/london-record-soc/vol2 (accessed 15 October 2019). The parishes are: St
     Olave Silver Street, St Stephen Coleman Street, St Perter Westcheap, St Nicholas
     Cole Abbey, St Vedast, St Pancras Soper Lane, St Nicholas Olave, Holy Trinity
     the Less, St Peter le Poor, St Nicholas Acons, St Stephen Walbrook, St Peter Paul's
     Wharf, St Olave Old Jewry, St Thomas the Apostle, St Swithin, and St Peter Cornhill.

9   King, *Natural and Political Observations* ..., 17, 22.

10   28, 881 according to William White, *History, Gazetteer and Directory of Norfolk* ...
     (Sheffield: William White, 3rd edn, 1864), 141.

11   King, *Natural and Political Observations*, 23.

12   Giuseppe A. Graglia, *A Plan for the Periodical Abolition of All Taxes* ... (London: B.
     Crosby, 1795), 16. Graglia is probably the Joseph Antoine Graglia who married Jane
     Tate at St James's Westminster in 1787 (www.ancestry.co.uk, accessed 21 November
     2019) and ironically, given that his *Plan* entailed taxing lodgers, may be the Joseph
     Graglia notified to the authorities as a foreigner lodging with James Weaver of 22
     Castle Street in 1797 (LMA: WR/A/008).

13   See *Populations Past: Atlas of Victorian and Edwardian Population*, https://
     www.populationspast.org/about/ (accessed 3 December 2019) and Anderson,
     'Households, Families and Individuals', 428.

14   Spence, *London in the 1690s*.

15 Ibid., 88, 91, 93, 96.

16 For background see 'Introduction', *London Inhabitants within the Walls 1695*.

17 The number of shoemaker lodgers at Timothy Simms's, St Swithin parish, is not specified.

18 Spence, *London in the 1690s*, 99.

19 *Roger Whitley's Diary 1684–97 Bodleian Library, Ms Eng Hist C 711*, Michael Stevens and Honor Lewington, eds (s.l., 2004), *British History Online,* http://www.british-history.ac.uk/no-series/roger-whitley-diary/1684-97/january-1685 (accessed 14 October 2019).

20 Revd Henry John Wale, MA, *My Grandfather's Pocket Book, from AD 1701 to 1796* (London: Chapman & Hall, 1883), 122, 178, 187, 200.

21 James Fretwell, *A Family History*, 163–243 in *Yorkshire Diaries and Autobiographies in the Seventeenth and Eighteenth Centuries* (Durham, London and Edinburgh: Surtees Society, 1877), 177, 191–2, 198.

22 John Strype, *A Survey of the Cities of London and Westminster* (London: J. Churchill *et al.*, 1720), https://www.dhi.ac.uk/strype/TransformServlet?page=book6_068 (accessed 20 November 2019).

23 LMA: WR/R/R/002.

24 *MC*, 6 July 1799.

25 J. M. Price, ed., *Joshua Johnson's Letterbook, 1771–4: Letters from a Merchant in London to His Partners in Maryland* (London: London Record Society, 1979), 17.

26 Joseph Emin, *The Life and Adventures of J.E., an Armenian* (London: for the author, 1792), 28, 31, 48.

27 *Curwen Journal*, I, 47.

28 *MC*, 22 December 1800.

29 *SofL*, 'General Introduction', XXVII, *Spitalfields and Mile End New Town*, ed. F. H. W. Sheppard, 1–13, *British History Online,* http://www.british-history.ac.uk/survey-london/vol27/pp1-13 (accessed 22 October 2019).

30 Emin, *Life and Adventures*, 48.

31 Derek Morris and Ken Cozens, *London's Sailortown, 1600–1800: A Social History of Shadwell and Ratcliff, an Early Modern Riverside Suburb* (London: East London History Society, 2014); Jerry White, *London in the Nineteenth Century: A Human Awful Wonder of God* (London: Bodley Head, 2016), 148–9; John Cremer, transcr. R. Reynell Bellamy, *Ramblin' Jack: The Journal of Captain John Cremer, 1700–74* (London: J. Cape, 1936), 212. On foreign sailors' accommodation see Rozina Visram, *Ayahs, Lascars and Princes: Indians in Britain 1700–1947* (London: Pluto, 1986).

32 *MC*, 12 November 1782.

33 'General Introduction', *Survey of London*, XXVII, 1–13; White, *London in the Eighteenth Century*, 67–8.

34 OBOL: trial of Jacob Jeggett, t17931204–45. Catherine Wheel Alley, scarcely wide enough for two people to pass, survives opposite Liverpool Street Station.

35 Peter Fryer, *Staying Power: The History of Black People in Britain* (London: Pluto, 1984), 232–3.

36 *Olla Podrida*, no. XXIX (29 September 1787), 171.

37 BL: Lansdowne 509B, 1749 Westminster by election scrutiny, ff. 369d–70, 503, 347d, 500, 348.

38 Both 'centrical' and 'West End' were terms used in *Chronicle* advertisements.

39 James Boswell, *The Life of Samuel Johnson LLD* (New York: Everyman, 1992, 1st pub. 1791), 537.

40 *MC*, 11 September 1782.

41 For improvements to London's streets see White, *London in the Eighteenth Century*, 40–1, and for house layouts Guillery, *Small House*.

42 Christoph Heyl, 'We Are Not at Home: Protecting Domestic Privacy in Post-Fire Middle-Class London', *London Journal* 27.2 (2002), 12–33.

43 *MC*, 16 September 1794.

44 BL: Lansdowne 509B, f. 139d. For urban conditions in the period see Emily Cockayne, *Hubbub: Filth, Noise and Stench in England* (New Haven CT: YUP, 2007).

45 *MC*, 30 May 1793, 2 June 1794, 16 June 1796.

46 Johnson's London addresses are listed in Boswell, *Life of Johnson*, 909–10 (fn.); John Forster, *The Life and Times of Oliver Goldsmith* (London: Bickers & Son, 5th edn, 1877); Charlotte Charke, *A Narrative of the Life of Mrs. C.C., Written by Herself* (London: Hunt & Clarke, 1827, 1st pub. 1755); James Boaden, ed., *Memoirs of Mrs. Inchbald: Including Her Familiar Correspondence*, 2 vols (London: Richard Bentley, 1833); Tate Wilkinson, *Memoirs of His Own Life*, 4 vols (York: Wilson, Spence & Mawman, 1790).

47 *MC*, 17 March 1797.

48 Penrose, *Haydon Autobiography*; Allan Cunningham, ed., *The Life of Sir David Wilkie …*, 3 vols (London: John Murray, 1843), I, 73; Ann Coppard was the widow of Revd William Hickes Coppard, non-resident vicar of East Dean and Westfield, Sussex, who died in 1808 (TNA: PROB 11/1477/116).

49 Angus Whitehead, '"I write in South Molton Street, what I both see and hear": Reconstructing William and Catherine Blake's Residence and Studio at 17 South Molton Street, Oxford Street', *British Art Journal* 11.2 (2010), 62–75. On the atmosphere of 'artistic London' see also Vic Gatrell, *The First Bohemians: Life and Art in London's Golden Age* (London: Penguin, 2013).

50 Swift, *Journal to Stella*.

51 Carl Van Doren, *Benjamin Franklin* (London: Cresset Press, 1946, 1st pub. 1939), 270, 411.

52 Max Byrd, 'Thomas Jefferson and Great Britain in Peace and War', 203–23 in *Guerres et Paix: La Grande-Bretagne du XVIII Siècle*, ed. Paul-Gabriel Boucé (Paris: Presses Sorbonne Nouvelle, 1998); *Thomas Jefferson Memorandum Books (1786)*, https://founders.archives.gov/documents/Jefferson/02-01-02-0020 (accessed 26 February 2019).

53 Susan and David Neave, eds, *The Diary of a Yorkshire Gentleman: John Courtney of Beverley, 1759–68* (Otley: Smith, Settle, 2001), 16–17, 56, 124.

54 See for example Clare Williams, trans., *Sophie in London in 1786: Being the Diary of Sophie von la Roche* (London: J. Cape, 1933), 'Introduction', 35–6.

55 William Byrd, Louis B. Wright, and Marion Tinling, eds, *The London Diary (1717–21) and Other Writings* (Oxford: OUP, 1958).

56 Emily Anderson, trans. and ed., *Letters of Mozart and His Family*, 2 vols (London: Macmillan, 1985, 1st pub. 1938), I, 25, 50.

57 Pierre-Jean Grosley, trans. Thomas Nugent, *A Tour to London, or, New Observations on England and Its Inhabitants*, 2 vols (London: Lockyer Davis, 1772), I, 23; Williams, *Sophie in London*, 35–6.

58 See Elizabeth McKellar, *Landscapes of London: The City, the Country and the Suburbs, 1660–1840* (New Haven CT: YUP, 2013).

59 Daniel Lysons, 'Putney' and 'Wandsworth', in *The Environs of London*, Vol. I, *County of Surrey* (London, 1792), 404–35 and 502–18. *British History Online,* http://www.british-history.ac.uk/london-environs/vol1/pp404-435 and http://www.british-history.ac.uk/london-environs/vol1/pp502-518 (accessed 29 October 2019).

60 *MC*, 21 February 1797.

61 *MC*, 14 April 1792.

62 Alexander Cruden, *The London-Citizen Exceedingly Injured …* (London: T. Cooper & A. Dodd, 1739), 5–7 and *The Adventures of Alexander the Corrector …*, 3 vols (London: for the author, 1754–5), I, 9.

63 Sarah Burton, *A Double Life: A Biography of Charles and Mary Lamb* (London: Penguin, 2004).

64 Alan Saville, ed., *Secret Comment: The Diaries of Gertrude Savile 1721–57* (Devon: Kingsbridge History Society, 1997), 41, 43, 47.

65 Forster, *Life of Goldsmith*, 172, 381.

66 *Curwen Journal*, Croydon reference: I, 177–9.

67 Boaden, *Inchbald Memoirs*, II, 70–1, 208; 'Colby Court, Kensington House and Kensington Court', in *SofL*, XLII, *Kensington Square to Earl's Court*, ed. Hermione Hobhouse (London, 1986), 55–76. *British History Online,* http://www.british-history.ac.uk/survey-london/vol42/pp55-76 (accessed 29 April 2020).

68 *Curwen Journal*, I, 177–9; *ODNB*: entry for Morland; Penrose, *Haydon Autobiography*, 286.

69   This is probably a result of the alphabetization which has removed the proximity of landlord/lady and lodger. The original document listing by household may contain more clues to landlords, but a full study is beyond the scope of this chapter as the data is outside the Georgian period and is used here as baseline evidence only.

70   Pottle, *Boswell's London Journal*, 317; *Curwen Journal, passim*.

71   Vickery, *Behind Closed Doors,* Ch. 1, 25–48, 'Thresholds and Boundaries at Home'.

72   Jane Whittle, 'A Critique of Approaches to "Domestic Work": Women, Work and the Pre-Industrial Economy', *Past & Present* 243.1 (2019), 35–70.

73   Graglia, *Plan*, 19.

74   Hunt, *Middling Sort*.

75   Anon. ('A Gentleman of Experience'), *The Economist* ... (London, 15th edn, 1781).

76   Anon. ('A German Gentleman'), *A View of London and Westminster: Or The Town Spy* (London: T. Warner, 1725), 9.

77   Francis Place, ed. Mary Thale, *The Autobiography of Francis Place (1771–1854)* (Cambridge: CUP, 1972), 173.

78   Michael Wynn Jones, *George Cruikshank: His Life and London* (London: Macmillan, 1978), 4–6; Michael Slater, *Charles Dickens* (New Haven CT: YUP, 2011), 14.

79   *MC*, 16 December 1778.

80   *MC*, 3 March 1785. Spence makes this point for the late-seventeenth century, *London in the 1690s*, 99.

81   For example, Chester Place, Kennington, *MC*, 14 April 1795 and, for 'new painted', 23 April 1796.

82   *MC*, 29 January 1785, 24 June 1799; on adaptable furniture and lodgers see Vickery, *Behind Closed Doors*, 286.

83   *MC*, 12 February 1800.

84   Teresia Constantia Muilman, *An Apology for the Conduct of Mrs Teresia Constantia Phillips* ..., 3 vols (London: for the author, 1748–9), I, 215–16; Laetitia Pilkington, *Memoirs of Mrs Laetitia Pilkington* ..., 3 vols (Dublin, 1748, 1749, 1754), II, 158.

85   *MC*, 26 August 1800.

86   Tim Hitchcock and John Black, eds, *Chelsea Settlement and Bastardy Examinations, 1733–66* (London: London Record Society, 1999), *British History Online*, http://www.british-history.ac.uk/london-record-soc/vol33 (accessed 20 November 2019), no. 290.

87   *MC*, 10 February 1792.

88   *MC*, 25 August 1783.

89   Hoh-Cheung and Lorna Mui, *Shops and Shopkeeping in Eighteenth-Century England* (Kingston Ontario: McGill-Queen's University Press, 1989), 119, 130.

90   Shelley Tickell, *Shoplifting in Eighteenth-Century England* (Woodbridge: Boydell & Brewer, 2018), 126–7.

91   *MC*, 19 April 1791; 12 September 1794; 29 April 1795; 23 April 1796 and 11 November 1797.

92   Ian Campbell Ross, *Laurence Sterne: A Life* (Oxford: OUP, 2001), 354 and Fourmantel's press advertisements e.g. *Public Advertiser*, 16 January 1768; Frank Brady and Frederick A. Pottle, eds, *Boswell in Search of a Wife 1766-9* (London: Heinemann, 1957), 176 (fn. 1), 322; Boaden, *Inchbald Memoirs*, II, 74; Thomas Chatterton, ed. Donald S. Taylor, *The Complete Works of Thomas Chatterton*, 2 vols (Oxford: Clarendon Press, 1971), I, 649; Jon Cook, *Hazlitt in Love: A Fatal Attachment* (London: Short Books, 2007), 21–3.

93   CWAC, A2269.

94   See Earle, *City Full of People,* especially 'Women without gainful employment', 150–5. Earle is one of those who regard lodger income as being outside 'gainful employment'.

95   *Curwen Journal*, II, 820, 822.

96   Edward Dutton Cook, 'Widow Hogarth and Her Lodger', *Once a Week* (29 December 1860), 10–13, 13.

97   Janet Todd, ed., *The Collected Letters of Mary Wollstonecraft* (London: Penguin, 2003), 50–3.

98   *MC*, 15 August 1783 and 28 September 1795.

99   Benjamin Franklin, ed. Ormond Seavey, *Autobiography and Other Writings* (Oxford: OUP, 1993), 48–9.

100   Todd, *Wollstonecraft Letters,* 62, 64–6.

101   Pottle, *Boswell's London Journal*, 63–4.

102   Weaver Lawrence French had six lodgers and Gregory Gregson, City Crier, seven.

103   John Burnett, ed., *Useful Toil: Autobiographies of Working People from the 1820s to the 1920s* (Harmondsworth: Penguin, 1974), 282–4.

104   CWAC, A2269. Barker also had premises at 42 Haymarket and it is not clear which was her residence.

105   *MC*, 15 April 1784.

106   John M. T. Ford, ed., *A Medical Student at St Thomas's Hospital, 1801–2, The Weekes Family Letters* (London: Wellcome Institute, 1987); *ODNB*: entry for Keats.

107   Boaden, *Inchbald Memoirs*, II, 70–1, 208, 215–16.

108   Printed handbills cited in Barbara Benedict, 'Advertising Women: Gender and the Vendor in the Print Culture of the Medical Marketplace', Ch. 26, 612–32 in Jennie Batchelor and Manushag Powell, eds, *Women's Periodicals and Print Culture in Britain, 1690-1820s: The Long Eighteenth Century* (Edinburgh: Edinburgh University Press, 2017), 622.

109   For a discussion of this among reasons for lodging see Wright, 'Sojourners and Lodgers'.

110   Spence, *London in the 1690s*, 99.

111   Raymond A. Anselment, ed., *The Remembrances of Elizabeth Freke, 1671–1714* (Cambridge: CUP, 2001); 'Albany', in *SofL, XXXI and XXXII, St James Westminster,*

Part 2, ed. F. H. W. Sheppard (London, 1963), 367–89. *British History Online*, http://www.british-history.ac.uk/survey-london/vols31-2/pt2/pp367-389 (accessed 7 October 2020).

112 For Lowe's see J. T. Smith, ed. Wilfred Whitten, *Nollekens and His Times ...*, 2 vols (London: John Lane, 1920, 1st pub. 1828), I, 174.

113 See David G. C. Allan, *The Adelphi Past and Present: A History and a Guide* (Basingstoke: Basingstoke Press, 2001); hotels listed in Ralph Rylance, ed. Janet Ing Freeman, *The Epicure's Almanack: Eating and Drinking in Regency London, the Original 1815 Guidebook* (London: British Library, 2013), 77, 99–100; Stephen Hoare, *Palaces of Power: The Birth and Evolution of London's Clubland* (Stroud: History Press, 2019).

114 Revd Montagu Pennington, *Memoirs of the Life of Mrs Elizabeth Carter* (London: Rivington, 1807), 164.

115 Rohan McWilliam, *London's West End: Creating the Pleasure District, 1800–1914* (Oxford: OUP, 2020), 42–3.

116 Thomas Jefferson Hogg, *The Life of Percy Bysshe Shelley ...*, 2 vols (London: J.M. Dent, 1933, 1st pub. 1858), II, 5.

117 Anon., *The Picture of London for 1809* (London: Richard Phillips, 1809), 356.

118 OBOL: trial of Mary Dobson, t17900113-28.

119 Anon., *The Thorough-bred Poor Gentleman's Book: or, How to Live in London on £100 a Year* (London: William Marsh, 3rd edn, 1835), 11.

120 Jon Bee, *A Living Picture of London for 1828 ...* (London: W. Clarke, 1828), 104.

121 *MC*, 23 June 1784.

122 The Albany rule was not always strictly enforced, however. See 'Albany', in *SofL, XXXI and XXXII*.

123 David Lemmings, *Professors of the Law: Barristers and English Legal Culture in the Eighteenth Century* (Oxford: OUP, 2000), 50, 295.

124 Burton, *Double Life,* 192.

125 Boswell, *Life of Johnson*, 909–10; Forster, *Life of Goldsmith*, 299.

126 For example, *MC*, 29 November 1794.

127 CWAC, A2269.

128 Dorothy Stroud, *Sir John Soane Architect* (London: Faber & Faber, 1984), 54, 58; Gillian Darley, *John Soane: An Accidental Romantic* (New Haven CT: YUP, 1999), 74, 95.

129 *MC*, 22 August 1794.

130 J. Curran, *Letters of [John Philpot] Curran to the Reverend H. Weston Written in the Years 1773 and 1774* (London: T. Hookham, 1819).

131 *MC*, 13 February 1792, 30 March 1795.

132 Ford, *Medical Student at St Thomas's*, 48–9.

133 Daniel Defoe, *The Great Law of Subordination Consider'd ...* (London: S, Harding, 1724), 11.

134   Wale, *Grandfather's Pocket Book*, 170. For Rivaz see www.ancestry.co.uk and *Journal of the House of Lords,* Vol. 31, 1765–7 (London: His Majesty's Stationery Office, 1767–1830), 21–30, *British History Online,* http://www.british-history.ac.uk/lords-jrnl/vol31/pp46-56 (both accessed 21 October 2019).

135   E. Olivier, *The Eccentric Life of Alexander Cruden* (London: Faber & Faber, 1934), 40.

136   *MC*, 11 September 1797.

137   *MC*, 21 March 1798, 6 February 1795.

138   *MC*, 29 December 1770, 2 February 1791, 1 October 1799.

139   *MC*, 17 June 1797.

140   *MC*, 21 October 1796.

141   *MC*, 3 July 1788.

142   Dorothy H. Woodforde, ed., *Woodforde Papers and Diaries* (London: P. Davies, 1932), 61.

143   McEwan and Sharpe, 'It Buys Me Freedom', 145.

144   Ibid., 161.

145   Penrose, *Haydon Autobiography*, 49.

146   E. E. Reynolds, ed., *The Mawhood Diary* (London: Catholic Record Society, 1956), 173–6.

147   Joseph Farington, ed. James Greig, *The Farington Diary*, 8 vols (London: Hutchinson, 1922–8), I, 270.

148   Simon Mason, *A Narrative of the Life and Distresses of Simon Mason, Apothecary* … (Birmingham: for the author, 1754), 90.

149   CWAC: A2269. Nihell was acquitted: OBOL: trial of Thomas Dempsey, Thomas Welch, James Delaney, Philip Corbet, Dennis Sherry, Andrew Nihil [*sic*], t17760417-59. When Nihell was buried on 27 January 1790 he was described as 'late a Prisoner from King's Bench' (register of St George the Martyr, Southwark, ancestry.co.uk, accessed 30 March 2020).

150   Williamson, *British Masculinity in the Gentleman's Magazine,* 114–17.

151   *GM*, July 1781, 344; July 1788, 659; July 1790, 673; July 1803, 696.

152   *GM*, July 1809, 681.

153   Penelope J. Corfield, *Power and the Professions in Britain 1700–1850* (London: Routledge, 2000, 1st pub. 1995), 230.

154   CWAC: A2269.

155   *GM* obituary, January 1792, 90.

156   *Pilkington Memoirs*, II, 9, 28, 95–6; Norma Clarke, *Queen of the Wits: A Life of Laetitia Pilkington* (London: Faber & Faber, 2008), 153.

157   John C. Hodges, *William Congreve the Man* (New York: Modern Language Association of America, 1941), 80.

158   Janet Todd, *The Secret Life of Aphra Behn* (London: André Deutsch, 1996), 123, 296.

159   CWAC: A2269.

160 See *ODNB* entries and Edward Edwards, *Anecdotes of Painters* (London: Cornmarket Press, 1970, facsimile edn, 1st pub. 1808), 220, 276; Claire Tomalin, *Mrs Jordan's Profession: The Story of a Great Actress and a Future King* (London: Penguin 2012, 1st pub. 1994), 41; *GM*, July 1808, 684–5; Samuel Johnson, eds Nicholas Seager and Lance Wilcox, *The Life of Mr Richard Savage* (Peterborough, Ontario: Broadview Press, 2016, 1st pub. 1744); *Mary Hays Life, Writings, and Correspondence*, http://www.maryhayslifewritingscorrespondence.com/mary-hays-correspondence/mary-hays-s-residences/1-upper-cumming-street-pentonville (accessed 15 November 2019).

161 Pottle, *Boswell's London Journal*, 327–8.

162 James Prior, *The Life of Oliver Goldsmith ...*, 2 vols (London: J. Murray, 1837), II, 321.

163 Nicholas Blundell, ed. J. J. Bagley, transcribed and annotated Frank Tyrer, *The Great Diurnal of Nicholas Blundell of Little Crosby, Lancashire*, 3 vols (Preston: Record Society of Lancashire and Cheshire, 1968–72), I, 37–8, 315.

164 Barbara Hurst, ed., *The Diaries of Sarah Hurst 1759–62: Life and Love in Eighteenth-Century Horsham* (Stroud: Amberley Publishing, 2009).

165 César de Saussure, trans. and ed. Mme van Muyden, *A Foreign View of England in the Reigns of George I and George II, 1725–9: The Letters of Monsieur César de Saussure to His Family* (London: J. Murray, 1902), 157, 165.

166 Carl Philipp Moritz, *Travels of Carl Philipp Moritz in England in 1782* (London: Humphrey Milford, 1924, 1st pub. in English 1795), 24.

167 Johanna Schopenhauer, trans. and eds Ruth Michaelis-Jena and Willy Merson, *A Lady Travels: Journeys in England and Scotland from the Diaries of Johanna Schopenhauer* (London: Routledge, 1988), 135–6.

168 Christian Augustus Gottlieb Goede, *The Stranger in England or, Travels in Great Britain ...*, 3 vols (London: Mathews & Leigh, 1807), I, 30.

169 *MC*, 19 October 1782; 6 May 1793.

170 Joanne Bailey, *Parenting in England 1760–1830: Emotion, Identity and Generation* (Oxford: OUP, 2012); Lisa Forman Cody, *Birthing the Nation: Sex, Science, and the Conception of Eighteenth-Century Britons* (Oxford: OUP, 2005).

171 William Howitt, *Homes and Haunts of the Most Eminent Poets*, 2 vols (London: R. Bentley, 1847), I, 129; *The Spectator*, no. 12 (14 March 1711).

172 Forster, *Life of Goldsmith*, 97.

173 *Inchbald Memoirs*, II, 40–1, 74.

174 *Curwen Journal*, II, 589, 787.

175 Gregory King estimated the ratio of women to men in London at 13:10 (King, *Natural and Political Observations*, 22) and the 1801 census also revealed a 'woman surplus', *A Vision of Britain through Time*, http://www.visionofbritain.org.uk/census/GB1801ABS_1 (accessed 15 November 2019).

176 Geoffrey E. Nuttall, ed., *Letters of John Pinney, 1679–99* (London: OUP, 1939), 51–2.

177 *George, London Life*, 174, see also Bridget Hill, *Women, Work and Sexual Politics in Eighteenth-Century England* (London: UCL Press, 1989).

178 Ben P. Robertson, ed., *The Diaries of Elizabeth Inchbald*, 3 vols (London: Pickering & Chatto, 2007), I, 185.

179 CWAC: A2269, A2270.

180 Earle, *City Full of People*, 150–1.

181 Swift, *Journal to Stella*, 298; *Curwen Journal*, II, 812; Place, *Autobiography*, 71.

182 Jacques Casanova de Seingalt, trans. Arthur Machen, *The Memoires of Casanova, Complete* (London: s.n., 1894), Episode 22, Ch. 8, http://www.gutenberg.org/files/2981/2981-h/2981-h.htm (accessed 15 November 2019).

183 Letter to William Godwin, 13 October 1795, Hays, *Life, Writings, and Correspondence*.

184 W. S. Lewis, ed., *Horace Walpole's Correspondence*, 48 vols (New Haven CT: YUP, 1937–83), XXIII, 287.

185 James Greig, ed., *The Diaries of a Duchess, Extracts from the Diaries of the First Duchess of Northumberland, (1716–76)* (London: Hodder & Stoughton, 1926), 90–1, with thanks to Meghan Kobza for this reference.

186 Naomi Tadmor, *Family and Friends in Eighteenth-Century England: Household, Kinship, and Patronage* (Cambridge: CUP, 2001).

Chapter 4

1 William Hutton, *A Journey from Birmingham to London* (Birmingham: Pearson & Rollason, 1785), 24–5.

2 David Love, *The Life, Adventures, and Experiences of David Love, Written by Himself* (Nottingham: Sutton & Son, 5th edn, 1825), 73.

3 Charles Richard Sanders, gen. ed., *The Collected Letters of Thomas and Jane Welsh Carlyle*, 45 vols (Durham NC: Duke University Press, 1970–7), V, 339.

4 *A Collection for Improvement of Husbandry and Trade* (London), 12 October 1694.

5 James Raven, *Publishing Business in Eighteenth-Century England* (Woodbridge: Boydell & Brewer, 2014), 118, 121.

6 Ivon Asquith, 'James Perry and the *Morning Chronicle*, 1790–1821' (unpublished PhD thesis, UCL, 1973), 316.

7 Ibid., 327; Raven, *Publishing Business*, 129–30.

8 *MC*, 16 January 1796.

9 Smith, *Nollekens and His Times*, I, 71–2.

10 *Morning Herald*, 5 July 1782. It is possible of course that 'F.F.' was also Taylor's lodger.

11 Bee, *Living Picture*, 105.

12 *Curwen Journal*, II, 588.

13 BM: D,2.4154.

14 Ibid., II, 564.

15 *London Daily Post & General Advertiser*, 13 September 1738.

16 Henry Fielding, *A Plan of the Universal Register-Office* (London: s.n., 1751), 10.

17 Miles Ogborn, *Spaces of Modernity: London's Geographies 1680–1780* (New York: Guilford Press, 1998), Ch. 6, 201–30, 'The Universal Register Office', 224.

18 *MC*, 16 August 1794.

19 *MC*, 24 July 1794.

20 Anon., *The New Cheats of the Town Exposed* ... (London: W. Clements, 1792), 45. See also Anon. ('Philanthropos'), *An Appeal to the Public against the Growing Evil of Universal Register-Offices* ... (London: for the author, 1757).

21 BM: 1951,0411.4.4 and 1893,0612.231.

22 Anon., *A Curious and Interesting Narrative of Poll House and the Marquis of C*******, (Late Lord T—-)* (London: J.L. Marks, n.d. ?1812), in Peakman, *Whore Biographies*, V, 396.

23 For example, BM: 1872,1012.4940, *Accommodation, or, Lodgings to Let at Portsmouth!!* (1808) and Library of Congress: *Retail Traders Not Affected by the Shop Tax* (1787).

24 Pottle, *Boswell's London Journal*, 55.

25 *General Advertiser*, 18 October 1750.

26 John Vanbrugh and Colley Cibber, *The Provok'd Husband; or, a Journey to London* (London: J. Watts, 1728), 13.

27 *Lady's Magazine*, 8 October 1777, 532–4; *Idler* no. 86 (December 1759).

28 Henry Fielding, *Miss Lucy in Town: A Sequel to The Virgin Unmasqued* (London: A. Millar, 1742), 2.

29 Saville, *Secret Comment*, 62.

30 *Curwen Journal*, II, 697.

31 *Inchbald Diaries*, II, 80–2, 236, III, 21, 70.

32 Hogg, *Life of Shelley*, I, 178.

33 For literacy, letter-writing and postal services see Susan Whyman, *The Pen and the People: English Letter Writers 1660–1800* (Oxford: OUP, 2009).

34 *Walpole Correspondence*, XXXVII, 184; IX, 333–4; X, 270–1.

35 J. E. Norton, ed., *The Letters of Edward Gibbon*, 3 vols (London: Cassell, 1956), I, 109.

36 Penrose, *Haydon Autobiography*, 13.

37 Tadmor, *Family and Friends.*

38 Angus Whitehead, 'William Blake's Last Residence: No. 3 Fountain Court, Strand, George Richmond's Plan and an Unrecorded Letter to John Linnell', *British Art Journal* 6.1 (2005), 21–30.

39   Wilbur L. Cross, *The Life and Times of Laurence Sterne* (New York: Macmillan, 1909), 198, 203.

40   Thomas Chatterton, ed. C. B. Willcox, *The Complete Works of Thomas Chatterton*, 2 vols (Cambridge: W. P. Grant, 1842), II, cxxii–iii; Charles Lamb, *The Letters of Elia*, 2 vols (London: J.M. Dent, 1909), I, 137; *Carlyle Letters*, V, 308–9, 318.

41   Anderson, *Mozart Letters*, I, 44–5.

42   James Albert Ukawsaw Gronniosaw, *A Narrative of the Most Remarkable Particulars in the Life of James Albert Ukawsaw Gronniosaw, an African Prince, as Related by Himself* (Bath: W. Gye, 1772), 26.

43   Henry B. Wheatley and Peter Cunningham, *London Past and Present …*, 3 vols (London: J. Murray, 1891), I, 519–20.

44   Martin Archer Shee, *The Life of Sir Martin Archer Shee …*, 2 vols (London: Longman, Green, 1860), I, 78–9, 171–2.

45   Emin, *Life and Adventures*, 58.

46   Grosley, *Tour to London,* I, 23.

47   Stobart, *Comforts of Home*, 10.

48   Henri Misson, *M. Misson's Memoirs and Observations in His Travels over England …*, trans. Mr Ozell (London: D. Brown, 1719), 145.

49   Kirsty Carpenter, *Refugees of the French Revolution: The French Émigrés in London, 1789–1802* (Basingstoke: Macmillan, 1999).

50   Abbé Tardy, *Manuel du Voyageur à Londres …* (London: W. & C. Spilsbury, 1800), 16.

51   *GM*, March 1807, 195–7; Carpenter, *Refugees*, 57.

52   Pottle, *Boswell's London Diary*, 64.

53   Ibid., 65.

54   Walter Thornbury, *The Life of J. M. W. Turner RA* (London: Chatto & Windus, 1877), 359.

55   John Nichols, *Illustrations of the Literary History of the Eighteenth Century*, 8 vols (London: Nichols, 1828), V, 318–19; 'Chitqua: A Chinese Artist in Eighteenth-Century London', Ch. 1, 15–84 in David Clarke, *Chinese Art and Its Encounter with the World* (Hong Kong: Hong Kong University Press, 2011). Boswell identifies the landlord as Marr (Brady and Pottle, *In Search of a Wife*, 317) and Charles Marr, hatter, Strand appears in vestry minutes for the parish of St Clement Danes for 1 May 1769 (CWAC: B1071).

56   Linda Colley, *Britons: Forging the Nation 1707–1837* (New Haven CT: YUP, 2005, 1st pub. 1992). Examples of abuse include violent protests against a group of French actors in winter 1749 and the events leading up to the trial for murder of Italian lexicographer Giuseppe Baretti (1719–89) in 1769. Baretti (who was acquitted on grounds of self-defence) said, in his defence, that a woman in the Haymarket who had assaulted him 'finding by my pronunciation I was a foreigner, she called

me several bad names in a most consumelious [*sic*] strain; among which, French bugger, d - ned Frenchman, and a woman-hater' (OBOL: trial of Joseph Baretti, t17691018– 9).

57   Nichols, *Illustrations*, V, 318–19.

58   Emin, *Life and Adventures*, 66.

59   Vincent Carretta, ed., *Letters of the Late Ignatius Sancho, an African* (Peterborough, Ontario: Broadview, 2015, 1st pub. 1782), 148, 231.

60   Prince Hoare, *Memoirs of Granville Sharp* (London: Henry Colburn, 1820), 33.

61   Sara Salih, ed., *The History of Mary Prince, a West Indian Slave* (London: Penguin, 2000, 1st pub. 1831), 38.

62   *GM*, March 1751, 122–5, 123.

63   *Curwen Journal*, II, 518.

64   White, *London in the Eighteenth Century*, 152–62.

65   Forster, *Life of Goldsmith*, 81.

66   OBOL: trial of Susan Grimes, t17250407–66.

67   Swift, *Journal to Stella*, 101.

68   Mason, *Narrative*, 71–2.

69   James Thomas Kirkman, *Memoirs of the Life of Charles Macklin ...*, 2 vols (London: Lackington & Allen, 1799), I, 32, 161–6.

70   Jefferies *v.* Duncombe (1809), 2 Campbell 3, 170 E.R. 1061.

71   Crisp *v.* Churchill, E.34 Geo. III cited in Lloyd *v.* Johnson (1798), 1 B. & P. 340.

72   Pilkington, in *Memoirs*, II, 100–1.

73   *Adventures of Alexander the Corrector*, I, 37; II, 35.

74   Trusler, *London Adviser*, 5–6.

75   Pottle, *Boswell's London Journal*, 55.

76   Hogg, *Life of Shelley*, I, 178; *Carlyle Letters*, V, 414.

77   *Curwen Journal*, I, 410; II, 588, 702.

78   *Carlyle Letters*, V, 414.

79   *Idler* 86; *Lady's Magazine*, 8 October 1777, 532–4.

80   Pilkington, in *Memoirs*, II, 159.

81   Pottle, *Boswell's London Journal*, 63–4; Brady and Pottle, *In Search of a Wife*, 317; Vickery, *Behind Closed Doors*, 180–1.

82   *Curwen Journal*, II, 697.

83   Lamb, *Letters of Elia*, I, 183.

84   Hogg, *Life of Shelley*, I, 178.

85   Ibid., I, 55; Serena Dyer, 'Masculinities, Wallpaper, and Crafting Domestic Space within the University, 1795–1914', *Nineteenth-Century Gender Studies* 14.2 (2018), 3–17. For wallpaper generally see Clare Taylor, *The Design, Production and Reception of Eighteenth-Century Wallpaper in Britain* (Oxford: Routledge, 2018).

86   *MC*, 29 November 1794. I therefore disagree with Vickery, '"Neat and Not Too Showey": Words and Wallpaper in Regency England', 201–22 in Styles and Vickery, *Gender and Material Taste*, 203, which lacks full archival evidence.

87 *Gibbon Letters*, I, 353.

88 Jonathan Swift, *Travels into Several Remote Nations of the World*, 4 parts (London: Benjamin Motte, 1726), II, 53.

89 *Curwen Journal*, II, 820.

90 *Carlyle Letters*, VI, 223.

91 LWL: 792.09.29.01+. The Blakes' rooms are described in Alexander and Anne Gilchrist, *Life of William Blake …*, 2 vols (London: Macmillan, 2nd edn, 1880), I, 305 and Whitehead, 'Blake's Last Residence'.

92 Frances Burney, *The Diary and Letters of Madame D'Arblay*, 3 vols (London: Viztelly & Co., 1890–1), I, 136–7.

93 Pottle, *Boswell's London Journal*, 63–4; Hogg, *Life of Shelley*, I, 178.

94 Place, *Autobiography*, 138, 115.

95 Ibid., 102, 109, 111; Franklin, *Autobiography*, 49; *Inchbald Diaries*, III, 98.

96 Pottle, *Boswell's London Journal*, 63–4.

97 Prior, *Life of Goldsmith,* II, 104.

98 Place, *Autobiography*, 158.

99 Saville, *Secret Comment,* 63.

100 Count Frederick Kielmansegge, trans. Countess Kielmansegg, *Diary of a Journey to England in the Years 1761–2* (London: Longman, Green, 1902), 19.

101 Trusler, *London Adviser*, 1–2.

102 Leigh, *New Picture of London …*, 343.

103 Trusler, *London Adviser*, 2; Tardy, *Manuel du Voyageur,* 16.

104 Paul V. and Dorothy J. Thompson, transcr. and intro., *The Account Books of Jonathan Swift* (Newark DE: Scolar Press, 1984), lxxxix.

105 *Curwen Journal*, I, 195.

106 Brady and Pottle, *In Search of a Wife*, 323.

107 Pottle, *Boswell's London Journal,* 327.

108 Franklin, *Autobiography.*

109 *Inchbald Diaries, passim.*

110 Place, *Autobiography,* 106, 111, 150–1.

111 Burton, *Double Life*, 362; sugar prices taken from the 'Estimates' in Anon., *A New System of Practical Domestic Economy* (London: Henry Colburn, 1823).

112 Franklin, *Autobiography*, 49.

113 Misson, *Memoirs*, 145–6.

114 *Inchbald Diaries*, I, *passim.*

115 LMA: WJ/SPD 77.

116 Yale Center for British Art: B1975.4.1027, Louis-Philippe Boitard, *Self-Portrait with Two Young Men* (*c.* 1730–40); Gatrell, *First Bohemians*, 149.

117 Gilchrists, *Life of Blake,* I, 323.

118 Hogg, *Life of Shelley*, II, 32, 33.

119 John Forster, *The Life of Charles Dickens*, 3 vols (London: Chapman & Hall, 1873–4), I, 35, 39.

120 Emin, *Life and Adventures*, 87. A groat was worth 4d.

121 Chynoweth, 'Domestic Service'; Smith, *Nollekens and His Times*, I, 87.

122 Moritz, *Travels*, 24; *Carlyle Letters*, VI, 8.

123 Sara Pennell, '"Great quantities of gooseberry pie and baked clod of beef": Victualling and Eating out in Early Modern London', Ch. 11, 228–49 in Griffiths and Jenner, *Londinopolis*, 237.

124 Pottle, *Boswell's London Diary*, 328; Cunningham, *Life of Wilkie*, I, 80.

125 Wheatley and Cunningham, *London Past and Present*, III, 107.

126 Forster, *Life of Goldsmith*, 49.

127 Anderson, *Mozart Letters*, I, 50.

128 Irvin Ehrenpreis, *Swift: The Man, His Works and the Age*, 3 vols (London: Methuen, 1962), II, 300–1, 556; Swift, *Journal to Stella*, 60, 429.

129 Pennington, *Memoirs of Carter*, 164.

130 D. E. Williams, *The Life and Correspondence of Sir Thomas Lawrence*, 2 vols (London: Colburn & Bentley, 1831), I, 96.

131 Love, *Life, Adventures and Experience*, 152.

132 *Curwen Journal*, II, 580–1.

133 *Inchbald Diaries*, III, 22.

134 Sutton, *Complete Guide*, 39.

135 Stobart, *Comforts of Home*, 3.

136 Swift, *Journal to Stella*, 34, 299, 466.

137 Van Doren, *Franklin*, 279.

138 Swift, *Journal to Stella*, 19, 29, 58–9.

139 *Inchbald Diaries*, I, 181.

140 Hawkins, *Life of Johnson*, 159.

141 Place, *Autobiography*, 109.

142 Swift, *Journal to Stella*, 102.

143 Pottle, *Boswell's London Journal*, 55, 199, 214.

144 Prior, *Life of Goldsmith*, II, 335.

145 William Hazlitt, *Liber Amoris, or, The New Pygmalion* (London: Chatto & Windus, 1985, 1st pub. 1823), 128.

146 Place, *Autobiography*, 157.

147 Ford, *Weekes Letters*, 218.

148 *Inchbald Diaries*, II, 98; III, 159.

149 For lodgers as quasi-servants see Meldrum, *Domestic Service*, 30,

150 Paul, *Landlord or Tenant*, 33.

151 *MC*, 10 February 1792.

152 *MC*, 9 March 1781.

153 Haywood, *Present for a Servant Maid*, 49.

154 Casanova, *Memoires*, Episode 22, Ch. 8 (accessed 15 January 2020).

155   John Beresford, ed., *Memoirs of an Eighteenth-Century Footman, John Macdonald: Travels 1745–79* (London: Routledge, 1927), 59.

156   *GM*, April 1761, 172.

157   CWAC: A2269.

158   Anderson, *Mozart Letters*, I, 44–5; Van Doran, *Franklin*, 270, 276. Franklin's American household contained a further four enslaved people, Jemima and Othello, Peter's wife and son, who were left behind, and two other men, George and John.

159   *Inchbald Diaries*, III, Diary of 1820, *passim*.

160   Pilkington, in *Memoirs*, II, 158.

161   Swift*, Journal to Stella*, 192; *Curwen Journal*, II, 675; Cunningham, *Life of Wilkie*, I, 282.

162   Wale, *Grandfather's Pocket Book*, 110–11.

163   *Curwen Journal*, II, 653, 704; Schopenhauer, *A Lady Travels*, 124.

Chapter 5

1   *Through-bred Poor Gentleman's Book*, 11.

2   Swift, *Journal to Stella*, 397.

3   Frederick L. Jones, ed., *Mary Shelley's Journal* (Norman OK: Oklahoma University Press, 1947), 25.

4   *Inchbald Diaries*, II, 52, 54.

5   Hazlitt, *Liber Amoris*, 144.

6   Ibid., 192.

7   Boswell, *Life of Johnson*, 432.

8   A. Candler, *Poetical Attempts by Ann Candler, a Suffolk Cottager, with a Short Narrative of Her Life* (Ipswich: John Raw, 1803), 9.

9   Hogg, *Life of Shelley*, I, 178.

10   Earle, *City Full of People*, 95–6.

11   Saville, *Secret Comment*, 47.

12   Burton, *Double Life*, 193.

13   Boaden, *Inchbald Memoirs*, II, 157.

14   Burton, *Double Life*, 254.

15   D. T. Egerton, *Fashionable Bores or Coolers in High Life* (London: Thomas McLean, 1824), no. 4.

16   Lamb, *Letters of Elia*, I, 285–6.

17   Saville, *Secret Comment*, 47.

18   *Curran Letters,* 33.

19 Charles Robert Leslie, *Autobiographical Recollections by the Late Charles Robert Leslie, RA*, 2 vols (London: J. Murray, 1860), I, 28–9.

20 Styles, 'Lodging at the Old Bailey'. See also Berg and Eger, eds, *Luxury in the Eighteenth Century*; Marie-Odile Bernez, 'Comfort, the Acceptable Face of Luxury: An Eighteenth-Century Etymology', *Journal for Early Modern Cultural Studies* 14.2 (2014), 3–21; Stobart, *Comforts of Home*; Vickery, *Behind Closed Doors*.

21 Wheatley and Cunningham, *London Past and Present*, II, 383.

22 Penrose, *Haydon Autobiography*, 46.

23 *Curwen Journal*, II, 699.

24 *Carlyle Letters*, VII, 144.

25 *Curwen Journal*, II, 653; Swift, *Journal to Stella*, 192.

26 Boaden, *Inchbald Memoirs*, II, 91.

27 Charke, *Narrative*, 42; Oliver Goldsmith, 'A Description of an Author's Bed Chamber', in *Poems and Plays by Oliver Goldsmith, MB* (Dublin: Price, Sleater *et al.*, 1785), 10.

28 *Gibbon Letters*, I, 353.

29 Forster, *Life of Goldsmith*, 299.

30 Chynoweth, 'Domestic Service', 164–5; Daniel Miller, *The Comfort of Things* (Cambridge: Polity, 2008), 91.

31 David Hussey and Margaret Ponsonby, *The Single Homemaker and Material Culture in the Long Eighteenth Century* (Farnham: Ashgate, 2012), 98; Vickery, *Behind Closed Doors*, 38, 46.

32 LMA: WJ/SPD/79.

33 CWAC: A2269 and A2270.

34 E.g. 14 March 1777, *Curwen Journal*, 314.

35 Ibid., II, 702–10, 839–41.

36 John Hollander, 'It All Depends', *Social Research* 58.1 (1991), 31–49, 31, 35, 45–6.

37 Ehrenpreis, *Swift*, II, 394.

38 Swift, *Journal to Stella*, 63, 74, 102, 324.

39 Ibid., 505, 285; Thompsons, *Account Books of Swift*, lxxxvii and *passim*.

40 Title of a 1971 novel by Anthony Powell.

41 LMA: WJ/SPD/110; CWAC: A2270.

42 William Congreve, ed. John C. Hodges, *Letters and Documents* (London: Macmillan, 1964), 5–6.

43 Hazlitt, *Liber Amoris*, 144.

44 George Speaight, ed., *Professional and Literary Memoirs of Charles Dibdin the Younger …* (London: Society for Theatre Research, 1956), 35; Richard Cumberland, *Memoirs*, 2 vols (London: Lackington, 1807), I, 148; Place, *Autobiography*, 126.

45 *Curwen Journal*, II, 882.

46 *Carlyle Letters*, V, 408; VI, 8, 36.

47   Boaden, *Inchbald Memoirs*, I, 300; II, 159–60, 215, 159.

48   Place, *Autobiography*, 111, 124.

49   Muilman, *Apology for the Conduct*, I, 176.

50   *Pilkington Memoirs*, II, 26; Clarke, *Queen of the Wits*, 161; *Inchbald Diaries*, II, 308, III, 100; Hazlitt, *Liber Amoris*, 128; Cook, *Hazlitt in Love,* 60.

51   *Carlyle Letters*, V, 408.

52   Ehrenpreis, *Swift*, II, 554; Margot Holbrook, *Where Do You Keep?: Lodging the Cambridge Undergraduate* (Great Malvern: Cappella Archive, 2006), 57.

53   Forster, *Life of Goldsmith*, 97; *Curran Letters*, 33; Leslie, *Autobiographical Recollections*, I, 248–9.

54   Ibid., I, 249.

55   Lamb, *Letters of Elia*, I, *291;* Burton, *Double Life,* 288.

56   *Pilkington Memoirs*, II, 43–4; Clarke, *Queen of the Wits*, 232.

57   Stobart, *Comforts of Home*, 9.

58   Karen Harvey, 'Men Making Home: Masculinity and Domesticity in Eighteenth-Century Britain', *Gender & History* 21.3 (2009), 520–40, 532.

59   Saville, *Secret Comment*, 47–8.

60   *Curwen Journal*, I, 81.

61   *Inchbald Diaries*, 177.

62   *Authentic Memoirs of the Life of Margaret Nicholson* … (London: James Ridgeway, 1786),17, 18–19.

63   *Curwen Journal*, I, 448; II, 811, 970, 1017.

64   The third occasion is at ibid., II, 602.

65   *Pilkington Memoirs* and *Inchbald Diaries, passim.*

66   *Pilkington Memoirs*, II, 35, 194.

67   Ibid., II, 194.

68   *Curwen Journal*, II, 699.

69   *Inchbald Diaries, passim;* Boaden, *Inchbald Memoirs,* II, 81, 248–7.

70   Moritz, *Travels*, 24.

71   Thomas Carter, *Memoirs of a Working Man* (London: Charles Knight, 1845), 185, 187, 188.

72   OBOL: trial of Charles Kinross, t17851019-62.

73   *Curwen Journal*, I, 512; II, 519.

74   Emin, *Life and Adventures,* 64, 87.

75   William Cowper, ed. T. Grimshawe, *Life and Works*, 8 vols (London: Saunders & Otley, 1835–6), I, 90.

76   Penrose, *Haydon Autobiography*, 98–9.

77   Hodges, *William Congreve*, 80–1.

78   Pottle, *Boswell's London Journal*, 88.

79   Hazlitt, *Liber Amoris*, 160.

80 Pottle, *Boswell's London Journal*, 88–9.

81 *Curwen Journal*, II, 741, 962; Wellcome Library: no. 11903i.

82 *Curwen Journal*, II, 802.

83 Thompsons, *Account Books of Swift*, 127.

84 John Money, ed., *The Chronicles of John Cannon Excise Officer and Writing Master*, 2 vols (Oxford, 2010), I, 99.

85 Cunningham, *Life of Wilkie*, I, 312, 319.

86 Thompsons, *Account Books of Swift*, 124.

87 Ralph S. Walker, ed., *James Beattie's London Diary, 1773* (Aberdeen: The University Press, 1946), 90.

88 *Curwen Journal*, II, 802.

89 *ODNB*: entry for Cowper.

90 Boaden, *Inchbald Memoirs*, I, 299; II, 33.

91 Cunningham, *Life of Wilkie*, I, 207, 312, 319, 338, 373.

92 *Carlyle Letters*, VII, 177; addresses on letters, e.g. Hays to William Godwin 13 October 1795 and Charlotte Smith to Hays 26 June 1800, http://www. maryhayslifewritingscorrespondence.com/ (accessed 29 January 2020).

93 Moritz, *Travels*, 30.

94 Kirkman, *Macklin Memoirs*, II, 86, 90.

95 On eighteenth-century celebrity see Mary Luckhurst and Jane Moody, eds, *Theatre and Celebrity in Britain, 1660–2000* (Basingstoke: Palgrave Macmillan, 2005), Luckhurst and Moody, 'Introduction', 3; Felicity Nussbaum, 'Actresses and the Economics of Celebrity, 1700–1800', Ch. 9, 148–68, 152 in Tom Mole, ed., *Romanticism and Celebrity Culture, 1750–1850* (Cambridge: CUP, 2009).

96 *London Daily Post & General Advertiser*, 20 February 1739.

97 Anderson, *Mozart Letters*, 56; *Public Advertiser*, 20 March 1765.

98 Boaden, *Inchbald Memoirs*, I, 231.

99 Lewis Melville, *The Life and Letters of Laurence Sterne*, 2 vols (London, ?1910) I, 249.

100 *British Mercury*, 37 (11 September 1790), 348; Ada Earland, *John Opie and his Circle* (London: Hutchinson, 1911), 29.

101 Cunningham, *Life of Wilkie*, I, 204, 296.

102 Jonathan Fiske, *The Life and Transactions of Margaret Nicholson* (London: J. Fiske, 1786); *Public Advertiser*, 8 August 1786 cited in Steve Poole, *The Politics of Regicide in England, 1760–1850* (Manchester: Manchester University Press, 2000), 80.

103 Johann Christian Fabricius, *Briefe aus London Vermischten Inhalts* (Dessau and Leipzig: Buchhlandlung der Gelehrten, 1784), 339–40, trans. Christoph Heyl in Heyl, 'We Are Not At Home', 17.

104 OBOL: trial of John Thompson, t17850406-31.

105 *Curwen Journal*, II, 960–1.

106 Jones, *Man of Manners*, 58.

107 *Pilkington Memoirs*, II, 28; 'An Impartial Hand' (Dorothea Wentworth), *Remarks on the Second Volume of the Memoirs of Mrs. Pilkington* ... (Dublin: s.n., 1749), 6.

108 Pierce Egan, *Finish to the Adventures of Tom, Jerry, and Logic* ... (London: G. Virtue, 1830), facing 119.

109 *Curwen Journal*, II, 891.

110 James Peller Malcolm, *Anecdotes of the Manners and Customs of London During the Eighteenth Century*, 2 vols (London: Longman, Hurst, Rees & Orme, 2nd edn, 1810, 1st pub. 1808), II, 415.

111 Johnson, *Life of Savage*, 112.

112 Boaden, *Inchbald Memoirs*, I, 272.

113 Pottle, *Boswell's London Journal*, 237–8.

114 Quennell, *Hickey Memoirs*, 174.

115 Vickery, *Behind Closed Doors*, 31.

116 Pottle, *Boswell's London Journal*, 242; Vickery, 'An Englishman's Home Is His Castle?'

117 Smith, *Nollekens and His Times*, II, 32–3.

118 Swift, *Journal to Stella*, 292.

119 *Curwen Journal*, II, 934.

120 Cruden, *London-Citizen Exceedingly Injured*, 3–5.

121 Ford, *Weekes Letters*, 233.

122 *Curwen Journal*, I, 164.

123 Ibid., II, 519, 919, 825.

124 Beresford, *Miseries of Human Life*, I, 254–5.

125 Johnson, *Life of Savage*, 110; J. T. Smith, *A Book for a Rainy Day* ... (London: s.n., 1845), 108–9.

126 *Curwen Journal*, II, 756.

127 Cozens-Hardy, *Neville Diary*, 191, 193, 195.

128 Cook, *Hazlitt in Love*, 72.

129 Cozens-Hardy, *Neville Diary*, 193.

130 Admiral Knowles *v.* Captain Gambier, *Trials for Adultery* ..., VI (London: S. Bladon, 1780), 25.

131 OBOL: trial of Eleanor Hughes and others, t17960622-8.

132 Van Doran, *Benjamin Franklin*, 404.

133 Richard Holmes, *Coleridge: Darker Reflections* (London: Flamingo, 1999), 119.

134 Cunningham, *Life of Wilkie*, I, 130.

135 Penrose, *Haydon Autobiography*, 28.

136 Swift, *Journal to Stella*, 249, 220

137 Boswell, *Life of Johnson*, 274; Hesther [sic] Lynch Piozzi, *Anecdotes of the Late Samuel Johnson* ... (Dublin: Moncrieffe *et al.*, 1786), 236.

138 *Curran Letters*, 34.

139 Prior, *Life of Goldsmith* II, 333, 335.

140 CWAC: A2269; Carter, *Memoirs*, 159–60.

141 *Carlyle Letters*, VI, 56.

142 *Ibid.*, VII, 209.

143 Jones, *Man of Manners*, 42–3.

144 Pottle, *Boswell's London Journal*, 223–4; Cruden, *Adventures*, I, 37; Money, *Cannon Chronicles*, I, 129; *Curwen Journal*, II, 286; *Inchbald Diaries*, II, 58, 174.

145 Pottle, *Boswell's London Journal*, 311–12.

146 Ford, *Weekes Letters*, 233.

147 *Curwen Journal*, II, 669.

148 Pottle, *Boswell's London Journal*, 317.

149 *Curwen Journal*, II, 861.

150 Cozens-Hardy, *Neville Diary*, 63–6.

151 Emin, *Life*, 58–9.

152 *Curwen Journal*, II, 702.

153 Prior, *Life of Goldsmith*, I, 135.

154 *Curwen Journal*, I, 172; II, 1002.

155 Hogg, *Life of Shelley*, II, 32.

156 Michael Griffin and David O'Shaughnessy, eds, *The Letters of Oliver Goldsmith* (Cambridge: CUP, 2018), 33.

157 Forster, *Life of Goldsmith*, 98–9.

158 Ford, *Weekes Letters*, 233, 217, 225.

159 Pottle, *Boswell's London Journal*, 88–9, 199.

160 Swift, *Journal to Stella*, 220; *Inchbald Diaries*, I, 277.

161 Saville, *Secret Comment*, 60; Pottle, *Boswell's London Journal*, 238, 317; *Curwen Journal*, II, 811, 969, 1004; Hazlitt, *Liber Amoris*, 157.

Chapter 6

1   *ODNB*: entry for Godwin.

2   *Carlyle Letters*, VII, 205.

3   Cozens-Hardy, *Neville Diary*, 312.

4   Lamb, *Letters of Elia*, II, 64.

5   *ODNB*: entry for Godwin.

6   Place, *Autobiography*, 176, 189–91, 202–3, 210 (fn.).

7   Carter, *Memoirs*, 207, 217, 218.

8   *GM*, July 1803, 693.

9   LMA: MJ/SP/1707/04/015, petition of Thomas Butcher.

10 Carter, *Memoirs*, 217.

11 CWAC, A2269.

12 F. J. Manning, ed., *The Williamson Letters, 1748–65: Being the Letters of Talbot and Christian Williamson* (Streatley: Bedfordshire Historical Record Society, 1954), 49–50. This was the fire which the Compton Street fundraisers used as a model (Chapter 1).

13 *Curwen Journal*, II, 867.

14 OBOL: trial of Ambrose Cook, t17840104–54.

15 Westminster Abbey Muniment Room: City of Westminster Coroners, Coroners' Inquests into Suspicious Deaths, 4 January–28 December 1796, in *London Lives, 1690–1800*, WACWIC652360336-39 (www.londonlives.org, version 1.1.17, June 2012, accessed 21 February 2020); for Higgins's occupation, OBOL: trial of Elizabeth Edwards, t18000709–61.

16 The words of Robert Southey: Burton, *Double Life*, 75.

17 Ibid., 75, 123.

18 Samuel Johnson, ed. E. L. McAdam jun., *Diaries, Prayers, and Annals* (New Haven CT: YUP, 1958), 39.

19 *Inchbald Diaries*, II, 274.

20 OBOL: trial of Mary Nott, t17960622–6.

21 Julian Hoppit, *Risk and Failure in English* Business, *1700–1800* (Cambridge: CUP, 1987).

22 Boaden, *Inchbald Memoirs*, II, 148.

23 Anon. (Oliver Goldsmith?), *The Mystery of the Supposed Cock-Lane Ghost Revealed* (London: W. Bristow, 1762).

24 NPG: Research programmes, 'Artists, Their Materials and Suppliers', https://www.npg.org.uk/research/programmes/artists-their-materials-and-suppliers/thomas-lawrences-studios-and-studio-practice/lawrences-studios (accessed 20 February 2020).

25 *London Gazette* (1825), II, 1594, 2114.

26 Emin, *Life and Adventures*, 78.

27 Cozens-Hardy, *Neville Diary*, 65–6.

28 Boaden, *Inchbald Memoirs*, I, 299–300.

29 Ibid., II, 157–60.

30 Colin Campbell, *The Romantic Ethic and the Spirit of Modern Consumerism* (Oxford: Blackwell, 2005, 1st pub. 1987).

31 *Franklin Autobiography*, 48.

32 *Curran Letters*, 31–2.

33 *Carlyle Letters*, V, 414, 426: VI, 8.

34 Cockayne, *Hubbub*.

35 *MC*, 6 July 1772.

36 Money, *Cannon Chronicles*, I, 129.

37 *Inchbald Diaries*, II, 217–18.

38 *Carlyle Letters*, VI, 8.

39 *Curwen Journal*, II, 837, 839.

40 Pottle, *Boswell's London Journal*, 167; Brady and Pottle, *Boswell in Search of a Wife*, 317, 322, 323.

41 *GM*, September 1750, 391.

42 Paul, *Landlord or Tenant*, 33; Walter Robinson, *The Landlord's Pocket Lawyer* ... (London: S. Bladon, 3rd edn, 1781), 49.

43 Bird, *Laws Respecting Landlords*, 49.

44 Tardy, *Manuel du Voyageur*, 17.

45 Congreve, *Letters*, 36–8.

46 Cruden, *Adventures,* II, 35.

47 Lamb, *Letters of Elia*, I, 183.

48 Burton, *Double Life*, 287.

49 Trusler, *London Adviser*, 6; Maxwell, *Housekeepers' Guide*, 40; Brady, *Plain Advice*, 25–6.

50 *Curwen Journal*, II, 549.

51 Pilkington, in *Memoirs*, II, 161.

52 *Curwen Journal*, I, 80–1; II, 519, 564, 822, 824.

53 Emin, *Life and Adventures*, 59, 70.

54 Boaden, *Inchbald Memoirs*, II, 73, 74, 91, 93, 157; *Inchbald Diaries*, III, 21–8.

55 Congreve, *Letters*, 36–8.

56 *Curwen Journal*, II, 601, 602, 970.

57 *Curwen Journal*, II, 602.

58 *Jefferson Memorandum Books* (accessed 26 February 2019); Cunningham, *Life of Wilkie*, I, 210

59 Holmes, *Darker Reflections*, 236.

60 Cruden, *Adventures*, II, 35.

61 Styles, 'Lodging at the Old Bailey'.

62 E.g. Maxwell, *Housekeepers' Guide*, 41.

63 OBOL: trial of Elizabeth Crimpshaw, t18050220-34.

64 Thomas Dibdin, *The Reminiscences of Thomas Dibdin*, 2 vols (New York: AMS Press, 1970, 1st pub. 1827), I, 317–18.

65 Holmes, *Darker Reflections*, 211–14, 221, 228.

66 Pottle, *Boswell's London Journal*, 214, 311–13, 17.

67 Ware, *Complete Body of Architecture*, I, 328; Conor Lucey, 'Marketing the Necessary Comforts in Georgian Dublin', 67–72 in Stobart, *Comforts of Home*.

68 *MC*, 9 November 1799, 2 January 1800.

69 OBOL: trial of Elizabeth Palmer, t17841020-32.

70 Malcolm, *Manners and Customs*, II, 401.

71 J. M. Beattie, *Policing and Punishment in London, 1660-1750: Urban Crime and the Limits of Terror* (Oxford: OUP, 2001), 'Jurors and Jury Practice', 264–76.

72 OBOL: trial of Daniel Macginniss, t17830117–1; TNA: HO 13/1, 330–1.

73 *Curwen Journal*, II, 969.

74 Pottle, *Boswell's London Journal*, 311–12.

75 Money, *Cannon Chronicles*, I, 94; Beresford, *Memoirs of John Macdonald*, 59–60.

76 John Black, 'Illegitimacy, Sexual Relations and Location in Metropolitan London, 1735–85', Ch. 7, 101–18 in Tim Hitchcock and Heather Shore, eds, *The Streets of London from the Great Fire to the Great Stink* (London: Rivers Oram, 2003), 113. On the sexualization of female servants see also Chynoweth, 'Domestic Service and Domestic Space'; Hill, *Servants* and Meldrum, *Domestic Service and Gender*.

77 Byrd, *London Diary*.

78 Beresford, *Memoirs of John Macdonald*, 59–60.

79 CWAC: St Martin-in-the-Fields Settlement Examinations, F5022, 129.

80 'Examinations, 1750–1766: nos 395–414', no. 396, in Hitchcock and Black, eds, *Chelsea Settlement and Bastardy Examinations, 1733–66*, 125–32. *British History Online*, http://www.british-history.ac.uk/london-record-soc/vol33/pp125-132 (accessed 5 March 2020).

81 Haywood, *Present for a Servant Maid*, 49.

82 *Farington Diary*, I, 185.

83 Quennell, *Hickey Memoirs*, 26, 175–9.

84 Cozens-Hardy, *Neville Diary*, 64–9, 73.

85 Cook, *Hazlitt in Love*, 21–3, 133.

86 Ibid., 15.

87 Hazlitt, *Liber Amoris*, 22, 35–6, 128, 135, 157; William Hazlitt, ed. Herschel Moreland Sikes, *The Letters of William Hazlitt* (London: Macmillan, 1979), 263.

88 Hazlitt, *Liber Amoris*, 34; *Hazlitt Letters*, 249.

89 Leonore Davidoff, 'Class and Gender in Victorian England: The Case of Hannah Cullwick and A. J. Munby', *Feminist Studies* 5.1 (1979), 86–141.

90 Hazlitt, *Liber Amoris*, 134–5, 269.

91 Ibid., 93–4, 163.

92 Letter to Patmore cited in Cook, *Hazlitt in Love*, 158.

93 Ibid., 189–91.

94 Penrose, *Haydon Autobiography*, 272.

95 Hazlitt, *Liber Amoris*, 20; Cook, *Hazlitt in Love*, 157; Penrose, *Haydon Autobiography*, 48, 272.

96 *Pilkington Memoirs*, II, 194, 207, 220, 223.

97 Muilman, *Apology*, II, 16–19.

98 Boswell, *Life of Johnson*, 261–2.

99 Edward Ward, *Dr Johnson Perusing the Manuscript of The Vicar of Wakefield* (exhibited at the Royal Academy, 1843).

100 Shee, *Life of Shee*, 171–2.

101   Anon., *A View of the Beau Monde: Or, Memoirs of the Celebrated Coquetilla* …
      (London: A. Dodd, 1731).

102   Anon., *The Uncommon Adventures of Miss Kitty F****r*, 2 parts (London: Thomas
      Bailey, 1759).

103   Frederick L. Jones, ed., *The Letters of Percy Bysshe Shelley*, 2 vols (Oxford:
      Clarendon, 1964), I, 139 (fn. 2), 331, 369.

104   Jones, *Mary Shelley's Journal, 39.*

105   Jones, *Letters of Shelley*, I, 395–464.

106   Richard Holmes, *Coleridge: Early Visions, 1772–1804* (London: HarperCollins,
      1998), 290; Earl Leslie Griggs, ed., *Collected Letters of Samuel Taylor Coleridge*,
      6 vols (Oxford: Clarendon, 1956–71), II, 424, 436.

107   Holmes, *Darker Reflections*, 221.

108   Penrose, *Haydon Autobiography*, 59, 117, 122,

109   Ibid., 143, 145, 213; Richard Henry Stoddard, ed., *The Life, Letters and Table Talk
      of Benjamin Robert Haydon* (New York: Scribner, Armstrong & Co., 1876), 47.

110   Penrose, *Haydon Autobiography*, 208, 286, 291.

111   *Pilkington Memoirs*, II, 142; *Curwen Journal*, II, 699.

Chapter 7

1   Davidoff, *Worlds Between*, 156–72.

2   George Gissing, ed. Paul Coustillas, *London, and the Life of Literature in Late
     Victorian England: The Diary of George Gissing, Novelist* (Hassocks: Harvester Press,
     1978).

3   The first such was the Public Health Act 1848 which limited the number of lodgers
     per house and promoted cleanliness, ventilation, and the segregation of the sexes,
     11 & 12 Vict. ch.63.

4   Stobart, *Comforts of Home*, 2.

5   Smith, *Nollekens and His Times*, II, 218–20.

6   Davidoff, *Worlds Between*, 155.

7   Quennell, *Hickey Memoirs*, 176.

8   White, *London in the Eighteenth Century*, 118–23.

9   Blackstone, *Commentaries*, I, Ch. 14, 410.

10   Sophie Carter, *Purchasing Power: Representing Prostitution in Eighteenth-Century
     English Popular Print Culture* (Aldershot: Ashgate, 2004), 55.

11   Adam Smith, *The Theory of Moral Sentiments* (New York: Barnes & Noble, 2004, 1st
     pub. 1759), 193.

Bibliography

Manuscript primary sources

British Library

Lansdowne 509B, Westminster by election scrutiny, 1749.

City of Westminster Archive Centre

A2269 and 2270, papers of the committee for the relief of the sufferers by fire, 1785.
B1071, vestry minutes, St Clement Dane, 1767–76.
F5022, settlement examinations, St Martin-in-the-Fields, 1729.

London Metropolitan Archives

MJ/SP/1707/04/015, petition of Thomas Butcher, 1707.
P92/SAV/178– 321. token books, St Saviour, Southwark, 1571–1643.
P92/SAV/1314–17, views of inmates of divided tenements, St Saviour, Southwark, 1593–5.
WJ/SPD 72–136, fire in Charles Street, Westminster, 1707.
WR/A/008, Westminster Sessions of the Peace: enrolment, registration and deposit, Jul. 1798.
WR/R/R/002, Return of lodgers in the parish of St Martin-in-the-Fields, Suffolk Street ward, November 1680.

Digital primary sources

17th and 18th Century Burney Newspapers Collection, https://www.gale.com/intl/c/17th-and-18th-century-burney-newspapers-collection.
Ancestry, www.ancestry.co.uk.
Chaucer, Geoffrey, *The Canterbury Tales*, (1342–1400), http://www.librarius.com/cantales.htm.

de Seingalt, Jacques Casanova, trans. Arthur Machen, *The Memoires of Casanova, Complete* (London: s.n., 1894), http://www.gutenberg.org/files/2981/2981-h/2981-h.htm.

Founders Online, https://founders.archives.gov/.

Hays, Mary, Life, Writings, and Correspondence, http://www.maryhayslifewritings correspondence.com/home.

Hitchcock, Tim and John Black, eds, *Chelsea Settlement and Bastardy Examinations, 1733– 66* (London: London Record Society, 1999), *British History Online*, http://www.british-history.ac.uk/london-record-soc/vol33.

Horwood, Richard, *Plan of the Cities of London and Westminster, the Borough of Southwark, and Parts Adjoining, Shewing Every House* (1792–9), http://www.romanticlondon.org/explore-horwoods-plan/#20/51.48906/-0.13119.

Journal of the House of Lords (London: His Majesty's Stationery Office, 1767–1830), *British History Online*, http://www.british-history.ac.uk/lords-jrnl.

London Inhabitants within the Walls 1695 (London: London Record Society, 1966), *British History Online*, http://www.british-history.ac.uk/london-record-soc/vol2.

London Lives, 1690–1800, www.londonlives.org.

Lysons, Daniel, *The Environs of London: Vol. I, County of Surrey* (London, 1792), *British History Online*, http://www.british-history.ac.uk/london-environs/vol1/.

Populations Past: Atlas of Victorian and Edwardian Population, https://www.populationspast.org/about/.

Proceedings of the Old Bailey, https://www.oldbaileyonline.org/.

Roger Whitley's Diary 1684–97 Bodleian Library, Ms Eng Hist C 711, Michael Stevens and Honor Lewington, eds (s.l., 2004), *British History Online*, http://www.british-history.ac.uk/no-series/roger-whitley-diary/1684-97/january-1685.

Strype, John, *A Survey of the Cities of London and Westminster* (London: J. Churchill *et al.*, 1720), https://www.dhi.ac.uk/strype/TransformServlet?page=book6_068.

Westlaw (online legal research service), used for researching civil cases, which are then cited using the legal report in which they were originally recorded, www.westlaw.co.uk.

Printed primary sources

Newspapers, periodicals and series

British Mercury.
Collection for Improvement of Husbandry and Trade.
General Advertiser.
Gentleman's Magazine.
Idler.
Lady's Magazine.
London Daily Post.
London Gazette.

Morning Chronicle.
Morning Herald.
Morning Post.
Newgate Calendar.
Olla Podrida.
Public Advertiser.
Rambler.
Spectator.
St James's Chronicle.
Times.

Published diaries, letters, autobiography and near-contemporary biography

Anon., *A View of the Beau Monde: Or, Memoirs of the Celebrated Coquetilla: A Real History, in Which Is Interspersed the Amours of Several Persons of Quality and Distinction* (London: A. Dodd, 1731).

Anon., *Memoirs of the Celebrated Miss Fanny Murray: Interspersed with the Intrigues and Amours of Several Eminent Personages, Founded on Real Facts*, 2 vols (Dublin: S. Smith, 2nd edn, 1759).

Anon., *The Uncommon Adventures of Miss Kitty F****r*, 2 parts (London: Thomas Bailey, 1759).

Anon., *Authentic Memoirs of the Life of Margaret Nicholson: Who Attempted to Stab His Most Gracious Majesty with a Knife* (London: James Ridgeway, 1786).

Anon., *A Curious and Interesting Narrative of Poll House and the Marquis of C******, (Late Lord T—)* (London: J.L. Marks, n.d. ?1812), in Julie Peakman, ed., *Whore Biographies, 1700–1825*, 8 vols (London: Pickering & Chatto, 2006).

Anderson, Emily, trans. and ed., *Letters of Mozart and His Family*, 2 vols (London: Macmillan, 1985, 1st pub. 1938).

Anselment, Raymond A., ed., *The Remembrances of Elizabeth Freke, 1671–1714* (Cambridge: CUP, 2001).

Batchelor, Jennie, and Megan Hiatt, eds, *The Histories of Some of the Penitents in the Magdalen-House, as Supposed to Be Related by Themselves* (London: Pickering & Chatto, 2007).

Beresford, John, ed., *Memoirs of an Eighteenth-Century Footman, John Macdonald: Travels 1745–79* (London: Routledge, 1927).

Blundell, Nicholas, ed. J. J. Bagley, transcr. and ann. Frank Tyrer, *The Great Diurnal of Nicholas Blundell of Little Crosby, Lancashire*, 3 vols (Preston: Record Society of Lancashire and Cheshire, 1968–72).

Boaden, James, ed., *Memoirs of Mrs. Inchbald: Including Her Familiar Correspondence*, 2 vols (London: Richard Bentley, 1833).

Boswell, James, *The Life of Samuel Johnson LLD* (New York: Everyman, 1992, 1st pub. 1791).

Brady, Frank, and Frederick A. Pottle, eds, *Boswell in Search of a Wife 1766–9* (London: Heinemann, 1957).

Burnett, John, ed., *Useful Toil: Autobiographies of Working People from the 1820s to the 1920s* (Harmondsworth: Penguin, 1974).

Burney, Frances, *The Diary and Letters of Madame D'Arblay*, 3 vols (London: Viztelly & Co., 1890–1).

Byrd, William, Louis B. Wright, and Marion Tinling, eds, *The London Diary (1717–21) and Other Writings* (Oxford: OUP, 1958).

Candler, A., *Poetical Attempts by Ann Candler, a Suffolk Cottager, with a Short Narrative of Her Life* (Ipswich: John Raw, 1803).

Carretta, Vincent, ed., *Letters of the Late Ignatius Sancho, an African* (Peterborough, Ontario: Broadview, 2015, 1st pub. 1782).

Carter, Thomas, *Memoirs of a Working Man* (London: Charles Knight, 1845).

Charke, Charlotte, *A Narrative of the Life of Mrs. C.C., Written by Herself* (London: Hunt & Clarke, 1827, 1st pub. 1755).

Congreve, William, ed. John C. Hodges, *Letters and Documents* (London: Macmillan, 1964).

Cook, Edward Dutton, 'Widow Hogarth and Her Lodger', *Once a Week* (29 December 1860), 10–13.

Cowper, William, ed. T. Grimshawe, *Life and Works*, 8 vols (London: Saunders & Otley, 1835–6).

Cozens-Hardy, B., ed., *The Diary of Sylas Neville 1767–88* (Oxford: OUP, 1950).

Cremer, John, transcr. R. Reynell Bellamy, *Ramblin' Jack: The Journal of Captain John Cremer, 1700–74* (London: J. Cape, 1936).

Cruden, Alexander, *The London-Citizen Exceedingly Injured: Or, a British Inquisition Display'd: In an Account of the Unparallel'd Case of a Citizen of London, Bookseller to the Late Queen, Who Was in a Most Unjust and Arbitrary Manner Sent on the 23d March Last, 1738, to a Private Madhouse* (London: T. Cooper & A. Dodd, 1739).

Cruden, Alexander, *The Adventures of Alexander the Corrector: Wherein Is Given an Account of His Being Unjustly Sent to Chelsea, … With an Account of the Chelsea-Academies, … To Which Is Added an Account of the Prophesies of Some Pious Ministers of the Gospel, … With Observations on the Necessity of a Reformation by Executing the Laws against Swearers*, 3 vols (London: for the author, 1754–5).

Cumberland, Richard, *Memoirs*, 2 vols (London: Lackington, 1807).

Cunningham, Allan, ed., *The Life of Sir David Wilkie, with His Journals, Tours, and Critical Remarks on Works of Art*, 3 vols (London: J. Murray, 1843).

Curran, J., *Letters of [John Philpot] Curran to the Reverend H. Weston Written in the Years 1773 and 1774* (London: T. Hookham, 1819).

D'Arblay, Mme (Frances Burney), *Memoirs of Doctor Burney* (Philadelphia PA: Key & Biddle, 1833).

de Saussure, César, trans. and ed. Mme van Muyden, *A Foreign View of England in the Reigns of George I and George II, 1725–9: The Letters of Monsieur César de Saussure to His Family* (London: J. Murray, 1902).

Dibdin, Thomas, *The Reminiscences of Thomas Dibdin*, 2 vols (New York: AMS Press, 1970, 1st pub. 1827).

Edwards, Edward, *Anecdotes of Painters* (London: Cornmarket Press, facsimile edn, 1970, 1st pub. 1808).

Emin, Joseph, *The Life and Adventures of J.E., an Armenian* (London: for the author, 1792).

Fabricius, Johann Christian, *Briefe aus London Vermischten Inhalts* (Dessau and Leipzig: Buchhlandlung der Gelehrten, 1784), 339–40, trans. Christoph Heyl in Christoph Heyl, 'We Are Not at Home: Protecting Domestic Privacy in Post-Fire Middle-Class London', *London Journal* 27.2 (2002), 12–33.

Fairburn, John, *Account of the Life, Death and Interment of John Williamson: The Supposed Murderer of the Families of Marr and Williamson; and Self-Destroyer* (London: J. Fairburn, 1812).

Farington, Joseph, ed. James Greig, *The Farington Diary*, 8 vols (London: Hutchinson, 1922–8).

Fiske, Jonathan, *The Life and Transactions of Margaret Nicholson* (London: J. Fiske, 1786).

Ford, John M. T., ed., *A Medical Student at St Thomas's Hospital, 1801–2, The Weekes Family Letters* (London: Wellcome Institute, 1987).

Franklin, Benjamin, ed. Ormond Seavey, *Autobiography and Other Writings* (Oxford: OUP, 1993).

Fretwell, James, *A Family History*, 163–43 in *Yorkshire Diaries and Autobiographies in the Seventeenth and Eighteenth Centuries* (Durham, London and Edinburgh: Surtees Society, 1877).

Gissing, George, ed. Paul Coustillas, *London, and the Life of Literature in Late Victorian England: The Diary of George Gissing, Novelist* (Hassocks: Harvester Press, 1978).

Goede, Christian Augustus Gottlieb, *The Stranger in England: Or, Travels in Great Britain; Containing Remarks on the Politics, Laws, Etc. of That Country*, 3 vols (London: Mathews & Leigh, 1807).

Greig, James, ed., *The Diaries of a Duchess, Extracts from the Diaries of the First Duchess of Northumberland, (1716–76)* (London: Hodder & Stoughton, 1926).

Griffin, Michael and David O'Shaughnessy, eds, *The Letters of Oliver Goldsmith* (Cambridge: CUP, 2018).

Griggs, Earl Leslie, ed., *Collected Letters of Samuel Taylor Coleridge*, 6 vols (Oxford: Clarendon, 1956–71).

Gronniosaw, James Albert Ukawsaw, *A Narrative of the Most Remarkable Particulars in the Life of James Albert Ukawsaw Gronniosaw, an African Prince, as Related by Himself* (Bath: W. Gye, 1772).

Grosley, Pierre-Jean, trans. Thomas Nugent, *A Tour to London, or, New Observations on England and Its Inhabitants*, 2 vols (London: Lockyer Davis, 1772).

Hawkins, Sir John, *The Life of Samuel Johnson, LLD* (London: Buckland, Rivington *et al.*, 1787).

Hazlitt, William, *Liber Amoris, or, The New Pygmalion* (London: Chatto & Windus, 1985, 1st pub. 1823).

Hoare, Prince, *Memoirs of Granville Sharp* (London: Henry Colburn, 1820).

Hogg, Thomas Jefferson, *The Life of Percy Bysshe Shelley: As Comprised in The Life of Shelley by Thomas Jefferson Hogg, the Recollections of Shelley and Byron by Edward John Trelawny, Memoirs of Shelley by Thomas Love Peacock*, 2 vols (London: J. M. Dent, 1933, 1st pub. 1858).

Hurst, Barbara, ed., *The Diaries of Sarah Hurst 1759–62: Life and Love in Eighteenth-Century Horsham* (Stroud: Amberley Publishing, 2009).

Hutton, William, *A Journey from Birmingham to London* (Birmingham: Pearson & Rollason, 1785).

Jackson, C., ed., *Yorkshire Diaries and Autobiographies in the Seventeenth and Eighteenth Centuries* (Durham, London and Edinburgh: Surtees Society, 1877).

Johnson, Samuel, eds Nicholas Seager and Lance Wilcox, *The Life of Mr Richard Savage* (Peterborough, Ontario: Broadview Press, 2016, 1st pub. 1744).

Johnson, Samuel, ed. E. L. McAdam jun., *Diaries, Prayers, and Annals* (New Haven CT: YUP, 1958).

Jones, Frederick L., ed., *Mary Shelley's Journal* (Norman OK: Oklahoma University Press, 1947).

Jones, Frederick L., ed., *The Letters of Percy Bysshe Shelley*, 2 vols (Oxford: Clarendon, 1964).

Kielmansegge, Count Frederick, trans. Countess Kielmansegg, *Diary of a Journey to England in the Years 1761–2* (London: Longman, Green, 1902).

Kirkman, James Thomas, *Memoirs of the Life of Charles Macklin Esq.: Principally Compiled from His Own Papers and Memorandums …*, 2 vols (London: Lackington & Allen, 1799).

Lamb, Charles, *The Letters of Elia*, 2 vols (London: J.M. Dent, 1909).

Leslie, Charles Robert, *Autobiographical Recollections by the Late Charles Robert Leslie, RA*, 2 vols (London: J. Murray, 1860).

Lewis, W. S., ed., *Horace Walpole's Correspondence*, 48 vols (New Haven CT: YUP, 1937–83).

Love, David, *The Life, Adventures, and Experiences of David Love, Written by Himself* (Nottingham: Sutton & Son, 5th edn, 1825.).

Manning, F. J., ed., *The Williamson Letters, 1748–65: Being the Letters of Talbot and Christian Williamson* (Streatley: Bedfordshire Historical Record Society, 1954).

Mason, Simon, *A Narrative of the Life and Distresses of Simon Mason, Apothecary: Setting Forth the Injurious Treatment He Hath Met with; with Many Other Transactions* (Birmingham: for the author, 1754).

Misson, Henri, *M. Misson's Memoirs and Observations in His Travels over England: With Some Account of Scotland and Ireland, Dispos'd in Alphabetical Order*, trans. Mr Ozell (London: D. Brown, 1719).

Money, John, ed., *The Chronicles of John Cannon Excise Officer and Writing Master*, 2 vols (Oxford, 2010).

Moritz, Carl Philipp, *Travels of Carl Philipp Moritz in England in 1782* (London: Humphrey Milford, 1924, 1st pub. in English 1795).

Muilman, Teresia Constantia, *An Apology for the Conduct of Mrs Teresia Constantia Phillips; More Particularly, that Part of It which Relates to Her Marriage with an Eminent Dutch Merchant, the Whole Authenticated by Faithful Copies of His Letters*, 3 vols (London: for the author, 1748–9).

Neave, Susan and David, eds, *The Diary of a Yorkshire Gentleman: John Courtney of Beverley, 1759-68* (Otley: Smith, Settle, 2001).

Norton, J. E., ed., *The Letters of Edward Gibbon*, 3 vols (London: Cassell, 1956).

Nuttall, Geoffrey F., ed., *Letters of John Pinney, 1679–99* (London: OUP, 1939).

Oliver, Andrew, ed., *The Journal of Samuel Curwen, Loyalist*, 2 vols (Cambridge MA: HUP, 1972).

Peakman, Julie, ed., *Whore Biographies, 1700–1825*, 8 vols (London: Pickering & Chatto, 2006).

Pennington, Revd Montagu, *Memoirs of the Life of Mrs Elizabeth Carter* (London: Rivington, 1807).

Penrose, Alexander P. D., ed., *The Autobiography and Memoirs of Benjamin Robert Haydon, 1786-1846* (London: G. Bell, 1927).

Pilkington, Laetitia, *Memoirs of Mrs Laetitia Pilkington: Written by Herself, Wherein Are Occasionally Interspersed All Her Poems*, 3 vols (Dublin, 1748, 1749, 1754).

Piozzi, Hesther [*sic*] Lynch, *Anecdotes of the Late Samuel Johnson, LLD During the Last Twenty Three Years of His Life* (Dublin: Moncrieffe *et al.*, 1786).

Place, Francis, ed. Mary Thale, *The Autobiography of Francis Place (1771-1854)* (Cambridge: CUP, 1972).

Pottle, Frederick A., ed., *Boswell's London Journal, 1762-3* (London: Futura, 1982, 1st pub. 1950).

Price, J. M., ed., *Joshua Johnson's Letterbook, 1771–4: Letters from a Merchant in London to His Partners in Maryland* (London: London Record Society, 1979).

Quennell, P., ed., *Memoirs of William Hickey* (London: Hutchinson, 1960).

Reynolds, E. E., ed., *The Mawhood Diary* (London: Catholic Record Society, 1956).

Robertson, Ben P., ed., *The Diaries of Elizabeth Inchbald*, 3 vols (London: Pickering & Chatto, 2007).

Salih, Sara, ed., *The History of Mary Prince, a West Indian Slave* (London: Penguin, 2000, 1st pub. 1831).

Sanders, Charles Richard, gen. ed., *The Collected Letters of Thomas and Jane Welsh Carlyle*, 45 vols (Durham NC: Duke University Press, 1970–77).

Saville, Alan, ed., *Secret Comment: The Diaries of Gertrude Savile 1721-57* (Devon: Kingsbridge History Society, 1997).

Schopenhauer, Johanna, trans. and eds Ruth Michaelis-Jena and Willy Merson, *A Lady Travels: Journeys in England and Scotland from the Diaries of Johanna Schopenhauer* (London: Routledge, 1988).

Shee, Martin Archer, *The Life of Sir Martin Archer Shee: President of the Royal Academy, FRS, DCL, by His Son*, 2 vols (London: Longman, Green, 1860).

Sikes, Herschel Moreland, ed., *The Letters of William Hazlitt* (London: Macmillan, 1979).

Smith, J. T., ed. Wilfred Whitten, *Nollekens and His Times: Comprehending a Life of That Celebrated Sculptor, and Memoirs of Several Contemporary Artists*, 2 vols (London: John Lane, 1920, 1st pub. 1828).

Smith, J. T., *A Book for a Rainy Day: Or, Recollections of the Events of the Last Sixty-Six Years* (London: s.n., 1845).

Speaight, George, ed., *Professional and Literary Memoirs of Charles Dibdin the Younger; Dramatist and Upward of Thirty Years Manager of Minor Theatres, Edited from the Original Manuscript* (London: Society for Theatre Research, 1956).

Stoddard, Richard Henry, ed., *The Life, Letters and Table Talk of Benjamin Robert Haydon* (New York: Scribner, Armstrong & Co., 1876).

Swift, Jonathan, ed. Abigail Williams, *Journal to Stella: Letters to Esther Johnson and Rebecca Dingley, 1710–13* (Cambridge: CUP, 2013).

Thompson, Paul V. and Dorothy J., transcr. and intro., *The Account Books of Jonathan Swift* (Newark DE: Scolar Press, 1984).

Todd, Janet, ed., *The Collected Letters of Mary Wollstonecraft* (London: Penguin, 2003).

von Archenholz, Johann Wilhelm, *A Picture of England: Containing a Description of the Laws, Customs, and Manners of England, Interspersed with Curious and Interesting Anecdotes*, trans. from the French (Dublin: P. Byrne, 1791, 1st pub. 1785).

Wale, Revd Henry John, MA, *My Grandfather's Pocket Book, from AD 1701 to 1796* (London: Chapman & Hall, 1883).

Walker, Ralph S., ed., *James Beattie's London Diary, 1773* (Aberdeen: The University Press, 1946).

Wilkinson, Tate, *Memoirs of His Own Life*, 4 vols (York: Wilson, Spence & Mawman, 1790).

Williams, Clare, trans., *Sophie in London in 1786: Being the Diary of Sophie von la Roche* (London: J. Cape, 1933).

Williams, D. E., *The Life and Correspondence of Sir Thomas Lawrence*, 2 vols (London: Colburn & Bentley, 1831).

Woodforde, Dorothy H., ed., *Woodforde Papers and Diaries* (London: P. Davies, 1932).

Other printed primary sources

Anon., 'An Impartial Hand' (Dorothea Wentworth), *Remarks on the Second Volume of the Memoirs of Mrs. Pilkington …* (Dublin: s.n., 1749).

Anon. ('Philanthropos'), *An Appeal to the Public against the Growing Evil of Universal Register-Offices, Otherwise Called Agency and Intelligence Offices for Masters and Servants; the Loan of Money; and Sale of Estates* (London: for the author, 1757).

Anon. (Oliver Goldsmith?), *The Mystery of the Supposed Cock-Lane Ghost Revealed* (London: W. Bristow, 1762).

Anon, *Low-Life: Or One Half of the World Knows Not How the Other Half Live ...* (London: John Lever, 3rd edn, 1764, 1st pub. c. 1752).

Anon., *Trials for Adultery, or, The History of Divorces: Being Select Trials at Doctors Commons ... from Year 1760, to the Present Time, Taken in Short-Hand by a Civilian*, 7 vols (London: S. Bladon, 1779–80).

Anon. ('A Gentleman of Experience'), *The Economist: Shewing, in a Variety of Estimates, from Fourscore Pounds a Year to Upwards of 800l. How Comfortably and Genteely a Family May Live with Frugality* (London, 15th edn, 1781).

Anon., *The New Cheats of the Town Exposed: or, The Frauds and Tricks of the Town Laid Open to Both Sexes* (London: W. Clements, 1792).

Anon., *Harris's List of Covent Garden Ladies, Or, Man of Pleasure's Kalender for the Year 1793* (London: 'H. Ranger', 1793).

Anon., *The Picture of London for 1809; Being a Correct Guide to all the Curiosities, Amusements, Exhibits, Public Establishments and Remarkable Objects, in or Near London* (London: Richard Phillips, 1809).

Anon., *A New System of Practical Domestic Economy* (London: Henry Colburn, 1823).

Anon., *West Port Murders; or an Authentic Account of the Atrocious Murders Committed by Burke and His Associates, Containing a Full Account of All the Extraordinary Circumstances Connected with Them* (Edinburgh: Thomas Ireland, jun., 1829).

Anon., *The Thorough-bred Poor Gentleman's Book; or, How to Live in London on £100 a Year* (London: William Marsh, 3rd edn, 1835).

Barnett, George E., ed., *Two Tracts by Gregory King* (Baltimore MD: Johns Hopkins Press, 1936).

Bee, Jon, *A Living Picture of London for 1828, and Stranger's Guide through the Streets of the Metropolis* (London: W. Clarke, 1828).

Beresford, James, *The Miseries of Human Life or, the Last Groans of Timothy Testy and Samuel Sensitive: With a Few Supplementary Sighs from Mrs Testy, with Which Are Now for the First Time Interspersed, Varieties, Incidental to the Principal Matter, in Prose and Verse, in Nine Additional Dialogues as Overheard by James Beresford*, 2 vols (London: W. Miller, 8th edn, 1807).

Bird, James Barry, *The Laws Respecting Landlords, Tenants and Lodgers: Laid Down in a Plain, Easy, and Familiar Manner; and Free from the Technical Terms of the Law, as Collected from the Several Reports and Other Books of Authority, up to the Commencement of the Present Easter Term* (London: W. Clarke, 1794).

Blackstone, William, *Commentaries on the Law of England*, 4 vols (London: Strahan & Woodfall, 1795, 1st pub. 1765–70).

Brown, John, *An Estimate of the Manners and Principles of the Times* (London: L. Davis & C. Reymers, 1757).

Burney, Frances, ed. Edward A. Bloom, *Evelina: Or, the History of a Young Lady's Entrance into the World* (Oxford: OUP, 2002, 1st pub. 1778).

Burney, Frances, eds Peter Sabor and Geoffrey Sill, *The Witlings* and *The Woman Hater* (London: Pickering & Chatto, 1997).

Chatterton, Thomas, ed. C. B. Willcox, *The Complete Works of Thomas Chatterton*, 2 vols (Cambridge: W.P. Grant, 1842).

Chatterton, Thomas, ed. Donald S. Taylor, *The Complete Works of Thomas Chatterton*, 2 vols (Oxford: Clarendon Press, 1971).

Child, Sir Josiah, *A New Discourse of Trade: Wherein Are Recommended Several Weighty Points* (Glasgow: Foulis, 1751, 1st pub. 1690).

Cleland, John, *Fanny Hill, or, Memoirs of a Woman of Pleasure* (London: Penguin, 1985, 1st pub. 1748–9).

Cobb, James, *The First Floor; a Farce in Two Acts* (London: C. Dilly, 2nd edn, 1787).

Defoe, Daniel, *The History and Remarkable Life of the Truly Honourable Colonel Jacque, Commonly called Colonel Jack*, 2 vols (Edinburgh: Ballantyne, 1810, 1st pub. 1722).

Defoe, Daniel, *The Fortunes and Misfortunes of the Famous Moll Flanders, &c.* (London: Penguin, 1989, 1st pub. 1722).

Defoe, Daniel, *Roxana, or, The Fortunate Mistress* (Oxford: OUP, 1996, 1st pub. 1724).

Defoe, Daniel, *The Great Law of Subordination Consider'd; or, the Insolence and Unsufferable Behaviour of Servants in England Duly Enquired* (London: S, Harding, 1724).

Defoe, Daniel, *A Tour Thro' the Whole Island of Great Britain: Divided into Circuits or Journies: Giving a Particular and Diverting Account of Whatever is Curious and Worth Observation*, 3 vols (London: G. Strahan, 1724–7).

Defoe, Daniel, *The Complete English Tradesman, in Familiar Letters: Directing Him in All the Several Parts and Progressions of Trade*, 2 vols (London: Rivington, 1726).

Defoe, Daniel, *A Plan of the English Commerce Being a Compleat Prospect of the Trade of This Nation, As Well the Home Trade as the Foreign* (London: Rivington, 1728).

De Quincy [sic], Thomas, *On Murder Considered as One of the Fine Arts and on War: Two Essays* (London: Doppler Press, 1980, 1st pub. 1827–9).

Dryden, John., *The Wild Gallant: A Comedy* (London: H. Herringman, 1669).

Dyce, Revd Alexander, ed., *The Works of Thomas Middleton*, 5 vols (London: Edward Lumley, 1840).

Egan, Pierce, *Finish to the Adventures of Tom, Jerry, and Logic in their Pursuits through Life in and Out of London* (London: G. Virtue, 1830).

Egerton D. T., *Fashionable Bores or Coolers in High Life* (London: Thomas McLean, 1824).

Fielding, Henry, *Miss Lucy in Town: A Sequel to The Virgin Unmasqued* (London: A. Millar, 1742).

Fielding, Henry, ed. David Blewett, *Amelia* (Harmondsworth: Penguin, 1987, 1st pub. 1751).

Fielding, Henry, *A Plan of the Universal Register-Office* (London: s.n., 1751).

Goldsmith, Oliver, 'A Description of an Author's Bed Chamber', in *Poems and Plays by Oliver Goldsmith*, MB (Dublin: Price, Sleater *et al.*, 1785).

Graglia, Giuseppe A., *A Plan for the Periodical Abolition of All Taxes, Raised by the Means of Collectors* (London: B. Crosby, 1795).

Grosart, Revd Alexander B., *The Works of Gabriel Harvey, for the First Time Collected and Edited with Memorial-Introduction, Notes and Illustration, etc.*, 3 vols (London: for private circulation, 1884–5).

Grose, Francis, *A Classical Dictionary of the Vulgar Tongue* (London: S. Hooper, 1785).

Haywood, Eliza, *A Present for a Servant Maid* (London: T. Gardner, 1743).

Johnson, Samuel, *A Dictionary of the English Language*, 2 vols (London: Rivington, 6th edn, 1785, 1st pub. 1755).

Jones, Erasmus, *The Man of Manners, or, Plebeian Polish'd, Being Plain and Familiar Rules for a Modest and Genteel Behaviour, on Most of the Ordinary Occasions of Life* (London: J. Roberts, 1737).

King, Gregory, *Natural and Political Observations and Conclusions upon the State and Condition of England* (mss 1696, 1st pub. George Chalmers, 1802) in George E. Barnett, ed., *Two Tracts by Gregory King* (Baltimore MD: Johns Hopkins Press, 1936), 11–56.

Leigh, Samuel, *Leigh's New Picture of London: Or, a View of the Political, Religious, Medical, Municipal, Commercial, and Moral State of the British Metropolis; Presenting a Luminous Guide to the Stranger, on All Subjects Connected with General Information, Business, or Amusement, to Which Is Subjoined, a Description of the Environs* (London: for the author, 1822).

Lichfield, Richard, *The Trimming of Thomas Nashe Gentleman* (London: Philip Scarlet, 1597).

Mackenzie, Henry, *The Man of Feeling* (London: Strahan & Cadell, 1783).

Malcolm, James Peller, *Anecdotes of the Manners and Customs of London During the Eighteenth Century*, 2 vols (London: Longman, Hurst, Rees & Orme, 2nd edn, 1810, 1st pub. 1808).

Mandeville, Bernard, *The Fable of The Bees: Or, Private Vices, Publick Benefits* (London: Edmund Parker, 1705).

Maxwell, John Irving, *The Housekeepers' Guide and Lodgers' Adviser, Being such Selections from the Law of Landlords and Tenants as Are More Immediately Interesting to Housekeepers and Lodgers* (London: Cox & Hughes, 1805).

Middleton, Thomas, *The Black Book*, in Revd Alexander Dyce, ed., *The Works of Thomas Middleton*, 5 vols (London: Edward Lumley, 1840).

Nashe, Thomas, *Have with You to Saffron Walden* (London: John Danter, 1596).

Nichols, John, *Illustrations of the Literary History of the Eighteenth Century*, 8 vols (London: Nichols, 1828).

Paul, John, *Every Landlord or Tenant His Own Lawyer* (London: Wm Strahan, 4th edn, 1778).

Peacham, Henry, ed. Virgil B. Heltzel, *The Complete Gentleman, The Truth of the Times; and The Art of Living in London* (Ithaca NY: Cornell University Press, 1962, 1st pub. 1622).

Reeve, Clara, *The Progress of Romance, through Times, Countries, and Manners; with Remarks on the Good and Bad Effects of It, on Them Respectively; in a Course of Evening Conversations*, 2 vols (Dublin: Price, Exshaw et al., 1785).

Richardson, Samuel, *Clarissa, or The History of a Young Lady* (London: Penguin, 2004, 1st pub. 1748).

Robinson, Walter, *The Landlord's Pocket Lawyer: Or, the Complete Landlord and Tenant: Containing the Whole Law Concerning Landlords, Tenants, and Lodgers, Explained in a Familiar Manner* (London: S. Bladon, 3rd edn, 1781).

Rylance, Ralph, ed. Janet Ing Freeman, *The Epicure's Almanack: Eating and Drinking in Regency London, the Original 1815 Guidebook* (London: British Library, 2013).

Shaw, Joseph, *Parish Law: Or, a Guide to Justices of the Peace, Ministers, Churchwardens, Overseers of the Poor, Constables, Surveyors of the Highways, Vestry-Clerks, and All Others Concern'd in Parish Business* (London: Henry Lintot, 8th edn, 1753).

Smith, Adam, *The Theory of Moral Sentiments* (New York: Barnes & Noble, 2004, 1st pub. 1759).

Smith, Adam, *The Wealth of Nations*, 2 vols (London: Penguin, 1999, 1st pub. 1776).

Smollett, Tobias, *The Adventures of Peregrine Pickle, in which are included Memoirs of a Lady of Quality*, 4 vols (London: for the author, 1751).

Sutton, Robert, *A Complete Guide to Landlords, Tenants, and Lodgers, Being a Methodical Arrangement of the Whole Law as It Now Stands, Respecting the Taking or Letting Lands, Houses, or Apartments* (London: Stratford, 1799).

Swift, Jonathan, *Travels into Several Remote Nations of the World*, 4 parts (London: Benjamin Motte, 1726).

Tallis, John, *London Street Views 1838–40* (London: London Topographical Society, 2nd edn, 2002, 1st pub. 1969).

Tardy, Abbé, *Manuel du Voyageur à Londres; ou Recueil de Toutes les Instructions aux Étrangers qui Arrivent dans Cette Capitale* (London: W. & C. Spilsbury, 1800).

Trusler, Revd John, *The London Adviser and Guide: Containing Every Instruction and Information Useful and Necessary to Persons Living in London, and Coming to Reside There* (London: for the author, 1786).

Vanbrugh, John and Colley Cibber, *The Provok'd Husband; or, a Journey to London* (London: J. Watts, 1728).

Ware, Isaac, *A Complete Body of Architecture, Adorned with Plans and Elevations from Original Designs by Isaac Ware; in Which Are Interspersed Some Designs of Inigo Jones*, 2 vols (Farnborough: Gregg, facsimile edn, 1971, 1st pub. London, 1768).

White, William, *History, Gazetteer and Directory of Norfolk: Comprising a General Survey of Norfolk and the Diocese of Norwich; and Separate Historical, Statistical, and Topographical Descriptions of All the Hundreds, Liberties, Unions, Boroughs, Towns, Ports, Parishes, Villages, Hamlets, and Manors* (Sheffield: William White, 3rd edn, 1864).

Willan, Robert, *Reports on the Diseases in London: Particularly during the Years 1796–1800* (London: R. Phillips, 1801).

Woodfall, William, *Law of Landlord and Tenant: To Which Is Added an Appendix of Precedents* (London: J. Butterworth, 4th edn, 1814).

Secondary sources

Digital secondary sources

Keene, Derek, Peter Earle, Craig Spence and Janet Barnes, 'Guide to the Source', in *Four Shillings in the Pound* Aid *1693/4: The City of London, the City of Westminster,*

Middlesex (London, 1992), *British History Online,* http://www.british-history.ac.uk/
   no-series/london-4s-pound/1693-4/guide-to-the-source.
National Portrait Gallery, Research programmes, 'Artists, Their Materials and Suppliers',
   https://www.npg.org.uk/research/programmes/artists-their-materials-and-
   suppliers/.
Oxford Dictionary of National Biography, https://www.oxforddnb.com/.
Survey of London, *British History Online*, http://www.british-history.ac.uk/survey-
   london/.
UCL Bloomsbury Project, https://www.ucl.ac.uk/bloomsbury-project/.
A Vision of Britain Through Time, http://www.visionofbritain.org.uk/.

Printed secondary sources

Allan, David G. C., *The Adelphi Past and Present: A History and a Guide* (Basingstoke:
   Basingstoke Press, 2001).
Anderson, Michael, 'Households, Families and Individuals: Some Preliminary Results
   from the National Sample from the 1851 Census of Great Britain', *Continuity &*
   Change, 3.03 (1988), 421–38.
Asquith, Ivon, 'James Perry and the *Morning Chronicle*, 1790–1821' (unpublished PhD
   thesis, UCL, 1973).
Baer, William, 'Planning for Growth and Growth Controls in Early Modern Northern
   Europe: Part 2: The Evolution of London's Practice 1580–1680', *Town Planning*
   Review 7.3 (2007), 257–77.
Bailey, Joanne, *Parenting in England 1760–1830: Emotion, Identity and Generation*
   (Oxford: OUP, 2012).
Baker, James, *The Business of Satirical Prints in Late-Georgian England* (Basingstoke:
   Palgrave Macmillan, 2017).
Barker-Benfield, G. J., *The Culture of Sensibility: Sex and Society in Eighteenth-Century*
   Britain (Chicago: University of Chicago Press, 1992).
Barry, Jonathan and Christopher Brooks, eds, *The Middling Sort of People: Culture,*
   Society and Politics in England, 1550–1800 (Basingstoke: Macmillan, 1994).
Batchelor, Jennie and Manushag Powell, eds, *Women's Periodicals and Print Culture in*
   Britain, 1690–1820s: The Long Eighteenth Century (Edinburgh: Edinburgh University
   Press, 2017).
Beattie, J. M., *Policing and Punishment in London, 1660–1750: Urban Crime and the*
   Limits of Terror (Oxford: OUP, 2001).
Benedict, Barbara, 'Advertising Women: Gender and the Vendor in the Print Culture
   of the Medical Marketplace', Ch. 26, 612–32 in Jennie Batchelor and Manushag
   Powell, eds, *Women's Periodicals and Print Culture In Britain, 1690–1820s: The Long*
   Eighteenth Century (Edinburgh: Edinburgh University Press, 2017).
Bennett, Tony and Diane Watson, eds, *Understanding Everyday Life* (Oxford: Blackwell,
   2002).

Berg, Maxine and Elizabeth Eger, eds, *Luxury in the Eighteenth Century: Debates, Desires and Delectable Goods* (Basingstoke: Palgrave, 2003).

Bernez, Marie-Odile, 'Comfort, the Acceptable Face of Luxury: An Eighteenth-Century Etymology', *Journal for Early Modern Cultural Studies* 14.2 (2014), 3–21.

Black, John, 'Illegitimacy, Sexual Relations and Location in Metropolitan London, 1735–5', Ch. 7, 101–18 in Tim Hitchcock and Heather Shore, eds, *The Streets of London from the Great Fire to the Great Stink* (London: Rivers Oram, 2003).

Boucé, Paul-Gabriel, ed., *Guerres et Paix: La Grande-Bretagne du XVIII Siècle* (Paris: Presses Sorbonne Nouvelle, 1998).

Briganti, Chiara, and Kathy Mezei, *Living with Strangers: Bedsits and Boarding Houses in Modern English Life, Literature and Film* (London: Bloomsbury, 2018).

Burton, Sarah, *A Double Life: A Biography of Charles and Mary Lamb* (London: Penguin, 2004).

Byrd, Max, 'Thomas Jefferson and Great Britain in Peace and War', 203–23 in Paul-Gabriel Boucé, ed., *Guerres et Paix: La Grande-Bretagne du XVIII Siècle* (Paris: Presses Sorbonne Nouvelle, 1998).

Campbell, Colin, *The Romantic Ethic and the Spirit of Modern Consumerism* (Oxford: Blackwell, 2005, 1st pub. 1987).

Carpenter, Kirsty, *Refugees of the French Revolution: The French Émigrés in London, 1789–1802* (Basingstoke: Macmillan, 1999).

Carpenter, Kirsty, 'The Novelty of the French Émigrés in London in the 1790s', Ch. 3, 69–90 in Debra Kelly and Martyn Cornick, eds, *A History of the French in London: Liberty, Equality, Opportunity* (London: University of London, 2013).

Carter, Sophie, *Purchasing Power: Representing Prostitution in Eighteenth-Century English Popular Print Culture* (Aldershot: Ashgate, 2004).

Chynoweth, Tessa, 'Domestic Service and Domestic Space in London, 1750–1800' (unpublished PhD thesis, Queen Mary University of London, 2016).

Clark, Anna, *Scandal: The Sexual Politics of the British Constitution* (Princeton NJ: Princeton University Press, 2004).

Clarke, David, *Chinese Art and Its Encounter with the World* (Hong Kong: Hong Kong University Press, 2011).

Clarke, Norma, *Queen of the Wits: A Life of Laetitia Pilkington* (London: Faber & Faber, 2008).

Cockayne, Emily, *Hubbub: Filth, Noise and Stench in England* (New Haven CT: YUP, 2007).

Cody, Lisa Forman, *Birthing the Nation: Sex, Science, and the Conception of Eighteenth-Century Britons* (Oxford: OUP, 2005).

Colley, Linda, *Britons: Forging the Nation 1707–1837* (New Haven CT: YUP, 2005, 1st pub. 1992).

Cook, Jon, *Hazlitt in Love: A Fatal Attachment* (London: Short Books, 2007).

Cooper, Di and Moira Donald, 'Households and "Hidden" Kin in Early-Nineteenth-Century England: Four Case Studies in Suburban Exeter, 1821–61', *Continuity & Change* 10.2 (1995), 257–78.

Corfield, Penelope J., 'Class by Name and Number in Eighteenth-Century Britain', *History* 72 (1987), 38–61.

Corfield, Penelope J., *Power and the Professions in Britain 1700–1850* (London: Routledge, 2000, 1st pub. 1995).

Cross, Wilbur L., *The Life and Times of Laurence Sterne* (New York: Macmillan, 1909).

Dabhoiwala, Faramerz, *The Origins of Sex: A History of the First Sexual Revolution* (London: Allen Lane, 2012).

Darley, Gillian, *John Soane: An Accidental Romantic* (New Haven CT: YUP, 1999).

Davidoff, Leonore, 'Class and Gender in Victorian England: The Case of Hannah Cullwick and A.J. Munby', *Feminist Studies* 5.1 (1979), 86–141.

Davidoff, Leonore, *Worlds Between: Historical Perspectives on Gender and Class* (Cambridge: Polity, 1995).

Doody, Margaret, 'Samuel Richardson: Fiction and Knowledge', Ch. 5, 90–119 in John Richetti, ed., *The Cambridge Companion to the Eighteenth-Century Novel* (Cambridge: CUP, 1996).

Dyer, Serena, 'Masculinities, Wallpaper, and Crafting Domestic Space within the University, 1795–1914', *Nineteenth-Century Gender Studies* 14.2 (2018), 3–17.

Earland, Ada, *John Opie and His Circle* (London: Hutchinson, 1911).

Earle, Peter, *The Making of the English Middle Class: Business, Society and Family Life in London, 1660–1730* (London: Methuen, 1989).

Earle, Peter, *A City Full of People: Men and Women of London, 1650–1750* (London: Methuen, 1994).

Ehrenpreis, Irvin, *Swift: The Man, His Works and the Age*, 3 vols (London: Methuen, 1962).

Ellis, Markman, *The Politics of Sensibility: Race, Gender and Commerce in the Sentimental Novel* (Cambridge: CUP, 1996).

Erickson, Amy, 'Eleanor Mosley and Other Milliners in the City of London Companies 1700–50', *History Workshop Journal* 71.1 (2011), 147–72.

Erickson, Amy, 'Esther Sleepe, Fan-Maker and Her Family', *Eighteenth-Century Life* 42.2 (2018), 15–37.

Fish, Stanley E., *Is There a Text in This Class? The Authority of Interpretive Communities* (Cambridge MA: Harvard University Press, 1980).

Forster, John, *The Life of Charles Dickens*, 3 vols (London: Chapman & Hall, 1873–4).

Forster, John, *The Life and Times of Oliver Goldsmith* (London: Bickers & Son, 5th edn, 1877).

Freeman, Janet Ing, 'Jack Harris and "Honest Ranger": The Publication and Prosecution of *Harris's List of Covent-Garden Ladies*, 1760–95', *The Library* 13.4 (2012), 423–56.

French, Henry R., 'The Search for the "Middle Sort of People" in England, 1600–1800', *Historical Journal* 43 (2000), 277–93.

Fryer, Peter, *Staying Power: The History of Black People in Britain* (London: Pluto, 1984).

Gatrell, Vic, *The First Bohemians: Life and Art in London's Golden Age* (London: Penguin, 2013).

George, Dorothy M., *London Life in the Eighteenth Century* (Harmondsworth: Penguin, 1966, 1st pub. 1925).

Greig, Hannah, and Giorgio Riello, 'Eighteenth-Century Interiors: Redesigning the Georgian', *Journal of Design History* 20.4 (2007), 273–89.

Griffiths, Paul and Mark S. R. Jenner, eds, *Londinopolis: Essays in the Cultural and Social History of Early Modern London* (Manchester: Manchester University Press, 2000).

Guillery, Peter, *The Small House in Eighteenth-Century London* (New Haven CT: YUP, 2004).

Harding, Vanessa, *People in Place: Families, Households and Housing in Early Modern London* (London: Centre for Metropolitan History, 2008).

Harding, Vanessa, 'Families and Housing in Seventeenth-Century London', *Parergon* 24.2 (2007), 115–38.

Harvey, Karen, 'Men Making Home: Masculinity and Domesticity in Eighteenth-Century Britain', *Gender & History* 21.3 (2009), 520–40.

Harvey, Karen, *The Little Republic: Masculinity and Domestic Authority in Eighteenth-Century Britain* (Oxford: OUP, 2012).

Heal, Sir Ambrose, *The London Goldsmiths 1200–1800: A Record of the Names and Addresses of the Craftsmen, Their Shop-Signs and Trade-Cards* (Cambridge: CUP, 1935).

Heath, Sue and Rachael Scicluna, 'Putting up (with) the Paying Guest: Negotiating Hospitality and the Boundaries of the Commercial Home in Private Lodging Arrangements', *Families, Relationships & Societies* 20.20 (2019), 1–18.

Heller, Benjamin, 'Leisure and the Use of Domestic Space in Georgian London', *Historical Journal* 53.3 (2010), 623–45.

Hembry, Phyllis, *The English Spa, 1560–1815* (London: Athlone, 1990).

Heyl, Christoph, 'We Are Not at Home: Protecting Domestic Privacy in Post-Fire Middle-Class London', *London Journal* 27.2 (2002), 12–33.

Hill, Bridget, *Women, Work and Sexual Politics in Eighteenth-Century England* (London: UCL Press, 1989).

Hill, Bridget, *Servants: English Domestics in the Eighteenth Century* (Oxford: Clarendon, 1996).

Hitchcock, Tim and Heather Shore, eds, *The Streets of London from the Great Fire to the Great Stink* (London: Rivers Oram, 2003).

Hoare, Stephen, *Palaces of Power: The Birth and Evolution of London's Clubland* (Stroud: History Press, 2019).

Hodges, John C., *William Congreve the Man* (New York: Modern Language Association of America, 1941).

Holbrook, Margot, *Where Do You Keep?: Lodging the Cambridge Undergraduate* (Great Malvern: Cappella Archive, 2006).

Hollander, John, 'It All Depends', *Social Research* 58.1 (1991), 31–49.

Hollows, Joanne, *Domestic Cultures* (Maidenhead: Open University Press, 2008).

Holmes, Richard, *Coleridge: Early Visions, 1772–1804* (London: HarperCollins, 1998).

Holmes, Richard, *Coleridge: Darker Reflections* (London: Flamingo, 1999).

Hoppit, Julian, *Risk and Failure in English* Business, *1700–1800* (Cambridge: CUP, 1987).

Howitt, William, *Homes and Haunts of the Most Eminent Poets*, 2 vols (London: R. Bentley, 1847).

Hunt, Margaret R., *The Middling Sort: Commerce, Gender, and the Family in England, 1680–1780* (Berkeley CA: University of California Press, 1996).

Hunter, J. Paul, 'The Novel and Social/Cultural History', Ch. 2, 9–40 in John Richetti, ed., *The Cambridge Companion to the Eighteenth-Century Novel* (Cambridge: CUP, 1996).

Hussey, David and Margaret Ponsonby, *The Single Homemaker and Material Culture in the Long Eighteenth Century* (Farnham: Ashgate, 2012).

Jauss, Hans Robert, trans. Timothy Bahti, *Toward an Aesthetic of Reception* (Minneapolis MN: University of Minnesota Press, 1982).

Jones, E. L., S. Porter and M. Turner, *Gazetteer of English Urban Fire Disasters, 1500–1900* (Norwich: Historical Geography Research Series 13, 1984).

Kelly, Debra and Martyn Cornick, eds, *A History of the French in London: Liberty, Equality, Opportunity* (London: University of London, 2013).

Kenlon, Tabitha, *Conduct Books and the History of the Ideal Woman* (London: Anthem Press, 2020).

Kevin Schurer and Tom Arkell, eds, 'Variations in Household Structure in the Late Seventeenth Century: Towards a Regional Analysis', Ch. 12, 253–78 in Schurer and Arkell, *Surveying the People: The Interpretation and Use of Document Sources for the Study of Population in the Later Seventeenth Century* (Oxford: Leopard's Head, 1992).

Lamb, Jonathan, *The Things Things Say* (Woodstock: Princeton University Press, 2011).

Laslett, Peter, ed., with Richard Wall, *Household and Family in Past Time: Comparative Studies in the Size and Structure of the Domestic Group Over the Last Three Centuries in England, France, Serbia, Japan and Colonial North America, with Further Materials from Western Europe* (Cambridge: CUP, 1972).

Lemmings, David, *Professors of the Law: Barristers and English Legal Culture in the Eighteenth Century* (Oxford: OUP, 2000).

Longstaffe-Gowan, Todd, *The London Square: Gardens in the Midst of Town* (New Haven CT: YUP, 2012).

Lucey, Conor, 'Marketing the Necessary Comforts in Georgian Dublin', 67–72 in Jon Stobart, ed., *The Comforts of Home in Western Europe 1700–1900* (London: Bloomsbury Academic, 2020).

Luckhurst, Mary and Jane Moody, eds, *Theatre and Celebrity in Britain, 1660–2000* (Basingstoke: Palgrave Macmillan, 2005).

McEwan, Joanne, and Pamela Sharpe, '"It Buys Me Freedom": Genteel Lodging in Late-Seventeenth- and Eighteenth-Century London', *Parergon* 24.2 (2007), 139–61.

McKellar, Elizabeth, *The Birth of Modern London: The Development and Design of the City 1660–1720* (Manchester: Manchester University Press, 1999).

McKellar, Elizabeth, *Landscapes of London: The City, the Country and the Suburbs, 1660–1840* (New Haven CT: YUP, 2013).

McKendrick, N., John Brewer and J. H. Plumb, *The Birth of a Consumer Society: The Commercialization of Eighteenth-Century England* (London: Hutchinson, 1983).

McWilliam, Rohan, *London's West End: Creating the Pleasure District, 1800–1914* (Oxford: OUP, 2020).

Meldrum, Tim, *Domestic Service and Gender: Life and Work in the London Household, 1660–1750* (Harlow: Longman, 2000).

Melville, Lewis, *The Life and Letters of Laurence Sterne*, 2 vols (London: S. Paul, 1910).

Miller, Daniel, *The Comfort of Things* (Cambridge: Polity, 2008).

Mole, Tom, ed., *Romanticism and Celebrity Culture, 1750–1850* (Cambridge: CUP, 2009).

Morris, Derek and Ken Cozens, *London's Sailortown, 1600–1800: A Social History of Shadwell and Ratcliff, an Early Modern Riverside Suburb* (London: East London History Society, 2014).

Mui, Hoh-Cheung and Lorna H., *Shops and Shopkeeping in Eighteenth-Century England* (Kingston Ontario: McGill-Queen's University Press, 1989).

Nussbaum, Felicity, 'Actresses and the Economics of Celebrity, 1700–1800', Ch. 9, 148–68 in Tom Mole, ed., *Romanticism and Celebrity Culture, 1750–1850* (Cambridge: CUP, 2009).

Ogborn, Miles, *Spaces of Modernity: London's Geographies 1680–1780* (New York: Guilford Press, 1998).

Olivier, E., *The Eccentric Life of Alexander Cruden* (London: Faber & Faber, 1934).

Pearson, Robin, 'The Impact of Fire and Fire Insurance on Eighteenth-Century English Town Buildings and Their Populations', Ch. 3, 67–93 in Carole Shammas, ed., *Investing in the Early Modern Built Environment: Europeans, Asians, Settler and Indigenous Societies* (Leiden: Brill, 2012).

Pennell, Sara, '"Great quantities of Gooseberry Pye and Baked clod of Beef": Victualling and Eating Out in Early Modern London', Ch. 11, 228–49 in Griffiths, Paul and Mark S. R. Jenner, eds, *Londinopolis: Essays in the Cultural and Social History of Early Modern London* (Manchester: Manchester University Press, 2000).

Poole, Steve, *The Politics of Regicide in England, 1760–1850* (Manchester: Manchester University Press, 2000).

Prior, James, *The Life of Oliver Goldsmith, MB: From a Variety of Original Sources*, 2 vols (London: J. Murray, 1837).

Raven, James, *Publishing Business in Eighteenth-Century England* (Woodbridge: Boydell & Brewer, 2014).

Richetti, John, ed., *The Cambridge Companion to the Eighteenth-Century Novel* (Cambridge: CUP, 1996).

Ross, Ian Campbell, *Laurence Sterne: A Life* (Oxford: OUP, 2001).

Roughead, William, ed., *Burke and Hare* (Edinburgh: Wm Hodge, 1921).

Rubenhold, Hallie, *The Covent Garden Ladies: Pimp General Jack and the Extraordinary Story of Harris's List* (Stroud: Tempus, 2005).

Schurer, Kevin and Tom Arkell, eds, *Surveying the People: The Interpretation and Use of Document Sources for the Study of Population in the Later Seventeenth Century* (Oxford: Leopard's Head, 1992).

Shammas, Carole, ed., *Investing in the Early Modern Built Environment: Europeans, Asians, Settler and Indigenous Societies* (Leiden: Brill, 2012).

Slater, Michael, *Charles Dickens* (New Haven CT: YUP, 2011).

Spence, Craig, *London in the 1690s: A Social Atlas* (London: Centre for Metropolitan History, 2000).

Steedman, Carolyn, 'Cries Unheard, Sights Unseen: Writing the Eighteenth-Century Metropolis', *Representations* 118.1 (2012), 28–71.

Stobart, Jon, ed., *The Comforts of Home in Western Europe 1700–1900* (London: Bloomsbury Academic, 2020).

Stroud, Dorothy, *Sir John Soane Architect* (London: Faber & Faber, 1984).

Styles, John, 'Lodging at the Old Bailey: Lodgings and their Furnishing in Eighteenth-Century London', 61–80 in John Styles and Amanda Vickery, eds, *Gender, Taste and Material Culture in Britain and North America, 1700–1830* (New Haven CT: YUP, 2006).

Styles, John and Amanda Vickery, eds, *Gender, Taste and Material Culture in Britain and North America, 1700–1830* (New Haven CT: YUP, 2006).

Summerson, John, *Georgian London* (New Haven CT: YUP, 2003, 1st pub. 1945).

Tadmor, Naomi, *Family and Friends in Eighteenth-Century England: Household, Kinship, and Patronage* (Cambridge: CUP, 2001).

Taylor, Clare, *The Design, Production and Reception of Eighteenth-Century Wallpaper in Britain* (Oxford: Routledge, 2018).

Thornbury, Walter, *The Life of J.M.W. Turner RA* (London: Chatto & Windus, 1877).

Tickell, Shelley, *Shoplifting in Eighteenth-Century England* (Woodbridge: Boydell & Brewer, 2018).

Todd, Janet, *Sensibility: An Introduction* (London: Methuen, 1986).

Todd, Janet, *The Secret Life of Aphra Behn* (London: André Deutsch, 1996).

Tomalin, Claire, *Mrs Jordan's Profession: The Story of a Great Actress and a Future King* (London: Penguin 2012, 1st pub. 1994).

Van Doran, Carl, *Benjamin Franklin* (London: Cresset Press, 1946, 1st pub. 1939).

Vickery, Amanda, '"Neat and Not Too Showey": Words and Wallpaper in Regency England', 201–22 in John Styles and Amanda Vickery, eds, *Gender, Taste and Material Culture in Britain and North America, 1700–1830* (New Haven CT: YUP, 2006).

Vickery, Amanda, 'An Englishman's Home Is His Castle? Thresholds, Boundaries and Privacies in the Eighteenth-Century London House', *Past & Present* 199 (2008), 147–73.

Vickery, Amanda, *Behind Closed Doors: At Home in Georgian England* (New Haven CT: YUP, 2009).

Visram, Rozina, *Ayahs, Lascars and Princes: Indians in Britain 1700–1947* (London: Pluto, 1986).

Watt, Ian, *The Rise of the Novel: Studies in Defoe, Richardson and Fielding* (Harmondsworth: Penguin, 1972, 1st pub. 1957).

Wheatley, Henry B. and Peter Cunningham, *London Past and Present: Its History, Associations, and Traditions*, 3 vols (London: J. Murray, 1891).

White, Jerry, *London in the Eighteenth Century: A Great and Monstrous Thing* (London: Bodley Head, 2012).

White, Jerry, *London in the Nineteenth Century: A Human Awful Wonder of God* (London: Bodley Head, 2016).

White, Jerry, *Mansions of Misery: A Biography of the Marshalsea Debtors' Prison* (London: Penguin Random House, 2016).

Whitehead, Angus, 'William Blake's Last Residence: No. 3 Fountain Court, Strand, George Richmond's Plan and an Unrecorded Letter to John Linnell', *British Art Journal* 6.1 (2005), 21–30.

Whitehead, Angus, '"I write in South Molton Street, what I both see and hear": Reconstructing William and Catherine Blake's Residence and Studio at 17 South Molton Street, Oxford Street', *British Art Journal* 11.2 (2010), 62–75.

Whittle, Jane, 'A Critique of Approaches to "Domestic Work": Women, Work and the Pre-Industrial Economy', *Past & Present*, 243.1 (2019), 35–70.

Whyman, Susan, *Sociability and Power in Late-Stuart England: The Cultural Worlds of the Verneys, 1660–1720* (Oxford: OUP, 2002).

Whyman, Susan, *The Pen and the People: English Letter Writers 1660–1800* (Oxford: OUP, 2009).

Williamson, Gillian, *British Masculinity in the Gentleman's Magazine, 1731–1815* (Basingstoke: Palgrave Macmillan, 2016).

Wright, S. J., 'Sojourners and Lodgers in a Provincial Town: The Evidence from Eighteenth-Century Ludlow', *Urban History* 17 (1990), 14–35.

Wynn Jones, Michael, *George Cruikshank: His Life and London* (London: Macmillan, 1978).

Index

Index235

Hamilton, Kitty 114, 159

Harivin, Mary 1, 3, 82

Harley, Robert Lord 123

Harris, Nancy 'Nanny' 160

Harris's List of Covent-Garden Ladies (directory of prostitutes) 37–9

Harvey, Gabriel 18–19

Harvey, Karen 126

The Little Republic 4

Harwood, Charles 53

Hawkins, John 10

Haydon, Benjamin 11, 59, 63, 93, 102, 121, 129, 139, 145, 162–3, 166

The Judgment of Solomon 166

Hays, Mary 79, 84, 131, 204 n.92

Haywood, Eliza 113, 159–62

Hazlitt, William 67, 117, 123–5, 130, 138–9, 144, 159, 161–2

Heath, Henry

Comfortable Lodgings 141

Notions of the Agreeable 130

heating and lighting

candles 30, 111, 139

coals/wood 111–12, 123

fire/fireplace 112

hearth 30, 80, 112, 129

house fire/fire risk 1–2, 5, 30, 50, 55, 67–8, 74, 77–9, 82, 85, 108, 113–14, 122–3, 129, 139, 147, 171, 174, 207 n.12

Heller, Benjamin 7

Hickey, William 77, 85, 136, 160, 172–3

Hiffernan, Paul 79

The Histories of Some of the Penitents in the Magdalen-House (Jennie Batchelor and Megan Hiatt) 33–4, 36, 47

Hogarth, Jane 68

Hogarth, William 22, 26, 28, 30, 47, 61, 68, 78

Distrest Poet 23, 35

Harlot's Progress 22, 34, 109

Industry and Idleness series 24

Picture of London 120

Hogg, Thomas Jefferson 90, 92, 104, 109, 118, 142, 157

Holcroft, Thomas 13

Hollander, John 122

homeless 19, 24, 147–8

Horwood, Richard 11

house collapse 147–8

households/householders 1–2, 5, 8, 15, 18, 37, 45, 52–3, 63–5, 68, 70, 72, 74, 81–2, 84–5, 108, 115, 120, 126, 132, 134–5, 144–5, 148, 171, 176 n.11

average size of (in London) 12, 51–2

budgets 64, 73, 79, 142–3, 145, 148

care/affection by (motherly) landladies 129–31

Georgian 136

houseful 3, 12, 120, 144, 149, 157, 174

respectable 144, 146, 160 (*see also* respectability)

servants 4, 113–14

taxes 50–1

widowed 51

house-hunting 145, 147

housekeeper/housekeeping 20, 64, 72, 74, 80, 82, 126, 145, 150

house rules 42–3, 106, 126, 128, 135, 139–40, 153, 156

houses in multiple occupation (HMO) 169

Hughes, Eleanor 138

Hunter, Anne 94

Hunter, John 94

Hunter, J. Paul 17

Hunt, George 64

Lodgings to Let Alone 27–8

Hunt, Margaret 22

Hurst, Sarah 80

Hutton, William 87

Inchbald, Elizabeth 7, 59, 63, 67–8, 71, 75, 79, 81, 83–4, 90–1, 94, 102, 104, 108, 111–14, 119, 121, 124–5, 127–8, 130–1, 135–7, 140, 143–4, 148–52, 154, 174

I'll Tell You What 133

inhabitants 15, 42, 49–50, 55, 62, 140

inhabited houses in England 51

initial welcome 143, 155

inventory 43, 154

Irving, George 93

Jefferson, Thomas 59, 80

Jeggett, Jacob 55, 188 n.34

Johnson, Esther 123

Johnson, Joshua 53, 77

9 781350 257016